EARLY
CHAMBER MUSIC

Da Capo Press Music Reprint Series

EARLY
CHAMBER MUSIC

By Ruth Halle Rowen

*New Preface and
Supplementary Bibliography by the Author*

DA CAPO PRESS · NEW YORK · 1974

Library of Congress Cataloging in Publication Data

Rowen, Ruth (Halle)
    Early chamber music.

    (Da Capo Press music reprint series)
    Reprint of the 1949 ed.
    Bibliography: p.
    1. Chamber music—History and criticism.
I. Title.
ML1100.R6   1974   785.7   68-8144
ISBN 0-306-71160-5

This Da Capo Press edition of *Early Chamber Music* is an unabridged republication of the first edition published in New York in 1949 by the King's Crown Press of Columbia University Press. It is reprinted by special arrangement with the author and includes a new preface and supplementary bibliography prepared by her for this edition.

Published by Da Capo Press, Inc.
A Subsidiary of Plenum Publishing Corporation
227 West 17th Street, New York, New York 10011

TO SY

Who saw this book through to completion

ACKNOWLEDGMENTS

*T*HE IMMEDIATE impetus for this work came from the seminars in musicology conducted by Professors Paul Henry Láng and Erich Hertzmann at Columbia University. It was at these meetings that I came into vivid contact with the fascinating problems connected with the early transformations of instrumental chamber music. When I chose to pursue the subject in detail, the complete support of Professors Láng and Hertzmann proved to be a guiding force of inestimable value. Furthermore, I am deeply indebted to Mr. Abraham Veinus for so willingly applying his expert talents toward shaping the revision of the manuscript. I wish to thank W. W. Norton and Company for permission to reproduce quotations from *Essay on the True Art of Playing Keyboard Instruments* by C. P. E. Bach, translated and edited by William J. Mitchell (to be published in the fall of 1948).

R. H. R.

New York City
October, 1948

CONTENTS

PREFACE TO THE 1974 EDITION

I **N THE** two centuries since chamber music began to be distinguished from church music or theater music, the private chamber of the princely entourage has given way to the modern concept of music in a "chamber" to which all may have access; and this concept has remained unchanged in the two decades since this book first appeared. The chamber musicians, chamber singers, and chamber virtuosos of old were called upon to perform for privileged guests. Our "chamber" today, whether it be an intimate concert hall, a room in someone's home, or a schoolroom, admits people from all walks of life and music of many media.

Whereas in the 1700's the term was self-limiting because of the social circumstances under which the music was performed, today we find that its meaning has been narrowed down in quite another way. Now, the term amalgamating the words "chamber" and "music" means less than the sum of its parts. "Chamber" music generally refers to instrumental but not to vocal works. As a medium in a specific sense, chamber music concentrates on solos and ensembles for diverse instrumental combinations. Those who champion the cause of vocal music, however, should not feel slighted. On the contrary, they should be delighted that the song, the madrigal, and the chamber cantata are not swallowed up by one all-inclusive, generic term.

While examining the roots of chamber music, rather than ignoring the other media, we should view their interesting relationships to it. As I reread *Early Chamber Music* from the vantage point of twenty years, I continue to think of it as a springboard for the exploration of many territories, further backward and forward in time, and unilaterally in depth. In addition to juxtaposing instrumental and vocal counterparts, other enterprising studies might involve the relation of the English fancy to the trio sonata, the penetration of the classical chamber style in the string quartet and combinations with piano, and the interplay of winds and strings. These are not virgin areas, as is evident from a perusal of the many excellent materials listed in the "Supplementary Bibliography" appended to this "Preface." However, reading, playing, sifting, and thinking may encourage other viewpoints, uncovering additional vistas.

Day by day my belief grows stronger that the concept of *the* definitive work is erroneous. A book on music that has come to be looked upon as definitive might retain its position if by some unfortunate accident the music and the treatises under discussion had disappeared, thus preventing the projection of fresh insights. However, as long as there is a thinking musician who has available to him valid materials, whether previously discovered or new, the possibility for the development of different, provocative theories exists. Any "definitive work," no matter how painstaking, penetrating, and perfect, cannot be the final, permanent word on the subject. On the contrary, the main service of each work is the opening up of paths to others. Therefore, the publishers of this reprint edition of *Early Chamber Music* have asked me to formulate a supplement to the "Bibliography" that appeared in the original edition, so as to render this book all the more useful for study and research today.

A quick perusal of the "Supplementary Bibliography" will turn up numerous articles challenging the authenticity of some compositions formerly attributed to the masters. Alan Tyson and H. C. Robbins Landon have assigned Opus 3 of Haydn to R. Hofstetter. Karl Geiringer has listed ten chamber works, traditionally attributed to J. S. Bach, whose authorship has recently been questioned. Charles Cudworth wonders about the authenticity of Pergolesi's *Sonata a tre.* Shocking as such discoveries are to the nervous system, we may be comforted by the fact that these works, whether or not composed by Bach, Haydn, or Pergolesi, are extant nevertheless, and are to be considered in the total gamut of musical creation. Conclusions are to be tempered in the light of new evidence. Often the corollary to the negative finding is a positive investigation. The solution does not lie in relegating the spurious compositions to the footnotes simply because they may not be by "master" composers, but in finding out more about the other works of the men whose compositions passed for creations of the great for two centuries.

The missing dimension in any book on music is the realization of the music itself. A reader without access to an adequate research library may not be in a position to reconstruct the musical situation from the few scattered examples offered in some book. This problem is gradually being alleviated by the publication of practical editions with a scholarly background. All too often, however, the editor of such works fails to provide the performer with the means for tracing the method leading to his conclusions. For example, it is tantalizing for the scholar to be confronted with the realization of a continuo part without indication of the figures, especially when he is told in the highly competent preface to the edition that the music at hand is not for keyboard, as was formerly supposed, but, rather, for violin and clavier. Further frustration is offered in cases where clavier music with optional instrumental parts or alternate combinations is published for keyboard alone. While the commercial publisher cannot be expected to print parts that will appeal only to a limited audience, there must be some recourse for the scholar other than a trip to the distant library which houses the manuscript or early print. Practical editions that show the scholarly process of the editor are a necessary adjunct to serious research.

In our zealous desire to examine the original, however, we must not forget the performer, who is equally anxious to bring the results of musicological research to life for the listener. A performer confronted with both the original and the various editorial solutions, all on one page, may give up on the scholarly edition and turn to a less complicated apparatus which, as an interpreter, he finds more inspiring because of its directness. The answer to this problem may be two complementary publications. *Parthenia In-Violata,* published in this fashion (see "Supplementary Bibliography"), exemplifies the virtues of collaborative efforts shared by a team of scholars, a library, and a commercial publisher. Cooperation between endowed or public institutions and commercial publishers, stimulated by scholarly research, though unusual, is not impossible.

The serious student must investigate much more music than an author is able to cite. Normally, as far as musical illustration is concerned, an author is limited to short examples interspersed through the book. In a work which is not aimed at esthetic justification, musical examples are more often chosen for their stylistic tendencies rather than for their emotional appeal to the author. Some of the works illustrated will necessarily be more musically satisfying than others to both the author and the reader. It is an old-fashioned assumption that those who delve into the mysteries of music have no feeling for the music they study. Constant reminders that the music is worthwhile and beautiful become clawing to the reader who has heard and played the music of the period, and is in a position to make value-judgments for himself. Those, on the other hand, who are not familiar with the music would rather seek from the author the sort of guidance that is likely to arouse meaningful insights.

Examination of the materials of the past twenty years reveals an interesting pattern between research and the direct presentation of music. Virtually every publisher of serious music has produced editions which are the result of scholarly research. The end products vary considerably, depending on the audience the publisher intended to capture. Music from the Baroque period, especially, is available in editions ranging from simple arrangements intended for modern instrumental instructional purposes and pleasure, to presentations making every effort to reconstruct the composer's exact intentions.

Musical editions in these various categories appear in the "Supplementary Bibliography," under "Scores and Musical Editions." Many of the scholars who have written on the vital trends in the history of chamber music have frequently edited the music they have written about. In some cases, the literary part of the investigation appears either as an introduction or an appendix to the published score. In other instances, it appears separately, either as a companion volume, or as an article in a periodical or festschrift. It is not surprising, therefore, that many of the editors whose names are found within the entries of "Scores and Critical Editions" also appear as authors in the listing of "Literature on Early Chamber Music." The merger of the talents of author and editor is a significant step toward the unification of chamber music scholarship.

So many materials are available today that it is somewhat problematic to attempt any kind of complete listing. Anyone who wants to locate the works of a given composer can find them readily in Anna H. Heyer's indispensable *Historical Sets, Collected Editions and Monuments of Music*, 2nd. ed. (1969). A sampling of masters' and doctoral dissertations has been included in the "Supplementary Bibliography." Authors of unpublished dissertations have often published articles on related subjects in journals more readily available to the reader. Perusal of such an article may often stimulate the reader to seek the more detailed, if less accessible, dissertation. Indices such as *The Music Index* and RILM are designed to furnish continuous bibliographical information in this area.

A number of theoretical works in the original bibliography of *Early Chamber Music,* which were rare and obtainable only in contemporary editions, have since been reprinted and are now to be found in the local music library and even in some homes. Among them are books by Quantz, Sulzer, Tartini, Wasielewski, and Zarlino, to name just a few. New critical editions of J. S. Bach, Beethoven,

Handel, Haydn, Mozart, and Schubert are making their way to the
library shelves as new volumes are issued; and even the voluminous
Telemann and Vivaldi are being conquered. Yet, though we have
much, we want and need more. Complete works of lesser-known
luminaries, such as Boccherini and Cambini, are joining or should
soon join the galaxy.

The rare materials themselves are becoming more accessible with
the publication of descriptive library catalogs. A thorough list of library catalogs may be found in Vincent Duckles' *Music Reference and
Research Materials,* 2nd. ed. (1968). Several of these up-to-date
catalogs, citing large amounts of chamber music, appear in the
"Supplementary Bibliography." The enterprising student may find
valuable leads in the musical titles mentioned in the compilations
of Davidsson, Duckles and Elmer, or Schnapper. Short of a visit to
Upsala; Berkeley, California; Great Britain; The Library of Congress in Washington; and The New York Public Library, he might
be able to send for a few pertinent microfilms. Methods of
musicological research are reaching new heights. The use of the
computer, the external examination of watermarks and erasures, the
comparison and codification of titles, are pinpointing details to the
scholar's delight. Compositions and composers who may have been
misidentified are being set aright. Chronology is being straightened
out. Yet, while accuracy is a sterling goal, we must learn to restrain
ourselves from getting so tangled in the details that we lose sight
of the broad trends.

In an area as elusive and expansive as chamber music, authorities
may never agree on the confines of the term. I could argue on either
side, for being more inclusive or more exclusive in the working
definition offered in the opening paragraphs of *Early Chamber Music.*
Some readers may feel that the feature of intimacy in compositions
for solo violin is not sufficient qualification for bringing this category
within the realm of chamber music. Others may agitate to include
additional areas. Aside from literature bearing directly on the
chamber works themselves, the "Supplementary Bibliography"
includes references to style, performance practice, individual instruments, letters and documents of composers, and library and thematic catalogs. Since it was not feasible to list all the Baroque and Classic Era chamber music published in the last twenty years, only music
series or parts of series are cited. The chronological limits of the
original bibliography have been expanded through the insertion of
references to some materials originating before 1600 and after the

1760's. Some items dealing with the *basse-dance* and lute music at one end, and Haydn, Mozart, Beethoven, and Schubert at the other, are also included. Citations of music from England, Spain, Sweden, Russia, and, in one instance, America, augment the items from Germany, Austria, Italy, and France. No doubt, I may have left out somebody's favorite author, editor, composer, or library. The oversight was unintentional. For books such as *Chamber Music* edited by Alec Robertson and *La Musique instrumentale de la Renaissance* edited by Jean Jacquot, which are in reality compilations of articles by experts in each phase of the subject, the author of each chapter would have been granted an individual entry, but for space limitations. Furthermore, the embryonic works which were on the way when this book went to press and may be out now, had to be overlooked. Unfortunately, a bibliography becomes outdated as soon as the last period has been typed. The reader is invited to add, to subtract, to expand, to play.

The immediate impetus for the expansion of the original bibliography came from Frederick Freedman, Music Librarian at Vassar College and General Editor of the Da Capo Press Music Reprint Series, to whom I am greatly indebted. I also wish to thank my colleagues at the City College of the City University of New York, including Melva Peterson, Music Librarian, as well as the staff of The New York Public Library's Research Library of the Performing Arts, at Lincoln Center, and the Columbia University Music Library for their competent and gracious service.

It is my hope that this reprint edition of *Early Chamber Music,* with its "Supplementary Bibliography," will provide a basis for continued research, discussion, and experimentation in the field which has meant so much to me through the years.

Ruth Halle Rowen

New York City

INTRODUCTION

*A*CCORDING TO modern conceptions, chamber music is instrumental music of an intimate, carefully balanced type, written for one or more instruments, one of which, at least, is a melodic instrument. Each part is performed by only one player.

Although the size of the concert room is a factor, "intimacy" refers primarily to the small number of performers, and to the manner of equating their parts so that no one instrument in the combination overpowers the others. To insure intimacy chamber style demands the presence of at least one melodic instrument, a species capable of more tonal delicacy than the chordal instrument. Latent within a chordal instrument like the piano is its ability to summon sufficient power to substitute for an orchestra. Hence, a composition for a single melodic instrument such as an unaccompanied violin belongs within chamber music, while one for a solo keyboard instrument does not.

This conception would have been disputed by mid-eighteenth-century theorists, whose notion of chamber music included intimate vocal as well as instrumental compositions. Their sense of chamber balance was somewhat different from our own, in that they recognized the practice of permitting one or more parts to dominate the remainder, and sanctioned the custom of doubling some parts in performance. It is the intention of this essay to focus upon that body of music from approximately 1600 to the early 1760s, which leads up to the establishment of our modern idea of chamber style.

The emergence of chamber music may be perceived best by first segregating the various elements which subsequently were consolidated into the so-called "classical" chamber style. In the initial period, during which the thorough bass was widely utilized, chamber music was differentiated according to medium, function, disposition and attributes of the instruments, fashion of composition, and solo instrumentation. Later, with the disappearance of the thorough bass, the integration of these elements culminated in the classical chamber style. The purpose of this book is to trace the rise and development of instrumental chamber style up to the point where it assumed definitively classical characteristics.

I: RELATIONSHIP OF STYLES

CONTRAST OF THE INSTRUMENTAL AND VOCAL MEDIUMS

*T*HROUGHOUT the vast Italian polyphonic literature of the sixteenth century the prevalence of the inscription "for voices or instruments" is proof of a deeply rooted reluctance to segregate the vocal from the instrumental medium. Performers of ensemble music were at liberty to make their own choice, which no doubt depended in part upon whether voices, instruments, or a mixture of the two were available. Although written directives of a more specific nature were rare during this period, Sylvestro Ganassi in his *Regola Rubertina* (1542) devoted a chapter to the procedure involved in transcribing vocal compositions for an ensemble of viols.[1] Similarly, Philippe de Monte, in the preface to his fifteenth book of five-part madrigals (Venice, 1592), declared that the works contained therein would also sound well on viole da gamba.[2] About the turn of the century the performance of vocal works instrumentally, as well as the composition of instrumental introductions and interludes to vocal works, motivated the crystallization of an independent instrumental ensemble style from which chamber music evolved.

Within the confines of pure instrumental music (i.e., music designed in the first place for instruments, not for voices), an analogous latitude was offered the performer in that the choice of specific instruments was left to his discretion. In Germany, however, composers were apt to specify their preference although they did not insist upon it. While Valentin Colerus in 1605 was content simply to advise the use of stringed instruments, Valentine Haussman, a year earlier, explicitly recommended the use of viols. Thus also Zacharias Füllsack and Christian Hildebrand published in Hamburg a collection containing many English compositions, entitled *Selected Pavanes and Galliards, for Five Parts, to Be Played on All Sorts of Instruments, and Especially on Viols* (1607).[3]

By the eighteenth century the instrumental medium per se was well clarified in the Italian and German mind, but the French persisted in

---

[1] Sylvestro Ganassi, *Regola Rubertina (1542)*, facsim. ed. Max Schneider (Leipzig, 1924), pp. 12–14.

[2] Otto Kinkeldey, *Orgel und Klavier in der Musik des 16. Jahrhunderts* (Leipzig, 1910), p. 182, note.

[3] *Ausserlesene Paduanen und Galliarden, zu 5 Stimmen, auff allerlei Instrumenten, und insonderheit auf Fiolen zu gebrauchen.*

leaning on vocal music to justify music with instruments. Sébastien de Brossard, for example, argued that instruments were invented either to imitate the voice artificially, to supplement its shortcomings, or to accompany and support it.[4] For several decades pure instrumental music was regarded with suspicion, curiously enough, because of its purity; because it could be manipulated, if the composer so desired, as an abstract idiom, complete and consistent within itself. The composer need no longer lean upon the "reproduction" or "imitation of nature," and this was a stage prop which the French were rather reluctant to discard. When verbal images were lacking, they favored music which incorporated imitative and picturesque effects, or music dependent on attitudes of the dance. Only toward 1750 was it generally granted that sentiment could be expressed in music without words. Instrumental music was centuries old before French aesthetes and philosophers recognized it as a separate language.[5]

In Germany, on the other hand, pure instrumental music had made such advances that its qualifying characteristics, in contrast to those of vocal music, were ripe for theoretical discussion by the time Mattheson wrote *Der vollkommene Kapellmeister* (1739). Mattheson listed seventeen distinctions between the two, headed by the observation that instrumental melody, "the young daughter," had more fire and freedom than vocal melody, "the serious mother." As opposed to vocal melody, instrumental melody was more choppy and punctuated in character; a fact attributable to its wider range which tended to promote extensive runs and leaps, and to its greater propensity toward dotted rhythms. "If the French," he wrote, "whom I consider, because of their inborn liveliness, great masters of instrumental music, would give up dots after notes, they would be like cooks without salt. Nevertheless, it is certain that such sharpened and pointed rhythms, beautiful and vigorous as they are with instruments, would seldom have an adequate effect in the throat of a singer." [6] The rhythm of an instrumental melody was closely associated with dance music more often than that of a vocal melody. Instrumental music, relying on pure and abstract sound, needed to adhere to a "geometrical" dance pattern more than vocal music, which derived its affective expression from the words.

Furthermore, Mattheson remarked that although the vocalist easily could sing in any key, the instrumentalist was restricted. Such a limita-

4 Sébastien de Brossard, *Dictionnaire de musique* (Paris, 1705), p. 223.
5 Lionel de la Laurencie, *L'École française de violon de Lully à Viotti* (Paris, 1922–1924), III, 191, 197.
6 Johann Mattheson, *Der vollkommene Kapellmeister* (Hamburg, 1739), p. 206.

tion was apparent in works like "fugues, counterpoints and canons," originally used for the instruction of boy vocalists, but by his time also adopted by instrumentalists. Works specifically designated for instruments included, among others, "the partite and other artistic works for the clavier; the corrente and gige for the violin; the so-called *subjecte* for the viola da gamba; the solos for the flute, and so forth." [7]

Mattheson, whose observations provide a concise background for an inquiry into the nature of eighteenth-century instrumental music, enumerated enough types of composition to indicate that the instrumental medium had already made its way. After devoting a chapter to the differences between vocal and instrumental melody, in the next chapter he summarized as follows: "In instrumental writing everything must be observed that the art of composition demands from vocal melodies, nay, often even more." [8] This sentence is the key to the relation between the two genres. Instrumental music could not ignore the vocal; rather, instrumental music was supposed to interpret the rules of vocal music on a broader scale.

In the course of time the two styles became more and more specialized, until each had its own supporters. As Charles Burney noted: "We never heard of Corelli, Geminiani, or Tartini attempting vocal melody, and the Music merely instrumental of the greatest vocal composers is often meagre, common, and insipid. There are limits set to the powers of every artist, and however universal his genius, life is too short for universal application." [9]

The same view was reflected in a letter from Italy written by Charles de Brosses, the first president of the parliament of Burgundy, to M. de Maleteste, adviser to the parliament of Dijon. "Tartini also complained," reported de Brosses, "of another abuse, that composers of instrumental music want to have a hand in writing vocal music, and vice versa. 'These two species,' he said to me, 'are so different, that what is proper for one, can hardly be proper for the other; each one must confine oneself to one's talent. I have,' he said, 'been solicited to compose for the theaters of Venice, and I never wanted to do it, knowing well that a gullet is not the neck of a violin. Vivaldi, who wanted to write in both genres, has always been hissed in one while he succeeded very well in the other.' " [10]

For Tartini the separation of the genres was so marked that he ex-

---

[7] *Ibid.*, p. 207.   [8] *Ibid.*, p. 223.
[9] Charles Burney, *A General History of Music* (London, 1776–1789), III, ix.
[10] Le Président de Brosses, *Lettres familières écrites d'Italie en 1739 et 1740* (Paris, 1858), II, 360 f.

pected a composer to choose primarily one or the other. An instrumental style from which chamber music could take its course had already been initiated.

FUNCTION OF MUSIC IN THE CHAMBER, CHURCH, AND THEATER

The early seventeenth-century musician held that music fulfilled three primary functions: to induce the listener toward worship in the church, to stir his emotions in the theater, and to entertain him in his private chamber. Since instrumental ensembles were employed in all three connections, it is evident that the theater and church as well as the chamber exerted an influence upon the development of an over-all instrumental ensemble style, and it is further evident that style was not an entirely autonomous factor, but a variable dependent, to a degree, upon the place of performance.

Whether chamber music was performed in the private salons of the landed gentry or in the public meeting places of the ordinary man, the relative restriction in the size of the room as compared with a church or a theater provided the composer with certain advantages which he was quick to exploit. His acoustical problems, for one thing, were considerably simplified in the sense that he did not have to concern himself with the possible echoes and the unpredictable reverberations of a church or a theater. He could deal with fleeting subtleties instead of broadly sculptured gestures, with no fear that his nuances of line or harmony would blur or be entirely swallowed by the acoustics of a large auditorium. Forkel cautioned the composer that church and chamber demanded a different approach to the handling of modulation. The practice of staying close to the tonic key and modulating out of it only with deliberation made good sense when a goodly number of performers were involved, and where the place of performance was a spacious building, like a church, where the large volume of sound dies away slowly. But such deliberation and conservatism in chamber music, far from indicating the composer's wisdom, might constitute proof of his mental poverty.[11]

Furthermore, the size of the room was a consideration—for Quantz, the first consideration—in the selection of a program. "In the choice of pieces," he advised, "a flutist, or any concert artist, must be guided not only by himself, his skill and his capacity, but also by the place where he plays, the accompaniment that assists him, the circumstances

---

[11] Johann Nikolaus Forkel, *Johann Sebastian Bach, His Life, Art, and Work* [*Über J. S. Bachs Leben, Kunst, und Kunstwerke,* 1802], trans. Charles Sanford Terry (London, 1920), p. 78.

under which he plays, and the listeners before whom he wishes to perform." The type of concerto one chose and the tempo at which one
performed it depended upon room size. As opposed to the kind of
concerto that was suitable for "a large place, where there is great
resonance, and where the accompanying instruments are very numerous . . . in a small room, where there are few instruments for
accompaniment, one may play concertos that have a *galant* and lively
melody and in which the harmony changes more quickly than by half
or whole measures. These concertos may be played faster than the
others." [12] .The demand for greater harmonic subtlety, greater fre-
quency of modulation in chamber music, was voiced by many writers;
and the performer was also continually enjoined to control his tone,
and to suit the level of his dynamics (loud and soft) in accordance with
the size of the audience and the nature of the place.

The furnishings of the room set aside for chamber music varied, of
course, with the taste, the income, and the social status of its owner.
But while the academic burgher often furnished his own relatively
modest chamber music room, and even the ordinary citizen had access
to small instrumental ensembles in the coffee house, the majority of
theorists make it clear that chamber music was envisioned amid aristocratic, not middle-class surroundings.

Johann Gottfried Walther in his *Musicalisches Lexicon* (1732) defined
Cammer-Music as "that which is usually performed in the apartments
of the great nobility." [13] These words were repeated almost verbatim
in the *Tractatus musicus compositorio-practicus* of Meinrado Spiess
(1745).[14] The word "chamber" itself referred generally to the men
responsible for the administration of a princely residence. Musical
affairs at the court were in the hands of a director who had under him
a body of chamber musicians, both performers and composers. The
director was entrusted with choosing the music to be performed, although it was generally assumed that he would favor his own work.
His position in chamber music was a strategic one; yet his status in the
aristocratic household was that of a domestic. Hawkins reveals this
status clearly in his account of how Giuseppe San Martini, a most
celebrated instrumentalist, fortunate enough to make contact with the
Prince of Wales, "was at length received into his family upon the footing
of a domestic, and appointed master or director of the chamber music

[12] Johann Joachim Quantz, *Versuch einer Anweisung die Flöte traversiere zu spielen*
(*1752*), reprint ed. A. Schering (Leipzig, 1906), chap. xvi, pars. 17–19.
[13] Johann Gottfried Walther, *Musicalisches Lexicon* (Leipzig, 1732), p. 130.
[14] R. P. Meinrado Spiess, *Tractatus musicus compositorio-practicus* (Augsburg,
1745), p. 161.

to his royal highness. In the course of this employment he composed a great number of Sonatas for the practice of the chamber." [15]

The "noble" background of chamber music persisted into the nineteenth century. Koch said rather bluntly in his *Lexikon* (1802): "Chamber music is in the real sense of the word, such music as is only customary in courts, and to which, since it is merely arranged for the private entertainment of the reigning prince, no one without special permission is allowed entrance as an auditor." [16] He continued with a graphic description of chamber music, as contrasted with church music and opera, in which the musical consequences of this limitation of audience and auditorium are indicated:

Since in chamber music the art was never especially directed towards expressing religious emotions as in the church, or moral emotions as in opera, but was intended only to serve the private pleasures of the reigning prince or of the court, and since, besides, it is only performed in a room and with one player to each part, the result of all these circumstances was that the older composers took greater pains with the art products for the chamber, nuanced them more finely, and assumed on the part of the performer greater technical finish than they considered appropriate in compositions for the church, or for the theater, partly on account of the size of the building, partly also on account of the larger number of performers for each part, etc. They imitated (so to speak) the painter who shades more finely and colors in greater detail a painting intended to be viewed from close by, than, for example, a ceiling painting which is far from the eye and in which not only would these nuances be lost, but also the effect of the whole be weakened. The composers treated the works intended for the chamber in a similar manner, and thus this type of composition achieved its own character, which is still indicated by the term chamber style.[17]

Nevertheless, even in the eighteenth century, chamber music reached other than aristocratic audiences. In spite of the fact that the citizen class was not generally invited to the halls of the nobility, the comparatively small expense of chamber performance made it possible for the ordinary music lover to enjoy such entertainment either at home, or in coffee houses and other rooms open to the public. Giorgio Antoniotto, before discussing private performances in Italy, related that elsewhere in Europe public chamber concerts flourished:

The simple instrumental chamber music comprehends all sorts of instrumental music, and sometimes intermixed with some favourite air or song of some opera; and this happens in almost all the countries of *Europe,* and it is often performed in public assemblies; excepting in *Italy,* where all sorts of chamber

[15] John Hawkins, *A General History of the Science and Practice of Music* (London, 1776), V; 370.

[16] Heinrich Christoph Koch, *Musikalisches Lexikon* (Frankfort on the Main, 1802), p. 820 f.   [17] *Ibid.,* p. 821.

music are performed in private, and in those particular assemblies of young
gentlemen, where the instrumental music is practised for pleasure and for
practice, every one who is capable of composing, exposes their musical compositions, which are almost all composed for the violino, flute, or oboe solo,
or in concertos with a principal instrumental part accompanied by the other
instruments.[18]

Only rarely did writers refer to public performances of chamber
music. It is interesting that while Antoniotto acknowledged the existence of public chamber concerts elsewhere, he noted that in Italy there
were no performances of this sort. This, coupled with his association
of Italian chamber practice with gentlemen of high social standing,
casts a significant light upon the Italian outlook. In Germany, when
native writers mentioned performances in public buildings, they did
not specifically designate them as chamber performances. Yet chamber
music was undoubtedly performed in public, particularly at student
gatherings modeled after the *collegium musicum* of Johann Friedrich
Fasch. In his autobiography published by Marpurg, Fasch tells about his
meetings, formed after he left the Leipzig Thomas-Schule, where he
studied under Kuhnau from 1701 to 1707. "I established a *collegium
musicum* in my lodgings on Sundays, after the ending of the Holy
Service. More and more students gradually came until there were twenty
persons." [19] It was probably the confined space of his dwelling and the
desire for monetary advancement that caused Fasch to look around for
a roomier and more lucrative place. Johann Adam Hiller apologized, in
retrospect, for Fasch's choice of location:

And what would that be, if not a coffee house? These houses were long the
sanctuary of music in Leipzig. Therefore Fasch deserves no blame for moving
his concert or *collegium musicum* (as it was then called) to the Lehmann coffee
house. He had the satisfaction of seeing it grow ever stronger, and his reputation grew with his concerts; so that, if the students had to serenade an incoming
chief chaplain to a prince, or wanted to celebrate the birthday of a burgomaster,
Fasch composed the music and his *collegium musicum* performed it.[20]

More intangible and perhaps more important than simply the phys-
ical characteristics of the hall and its social setting were considerations
involving the style of the music. A small room, in itself, did not automatically endow a work performed in it with the characteristics of
chamber style; nor, conversely, did bona fide chamber music lose its

[18] Giorgio Antoniotto, *L'Arte Armonica; or, A Treatise on the Composition of
Musick* (London, 1760), p. 109.
[19] Friedrich Wilhelm Marpurg, *Historisch-kritische Beyträge zur Aufnahme der
Musik* (Berlin, 1754), III, 125.
[20] Johann Adam Hiller, *Lebensbeschreibungen berühmter Musikgelehrten und
Tonkünstler neurer Zeit* (Leipzig, 1784), p. 60.

identity when performed in places other than the chamber. Mattheson was well aware of this:

It must not be supposed that the word church is used here only with respect to the mere place and the time, in classifying the type of writing; the true meaning lies elsewhere entirely, namely in the purpose of the divine service itself, in the spiritual rites and in the real devotion or edification, not in the building or the walls of the temple: for, where God's word is taught and heard, be it sung or spoken, there is indisputably God's house. When Paul preached in Athens, the stage was his church.

Similarly with the theater and the chamber: neither place nor time comes especially into consideration here. A sacred piece as well as a *Tafel-Concert* [21] can be performed in a hall. Therefore it is good to identify the chamber style by means of the adjective "domestic," whenever moral customs and matters are the objectives. In the same sense, the moralist Sirach is called a domestic tutor; not on account of the domiciles [where he taught], nor the time and place, but on account of the particular or private instruction in good breeding and manners.[22]

Mattheson carried his argument to the point of insisting that a mere change in place of performance could not alter the essential style of a composition. He instanced Corelli, whom he considered the "incomparable" master of instrumental chamber music, whose chamber sonatas he heard with great enjoyment performed by an organist and a group of violins in a church in Holland during vespers.[23] In discussing this church performance, Mattheson still continued to treat specifically of *Kammer-Styl*.

In general, the attributes which identified chamber style by contrast to the musical styles of church and opera were, as Spiess enumerated them, fluency, delicacy, charm, and balance.[24] As Scheibe observed, "The ultimate purpose of the chamber style is above all, to delight and enliven the auditors. It [this style] is thus used for splendor, joy and laughter. . . . From this can be determined the general character of chamber music. It must be above all lively and penetrating." [25]

According to Mattheson, the chamber style embraced several categories, the *Symphoniacus Stylus, Stylus Madrigalescus, Melismaticus Stylus, Canonicus Stylus,* and *Choraicus Stylus*. Species dealing with instrumental music in particular were the *Choraicus Stylus* and the *Symphoniacus Stylus*. The *Choraicus Stylus,* deriving its name from *chorus,* Latin for a group dance in a ring, included the dances of various nations, France, Italy, Scotland, England, Poland, and Germany.

21 *Tafelmusik* or *Musique de Table,* music played at mealtime to entertain the nobility, limited the function of chamber music to a specific purpose.
22 Mattheson, *op. cit.,* p. 69.   23 *Ibid.,* p. 91.   24 Spiess, *op. cit.,* p. 162.
25 Johann Adolph Scheibe, *Critischer Musikus* (Leipzig, 1745), I, 379.

There were as many facets to the choraic style as there were types of dances in rooms, salons, and large halls.[26]

Mattheson dealt with the *Symphoniacus Stylus* at length because he thought it was one of the most important in chamber music. In *Das neu-eröffnete Orchestre* he asserted: "*Symphonie, Simphonia* means in general all that sounds together, but in particular it means a composition that is played on instruments alone. In this type of composition a composer has complete freedom and is not bound to any number or grouping of performers, but may choose as many and whichever he pleases according to his own taste. However, no formless chaos should result." [27]

He amplified this vague definition in his *Beschützte Orchestre,* where the symphony as a type of composition came under the heading of *Symphoniacus Stylus* along with the concerto grosso, overture, sonata, and suite. To the *Symphoniacus Stylus*

belong the allemandes, etc., for the clavier, lute, viola da gamba, violin, etc., the courantes, sarabandes, gavottes, gigues, etc., in a word, all suites, whether for many instruments or few. If they are for few instruments and consist of solos, they belong to the *Stylus Phantasticus,* which is here subordinate to the *Symphoniacus.* . . . The above-mentioned dance-types which are counted among the *Stylus Symphoniacus* are artistically elaborated and may not really be used for dancing. They have perhaps only the tempo of the above-mentioned dances but are far nobler than the dance. An allemande for dancing and one for playing are as different as heaven and earth, and so are the other dances, except the sarabandes which are only slightly different.[28]

The subdivision of the *Stylus Symphoniacus* called *Stylus Phantasticus,* in its restriction to a small number of instruments, coincides with the notion that chamber music has one instrument to a part. As early as 1650 Athanasius Kircher had described a *Stylus Phantasticus* along with the other types later listed by Mattheson. The source from which Mattheson derived his observations is plain. According to Kircher, "The *Phantasticus Stylus* apt for instruments is the most free and un- fettered method of composing. It is bound in no ways, neither by words nor by a cantus firmus [*subiecto harmonico*] [29] and is arranged to show ingenuity and to teach the inherent logic of harmony, the inventiveness of harmonic cadences, and fugal technique. It is divided into types commonly called *fantasias, ricercari, toccatas, sonatas.*" [30]

[26] Mattheson, *op. cit.,* p. 92.

[27] Johann Mattheson, *Das neu-eröffnete Orchestre* (Hamburg, 1713), p. 171.

[28] Johann Mattheson, *Das beschützte Orchestre* (Hamburg, 1717), p. 137 f.

[29] Cf. Erich Katz, *Die musikalischen Stilbegriffe des 17. Jahrhunderts* (Freiburg, 1926), p. 45.

[30] Athanasius Kircher, *Musurgia universalis sive ars magna consoni et dissoni* (Rome, 1650), I, 585.

Mattheson also referred to the grace of the cadences in the *Stylus Phantasticus* as one way in which to distinguish that style from the *Stylus Symphoniacus* in general. The latter had no "dexterity and elegance" in the cadences.[31] Besides, Mattheson discussed the characteristics of the instruments that played a part in the *Stylus Symphoniacus*. To each instrument he attributed its own effect and for each there was a subdivision under this style. "The violin style is usually somewhat fresh. The flute, especially the transverse flute style is sad and melancholy." [32]

Even though Mattheson's inclusion of dances both in the choraic and symphonic styles might at first appear inconsistent, his line of reasoning is secure. It must be remembered that the *Stylus Choraicus* involved actual dancing, while the dances associated with the *Stylus Symphoniacus* were abstract, conceived without reference to dancers. Among the abstract instrumental dances were allemandes, courantes, sarabandes, and gigues, which, beginning in the late sixteenth century, were grouped into suites.

Minuets, passepieds, gavottes, bourrées, rigaudons, and numerous other dances were introduced to the suite in the course of the seventeenth century. Most significant is the minuet, which still persists in chamber music under its old title. Sébastien de Brossard outlined the pattern of the minuet, a

very gay dance, which originally comes to us from Poitou. One should, in imitation of the Italians, use the sign $\frac{3}{8}$ or $\frac{6}{8}$ to mark the movement, which is always very gay and very lively, but the usage of marking it by a simple 3 or triplet of black notes has prevailed. The melody of that dance ordinarily has two periods which are each played twice. The first has 4 or at most 8 measures of which the last should fall on the dominant, or at least on the mediant of the mode, and never on the finale, unless it be a rondo. The second period is ordinarily eight measures long of which the last should fall on the final of the mode, and is a dotted white note or a whole measure.[33]

Mattheson confirmed this origin and definition of the minuet, although he did not support Brossard in limiting the key patterns at the end of the first period.[34] He seemed to foresee the manifold designs of the Haydn minuets, which in many cases have a first section ending on the tonic.

On the other hand, the question of modulation was ignored completely by Jean le Rond d'Alembert who in 1752 summarized Rameau's work. The only new feature in his definition was the possibility of in-

[31] Mattheson, *Das beschützte Orchestre*, p. 128.   [32] *Ibid.*, p. 117.
[33] Brossard, *op. cit.*, p. 45.
[34] Mattheson, *Das neu-eröffnete Orchestre*, p. 193 f.

creasing the length of the period to twelve measures.[35] D'Alembert classified other dances in relation to the minuet. He called the sarabande a slow minuet and the courante a vigorous sarabande. Moreover, the passepied was a "fast minuet which does not commence with a downbeat, as the ordinary minuet; but which has two periods beginning on the up-beat." [36]

In the second half of the seventeenth century the combination of minuet and trio reflected an affinity which had already developed in France between the gavotte and musette.[37] The musette had three parts with a drone bass performed by a bagpipe. When the musette was brought into the court drawing room, two oboes and a bassoon substituted for the bagpipe, an outdoor, rustic instrument. Translated into chamber music terms, the flavor of the musette's three parts remained in the trio, but with different instrumentation. Thus, the trio sometimes consisted of a simple melody accompanied by a single or double organ point. Throughout the eighteenth century the minuet remained urban and the trio countrified.

The free compositions of the *Symphoniacus Stylus* came to the fore when too much of a diet of "dance pieces without dance" became tiresome. Two types of instrumental introductory movement achieved importance in large works. The French wrote "overtures" and the Italians, "symphonies." Theorists reiterated that the real function of the French overture or the Italian symphony was to introduce an opera or other stage work. Eventually the symphony gained importance in each of the three categories under discussion. Scheibe commented:

Ever since operas in Italy have reached their full bloom, they have been introduced with a type of instrumental piece which is performed before the raising of the curtain. It prepares the listeners for the whole opera in a suitable and meaningful way. These pieces are called symphonies. Not very long ago they were introduced to us in Germany, where I may almost say they have been brought to their greatest perfection. Although they really owe their origin to the opera, they have by no means been confined to it; because of their beauty they have been used not only for all vocal compositions, but also outside of the theater, and even in the church, and besides that without any relation to vocal music, merely alone as ordinary instrumental pieces. They have been thus used in the chamber with more than slight profit and pleasure.

There are really three genres of symphony; they are used, namely, as church pieces, as theatrical and other vocal pieces, and finally also as special purely

[35] J. d'Alembert, *Élémens de musique théorique et pratique suivant les principes de M. Rameau, éclaircis, développés et simplifiés* (Lyon, 1779), p. 209.
[36] *Loc. cit.*
[37] Eric Blom, "The Minuet-Trio," in *Music and Letters,* XXII (1941), 163.

instrumental pieces, not connected with vocal pieces, as I have already re-marked. Thus, there are sacred, theatrical, and chamber symphonies.[38]

A long work, such as an opera, oratorio, or suite, might well demand an instrumental introduction of more than one movement. The manner in which these prefatory movements were assembled at first varied with the French and the Italians. The French overture was based on a slow movement followed by a fast one, a succession championed by Lully, whereas the Italian symphonic pattern, associated with Alessandro Scar-latti, had three movements—fast, slow, fast. These were the fundamental patterns, which the composer, of course, modified in accordance with his plan for the remainder of the work. A symphony before an opera did not necessarily have three movements, even in Italy. It could have one, two, or three movements, depending on how the opera began. Theorists de-plored automatic composition according to the basic overture patterns, complaining that the stereotyped fast, slow, fast succession did not al-ways suit the opera in question.

Sometimes a chamber symphony preceded a vocal work such as a serenata or a cantata. A serenata addressed to a loved one demanded a symphony of a different cast from a cantata written to celebrate the birth-day of a great man. Nor could the composer use the same sort of tech-nique for a chamber symphony as for a theatrical symphony. "In the chamber symphony," advised Scheibe, "one should use more harmonic elaboration, or in general more harmony and more industry and energy. Such a symphony must be more full-voiced and worked out with more artistry than a theatrical symphony. In the former one must give the mid-dle parts more to do and they must be brought into prominence here and there in an especially skillful manner." [39]

In the field of chamber music, symphonies that stood alone, without being attached to a cantata, suite, or other longer work, came to be known as "concert symphonies." The concert symphony derived partly from those opera symphonies which had no reference to the operas which followed, and partly from church symphonies that were musical entities. Burney reports that at Turin, where symphonies were performed in church every morning at the low mass, the priest rendered the service in such a low voice that the instruments drowned him out.[40]

A church symphony, even if self-contained, was more subject to extra-musical influences than a chamber symphony, which was governed al-most entirely by "the fire of the composer" and "his vivacity and genius for inventing, expounding and animating a melody." [41] Yet, in actual

---

[38] Scheibe, *op. cit.*, II, 569 f.   [39] *Ibid.*, II, 620.   [40] Burney, *op. cit.*, p. 62 f.
[41] Scheibe, *op. cit.*, II, 622.

practice, just as the majority of church and opera symphonies had several characteristic designs, so in the concert symphony too, the composer adhered to the basic symphonic patterns. The chamber symphony as a whole could consist of "a lively or fast movement, as well as a slower one, without special division and without repetition of the first part." [42] The individual symphonic movement might either be divided into the two closed sections of a typical suite movement, or progress unbroken until the conclusion. Until well into the eighteenth century, the pattern of the symphony was altered according to its function. One of the principal canons of taste in composition was the success with which the flavor of the music was matched to the locale of performance. Music for the chamber had its own specific requirements out of which evolved technical procedures, tonal and emotional textures, and patterns of design characteristically different from those obtaining either in church or theater music.

[42] *Ibid.,* p. 623.

II: DISPOSITION OF INSTRUMENTS

THOROUGH BASS

*T*HE DISPOSITION of instruments in eighteenth-century chamber music was closely bound to one of the basic practices of the period—the art and science of the thorough bass (*Generalbass, basso continuo*): a term which refers to the lowest part of a composition over which a harmonic skeleton or outline summary of the remaining upper voices was superimposed. This harmonic outline was usually indicated by numerals above each of the important bass notes, showing the intervals to be reckoned upward from the bass. It was a kind of harmonic shorthand which the thorough-bass performers of the period deciphered readily, and usually at sight. Obviously, only a chordal instrument like the harpsichord or a member of the lute family could manage a thorough-bass part, for only such an instrument could render simultaneously the bass line and the harmonies which lay above it. One or more stringed instruments supplemented the chordal instrument in order to reinforce the all-essential bass line. The chordal instrument was usually the harpsichord, less often the organ, clavichord, theorbo, or harp; while the stringed instrument to support the bass line was the viola da gamba, cello or violone.

To understand the components of the thorough bass, it is necessary to take into account the division of instruments into two categories customary at the time. There were instruments which could most readily perform the harmony ("chordal" or "fundamental" instruments), and those which were best suited to performing the melody ("ornamental" instruments). Agostino Agazzari described this classification in *Del suonare sopra il basso con tutti stromenti & uso loro nel concerto,* 1607 (On Playing above the Bass with All Instruments and Their Use in Concert). But we quote from a somewhat later work—the third volume of Michael Praetorius' *Syntagma musicum* (1619)—where Agazzari's trend of thought is amplified and developed.

Omnivoca [multi-voiced], or Fundamental Instruments are those which are able to guide and handle all of the voices or parts of any composition [Praetorius *Gesang;* Agazzari *concerto*], and thus maintain the whole body and complete harmony of all voices or parts, the middle as well as the lower, both in vocal and instrumental music; they are: organs, positives, regals, strong harpsichords with two, three and four stops.

And here may also be added spinets, lutes, theorbos, double-harps, great cithers, lyres, etc., when one uses them as Fundamental Instruments, usually only for soft and intimate music in one, two or three parts. But in vigorous rushing music, [to be played] by many and several persons, it is better to use them as Ornamental Instruments.

Univoca [one-voiced], or Ornamental Instruments are those which are apt to make the harmony lovelier and more sonorous in a composition, as it were, with pleasantry (*schertzando*, as they say in Italian) and counterpoint, as well as to embellish and decorate the composition. They are all simple instruments, which can only produce and conduct a single part, and are divided into wind or stringed instruments; in Italian: *Instrumenti di fiato & Chorde;* in German: wind instruments such as cornets, flutes, trombones, bassoons, etc., and stringed instruments such as violins, etc.

And, as has been said before, to these Ornamental Instruments A. Agazzari also added spinets, lutes, theorbos, etc. (if they are not used as Fundamental Instruments, but only for decoration and padding of the middle parts).[1]

Spinets, lutes, and theorbos appeared in both groups because, notwithstanding the fact that they could play chords, they could also take part in the melodic decoration. As ornamental or melodic instruments they had their own technical and stylistic characteristics, and as fundamental or chordal instruments they performed a duty which was the most distinctive feature of seventeenth- and early eighteenth-century chamber music. Agazzari considered the keyboard instrument, which provided the harmonic framework by playing all the parts, as the backbone of the composition. The simple lines of this harmonic skeleton were reinforced by melodic instruments, each superimposing ornaments on a given part. With regard to the technique of accompaniment then in the process of formation, this method of reinforcement was applied to the bass part in particular. When the accompaniment was entrusted to the fundamental instrument, with melodic instruments participating only in the performance of the bass, the thorough-bass concept was codified.

Looking at it from the vantage point of the historian, the thorough bass embodied two principles contrary to modern ideals of chamber music. In the first place, the thorough bass denied individuality to the inner parts, whereas chamber music now stresses the interplay of all the parts, each carefully delineated and each possessing a measure of independence. Furthermore, the *continuo* bass was doubled and often tripled, whereas in modern chamber music there is only one instrument to a part. Still, in the history of instrumental music, the thorough-bass phase was an inevitable consequence of the disintegration of Renaissance part writing, and after certain elemental musical phenomena (such as chord succession and the relationship of parts in various reg-

[1] Michael Praetorius, *Syntagma musicum*, ed. Eduard Bernoulli (Leipzig, 1916), III, 94 f.

isters) had been realized and exploited, the practice led to a musical literature as rich as it is extensive.

A harmonic approach is prone to regard the inner voices as fillers and to embody the essence of a composition in the two outside voices. During the thorough-bass era this characteristic was carried to its logical conclusion. With the composer concentrating on the construction of the outer parts, any well-trained accompanist was qualified to supply the inner parts extemporaneously. So far as the bass was concerned, the composer used it mainly to establish the key and clarify the modulations, not to unfold an elaborate line. For such a purpose, reinforcement of a simple bass was a better solution than a weak presentation of an ornate bass.

Historically, this slighting of the middle voices had its roots deep in the sixteenth century. The Spanish theorist, Sancta Maria, in his *Arte de Tañer Fantasia*, 1565 (Art of Playing Fantasies) described how four-voice chords were built from the outer voices and were counted from the bass to the soprano.[2] The middle voices served only to accompany and supplement the outer voices. The fact that Sancta Maria called a chord of three, four, or more voices a *consonancia*, in itself showed that for him consonance and dissonance were determined only by the bass and upper voice. A distinction was already being made between main and subsidiary voices, with the position and direction of the main voices governing the course of the others. It now remained for the possible directions in which the subsidiary voices might move, to be codified so that, even when these voices were not written down, the performer could derive them improvisationally with ease.

One of the sources for the extempore playing of harmonies is the *Tratado de glosas sobre clausulas y otros generos de puntos en la musica de violones* (Treatise on the Ornamentation of Cadences and Other Kinds of Notes in the Music for Viola da Gamba) by Diego Ortiz, published at Rome in 1553. Ortiz discussed and illustrated three plans for combining the gamba with the harpsichord. The first scheme, with both players improvising, is not pertinent here. More to the point with regard to reduced emphasis on the middle parts is the second possibility, where an embellished melody was performed on the viol while the harpsichord accompanied by realizing a given bass, and the third method, which consisted of making a condensed score on two staves, of a madrigal, motet, or any other many-voice piece, and playing it on the harpsichord while one of the parts was being performed with ornamental elaborations on

[2] Max Schneider, *Untersuchungen zur Entstehungsgeschichte des Basso continuo und seiner Bezifferung* (Leipzig, 1917), p. 44, note.

the viol. In the third type the accompaniment was written out, whereas in the second it was improvised. The solo part in both cases had the flavor of a written-out improvisation.

Still another source for harmonic improvisation stemmed from sixteenth-century lute music. When lutenists tried to reproduce vocal polyphony, because of the very nature of their instrument, the music had to be altered. Although successive imitative entrances could be delineated, complete independence of parts could not be retained throughout the entire composition. In lute reproductions the melody-bearing voice was in the highest register, and the remaining voices were reduced to a chordal, quasi-polyphonic wickerwork. Since essentially the lutenist had to fake if he wanted to represent a full polyphonic composition on his stringed instrument, the practice arose whereby the first lute, playing the treble, was accompanied by a second lute which supplied the harmonic framework in a given rhythmic pattern.[3] Thus the lute, while consolidating contrapuntal pieces into a harmonic expression, reduced the rank of the inner parts.

The third source, and probably the principal one, for accompanying over a given bass, came from the disputed field of instrumental accompaniment during the so-called "a cappella era." While accompanying a many-voice composition, the organist had before him the vocal basses written on staves one above the other, with the notes placed so that the staves could be read simultaneously. For instance, in the case of an eight-part double-choir motet with two bass voices, one bass was put directly over the other in the organ part. The earliest printed organ basses appeared with the eight-part motets of Giovanni Croce (1594) and the eight-part Concerti ecclesiastici of Adriano Banchieri (1595). When compositions had three choirs, three basses were given in the organ part.[4] As he read, the organist played the note which was momentarily the lowest tone of the combined basses. Hypothetically, the next move was for the organist to work out the bass line beforehand by writing this "general bass" on one staff.

Aid toward deducing the right hand of the organ part, although infrequent, was sometimes supplied. In a composition for many choirs, in those places where all but one choir was silent, instead of wasting the space on one of the staves of the organ part by putting rests there, both staves occasionally were utilized by quoting the soprano, as well as the bass, of the choir in use. Or else, when a section of a work for multiple

[3] Ernst Ferand, Die Improvisation in der Musik (Zürich, 1938), p. 378.

[4] Otto Kinkeldey, Orgel und Klavier in der Musik des 16. Jahrhunderts (Leipzig, 1910), p. 201.

choirs called for only one choir, the four voices of the choir were at times written as a score for the organist. There are also rare examples where a full eight-voice score was printed.[5]

When only the soprano and the bass appeared in an abbreviated score, the placement was comparable to the German organ tablatures of the fifteenth and sixteenth centuries. Contrary to our modern scores, the voices in these tablatures did not ascend in order from the lowest voice at the bottom of the page to the highest voice on top. Instead, in the old German organ tablature, the discant (or highest voice) was noted on a staff on top of the page; immediately beneath it lay the bass, written in letters; and under these two voices were the alto and tenor, also in letters. This organization of the organ tablature corresponded to the customary order of the voices in the choir books in Germany, Italy, and Spain, where the discant and bass were on the left side of the page, while the alto and tenor were on the right. From the notation of the bass directly under the discant, a thorough-bass practice may be implied if one assumes that the organist concentrated above all on these two voices. In fashioning the harmony he relied much more heavily on the outer than the inner voices.[6] It is the same principle as was mentioned above; the outer voices were definitive. Without the soprano voice or some other guide, such as numerals, the problem of reconstructing the harmony even from a composite, prepared organ bass must have been perplexing.

Actually, the Italian and French organ tablatures were not so clumsy as those in Germany. In Italy and France keyboard compositions were notated with all the voices compressed to occupy two staves in a manner similar to our piano scores today. However, since the organist in the late sixteenth century was often confronted with choir books or even vocal part books when he was called on to accompany, he felt the need for a short-cut method, quicker and more convenient than constructing a separate organ tablature for each vocal composition. Ludovico Viadana in his *Cento Concerti Ecclesiastici, a Una, a Due, A Tre, & Quatro Voci. Con il Basso continuo per Sonar nell'Organo* (1602) looked to the principle of the earlier organ basses in an attempt to simplify performance with voices and organ accompaniment. In the preface to this work, Viadana explained that he wrote these concertos for performance by varying combinations of vocalists and the thorough bass, since a full complement of singers was not always on hand. With the earlier organ basses the entire quota of singers had to be present nonetheless, but with Viadana's system the keyboard instrument was qualified to make up for a deficiency in the vocal parts. "Anyone who might want to sing this sort of music without

---

[5] *Ibid.*, p. 198. [6] *Ibid.*, p. 190.

organ or clavier," wrote Viadana, "will never obtain a good effect; on the contrary, for the most part dissonances will be heard." [7]

Reasons for welcoming the thorough bass began to accumulate. The central sphere of influence was Rome where theorists and composers alike participated in the creation of the *basso continuo*. In 1597, the year that Viadana made the acquaintance of Agazzari in Rome, Caccini and Peri were also working in that city. Perhaps Caccini and Peri knew of Viadana's work in advance of its publication in 1602: a plausible possibility since Viadana asserts, in his preface, that he had composed his concertos five or six years prior to their appearance in print. Agazzari, drawing from sources in addition to the *Concerti ecclesiastici* of Viadana, presented three reasons why musicians accompanied from a bass. The first was the monodic style. Since one or few voices were used, in contrast to the old contrapuntal compositions with many voices, neither a score nor tablature was necessary; a figured bass could suffice. Secondly, when the keyboard player relied only upon the tablature, he had trouble in trying to follow so many parts at once. Thirdly, a simple matter of space: should an organist desire complete compositions he "would need a larger library than a Doctor of Laws." [8]

At first the Germans, French, and English were all wary of the Italian *basso continuo*. When the figured bass reached southern Germany shortly after it appeared in Italy, German suite composers disdained it as an unnecessary adjunct to music with independent parts. Yet, four years after Hermann Schein wrote the suite collection *Banchetto musicale* (1617), for four and five real parts,[9] Samuel Scheidt composed dances for the same number of parts with the addition of a figured *basso continuo*.[10] On German soil, Gaspard Vincent, a French organist, published the third volume of Abraham Schadaeus's *Promptuarium musicum* (Speyer, 1613), a collection of motets with thorough bass, and added figured basses of his own, to Lasso's *Magnum opus musicum* (Würzburg, 1625). In general, however, the use of the thorough bass was as unappealing to the French on their home territory as it was to the English. Richard Deering, an English composer, supplemented his *Cantiones sacrae* for five voices with a figured bass part for organ. But the work was published by Phalèse in Antwerp (1617), and Deering, moreover, was educated in Italy. Such instances of early English interest in thorough bass are isolated and

---

[7] Schneider, *op. cit.*, p. 8.

[8] F. T. Arnold, *The Art of Accompaniment from a Thorough-Bass* (London, 1931), p. 73; Kinkeldey, *op. cit.*, p. 221.

[9] *Johann Hermann Schein Sämtliche Werke*, ed. Arthur Prüfer (Leipzig, 1901), Vol. I.

[10] *Samuel Scheidts Werke*, ed. Gottlieb Harms (Hamburg, 1928), Vol. II.

rather premature. More important than the possible influence they exerted was the interest in thorough bass promoted by the English teaching of it in the last quarter of the seventeenth century. Nevertheless, as late as 1728 Roger North still confessed, "the masters never trusted ye organist with his thro base, but composed his part." [11]

TRIO SONATA

Acceptance of the thorough bass was first confirmed in chamber practice by the overwhelming interest shown in the trio sonata, a species of composition characterized by two treble parts, a bass part for one or more bass instruments reinforced by the keyboard *continuo*, and the absence of a written tenor part. (The empty space thus created in the tenor region was to be filled with the chords and passage work of the keyboard *continuo*.) A survey of the works within this frame reveals two types of trio sonata, distinguishable according to the delineation of the bass. Some had a bass line which served only as a harmonic foundation, not as a participant in the melodic activity. With the tenor missing and the bass utilitarian, these trio sonatas concentrated their attention on the two upper parts. Other trio sonatas had all three parts engaged in melodic activity.[12]

The distribution of parts in the trio sonata may be traced to such sources as the vocal *canzonetta* and the instrumental *canzone*. In the mid-sixteenth century, before the *basso continuo* came into being, the union of two high voices and a lower voice was one of several accepted combinations in the composition of *canzonette* for three voices. Annibale Stabile (1591), Paolo Bellasio (1592), Giovanni Maria Nanino (1593), and Adriano Banchieri (1603) often allotted the three voices of their *canzonette* to two sopranos, similarly handled either together or in succession, and a bass.[13]

Transcriptions of *canzonette* for harpsichord and lute were not only improvised, but actually written down. Simone Verovio from 1586 to 1595 published a series of works containing, besides their original vocal setting, a transcription for harpsichord and a second transcription for lute. Kinkeldey reprinted a composition by Felice Anerio from the collection *Diletto spirituale; canzonette a tre et a quattro voci composte da diversi eccelentissimi musici; raccolta da Simone Verovio, intagliate et stampate dal medesimo con l'intavolatura del cimbalo et liuto*, Rome,

[11] Roger North, *The Musicall Gramarian*, ed. Hilda Andrews (London, 1925), p. 28.
[12] See p. 95 f. for the correlation of these types with the *sonata da camera* and *sonata da chiesa*.
[13] Romeo Bartoli, *Composizioni vocali polifoniche a due, tre e quattro voci sole dei secoli XVI e XVII* (Milan, 1917).

1586 (Spiritual Delight; Canzonette for Three and Four Voices Composed by Divers Most Excellent Musicians; collected by Simone Verovio, engraved and printed by the same with tablature for harpsichord and lute).[14] The vocal parts were placed one beneath the other on the left side of the open book. Opposite were the instrumental transcriptions, transposed down a fourth or a fifth for clavier, and then in the original position for lute. Kinkeldey pointed out that, because competent performers could have played on a chordal instrument while reading the vocal parts, the transcriptions must have been made for dilettantes.[15] Comparison with the vocal original reveals the fact that in the clavier transcription a fourth part, a tenor, was added to the two sopranos and bass. Besides, the final chords at cadences were completed and the concluding measures were supplied with notes beyond the bounds of a strict four-voice setting. Obviously, the transcriber felt that the three voices of the vocal *canzonetta* required reinforcement when performed on a clavier. Foreshadowings of the keyboard instrument's role in the thorough bass were already at hand.

Aside from the practice of transcribing an entire *canzonetta* for a chordal instrument, throughout the sixteenth century in Germany as well as in Italy it was the custom to reproduce one or more individual voices of a *canzonetta* on melodic instruments. This usage still obtained in the instructions which J. H. Schein gave for his *Waldliederlein* (1621, 1626, and 1628).[16] These secular songs, designated for two sopranos and a bass, two tenors and a bass, or for soprano, tenor, and bass—the same combinations as were prevalent in the Italian *canzonetta*—might be performed either vocally or with a mixture of voices and instruments.

With regard to the use of instruments in the *canzonetta*, there was a practice more advanced than that of leaving the option to the performer. Certain crossbreed *canzonette* had sections called "ritornelli," which were definitely assigned to instruments. In the preface to his *Scherzi musicali* for three voices (1607) Claudio Monteverdi gives specific instructions for performance of the instrumental ritornello: "Before beginning to sing, the Ritornello should be played twice. The Ritornelli should be played at the end of every stanza, in the sopranos by two violins [*Violini da braccio*], and in the bass by the chitarrone, or harpsichord, or some other similar instrument." [17] So far as the evolution of chamber instrumentation is concerned, the Monteverdi scherzi showed the link between the similar disposition of parts in the vocal and instrumental mediums. If instruments were to perform the vocal sections of a three-voice scherzo,

---

[14] Kinkeldey, *op. cit.*, p. 280.   [15] *Ibid.*, p. 126.   [16] Schein, *op. cit.*, Vol. II.
[17] Claudio Monteverdi, *Tutte le opere*, ed. G. F. Malipiero (Asolo, 1926), Vol. X.

the composition would have trio sonata instrumentation throughout.

In addition to the *canzonetta,* other sources for the distribution of instruments in the trio sonata were the instrumental *canzone* and *ricercare* of the late sixteenth century. The two uppermost parts of *canzone* and *ricercare* often showed the tendency toward interplay in the same register already apparent in the *canzonetta* and soon to be featured in the trio sonata. Whereas in the *canzonetta* composers were not apt to lavish melodic attention on the bass, in the *canzone* and *ricercare* they frequently developed a bass line which rivaled the upper parts in melodic activity. Furthermore, although there was no "tenor part" in the type of *canzonetta* just discussed, tenor lines were present in the *canzone* and *ricercare.* How the tenor lines were obscured during conversion to the trio sonata—how in some cases they were omitted in view of the thorough bass, and how in other cases they were absorbed by the other parts—are processes reserved for discussion until the essential characteristics of the *canzone* and *ricercare* have been noted. Although *canzone* and *ricercare* eventually merged, in an early stage their backgrounds were distinct; the instrumental *canzone* was derived from secular vocal compositions, and the *ricercare* was drawn from the motet.

In spite of a rich vocal literature of their own, the Italians looked toward France for help in modeling the instrumental *canzone.* As instrumental prototypes, Italian vocal compositions were either too barren without the words, or else they relied too heavily on the relation between text and music to abandon the text completely.[18] The *canzonetta,* a source for the distribution of instrumental parts, could not exist as an instrumental composition in its own right because the content of the music was not strong enough to stand alone without the text. Likewise, the madrigal, an important source of influence for the instrumental *canzone,* was too greatly dependent on the words to be completely satisfying without them. On the other hand, in the French chanson the Italians found melodic content with a tendency toward natural formal divisions, a scheme acceptable for instrumental music.

Chansons were transcribed for lute, then for organ and clavier. Attaingnant, the Parisian publisher, printed *Dixneuf Chansons musicales reduictes en la tablature des orgues, espinettes, manicordions, et telz semblables instrumentz musicaulx* (1530). Girolamo Cavazzoni converted *Falt d'argens,* one of the thirty-three French chansons published by Attaingnant in 1529, into an organ *canzone* (1543).[19] Somewhat later the

---

[18] Alfred Einstein, "Zur deutschen Literatur für Viola da Gamba," *Publikationen der Internationalen Musikgesellschaft, Beihefte, Zweite Folge,* I (1905), 9.
[19] Luigi Torchi, *L'arte musicale in Italia* (Milan, 1897–1900), III, 24.

parts of the instrumental *canzone,* originally all played on one organ, were distributed among four melodic instruments. Florentio Maschera in 1584 wrote *canzoni* which may have been for organ, but were possibly conceived for a combination of stringed instruments, a conjecture substantiated by the fact that these *canzoni* were printed in four part books.[20]

A *canzone* had from one to twelve sections, each based on its own motive, meter, and tempo. Some of the sections were repeated immediately, and others were repeated after intervening sections, a fact which Praetorius noted in his discussion of the form. Having described the vocal *canzone,* Praetorius added,

There are also those without text with short fugues and agreeable fantasias, composed for four, five, six, eight, etc., voices. The opening Fuga is mostly repeated at the end as a close: these are also called *canzoni.* Many such beautiful *canzoni* with few and several voices were published in Italy by Giovanni Gabrieli.[21]

Like the *canzone,* the *ricercare* also worked with several motives or themes in turn, but whereas the *canzone* grew up with the organ, the *ricercare* received more nourishment from the lute. Since the lute could not reproduce all the voices of a vocal setting at once, the first *ricercari* were freely founded pieces very much hindered by technical deficiency. In 1536 Luiz Milan, the Spanish lute master, wrote *ricercari* which wavered between three, four, and two parts. A few decades later, composers of Italian *ricercari* for keyboard or stringed instruments clearly differentiated all the parts, tossing imitations from one part to another whenever a new motive appeared. While imitative writing achieved rank as the main characteristic of the *ricercare,* a paradox developed. In vocal music the successive introduction of the voices was often inherently related to the text lines, i.e., when a new line of text appeared, it was logical to couple it with a new motive. However, in instrumental music, this constant change of motive was superfluous. Nevertheless, display of an abundance of themes persisted in the *ricercare.* Instead of the *canzone's* closed sections with changes in meter and tempo, the sections of the *ricercare* often overlapped, with themes of a following phrase starting when the preceding one was not yet finished.

Imitative writing was eventually carried over from the *ricercare* to the *canzone.* Praetorius, who used only one definition for both fugue and *ricercare,*[22] showed the effect of the fugue on the *canzone* in the passage

---

[20] J. W. v. Wasielewski, *Die Violine im XVII Jahrhundert und die Anfänge der Instrumentalkomposition* (Bonn, 1874), p. 5.   [21] Praetorius, *op. cit.,* III, 29.
    [22] *Ibid.,* III, 34.

quoted above. As the *canzone* drew from the *ricercare* and dance music a type of composition with qualities ripe for transference to the trio sonata resulted. From the *ricercare* the newer instrumental *canzone* derived two treble parts in close imitative rapport, and from dance music it contracted a bass part devoted to establishing the harmony. During the period of transition Claudio Merulo wrote a five-part *canzon da sonar* containing passages with two treble instruments imitating each other, sometimes at the unison, and other passages with all the instruments in pure chordal successions, a type of material which might easily be handled by a thorough bass.[23]

As opposed to the effect of imitative writing on the *canzone,* there was also the influence of dance music, where the middle voices were so secondary in importance that a composition could be reconstructed from the outer parts alone. Praetorius indicated the small esteem accorded to the inner parts of dance music in the preface to his *Terpsichore* (1612), a work containing French dances and songs. For most of them only the treble parts were brought to Germany. When only the treble was given, Praetorius added the bass and two or three middle parts and affixed his name to the whole composition. However, when provided with both the cantus and bass, he restored the middle parts, and was content merely to write *Incerti* over the composition.[24] The cantus and bass together were so definitive that referring to the composition as his own would have been misrepresentation. Adding the inner lines was hack work; yet, since the reconstructed parts may not have been exactly what the original composer had in mind, Praetorius called such a composition "of uncertain author."

By two contrasting means, omission and absorption of parts, a *canzone* could be transformed into a trio sonata. Until the end of the seventeenth century prefatory instructions allowed players to leave out one, two, or three middle parts of a composition in which all the parts were noted.[25] It was evident that the deficiency in inner parts was to be recompensed extemporaneously by the accompanist. This practice continued long after the right to do so was indicated in the prefaces. In Sulzer's dictionary of 1792 appears the statement, "The middle voices, which are merely there for the sake of the harmony, may be omitted without mutilating or spoiling the piece; they can in some measure be replaced by the thorough bass." [26]

[23] Hugo Riemann, *Musikgeschichte in Beispielen* (Leipzig, 1912), p. 98.

[24] *Gesamtausgabe der musikalischen Werke von Michael Praetorius,* ed. Günther Oberst (Wolfenbüttel-Berlin, 1929), XV, xi.   [25] See p. 83 f.

[26] Johann George Sulzer, *Allgemeine Theorie der schönen Künste* (Leipzig, 1792–1799), III, 536.

Where the accompanist made amends for the real parts which were omitted, the question arises whether the parts he supplied approximated the original ones, or whether the missing parts lost their individuality to the composite harmony. At first the middle voices retained their identity completely. Viadana's thorough bass was not an improvisational art. The keyboard player filled in with previously determined parts which were supposed to duplicate the relative position of the intervals in the original composition. Viadana explained:

No tablature was made for these concertos, not to avoid the work, but to facilitate their performance by the organist. Not everyone would play from a tablature at sight; the majority would consider it easier to play from a Partitura [an organ bass]. Therefore the organists may make the said tablature at their own convenience, which, to tell the truth, is much better.[27]

In other words, Viadana advised the organist to make a tablature so that he would be sure to add the missing voices correctly. A tablature was necessary for the placement of the intervals since Viadana did not use many figures. The scarcity of numerals caused printers to mistake for flats the sixes scattered here and there in his work.[28] As shown in the above quotation, Viadana, still relying on the composite voices to establish the changing harmonies, claimed that his reason for omitting the construction of a tablature was not based on the desire to save effort. Nevertheless, if the thorough bass was to succeed as a method of abbreviation by eliminating the time consumed in writing down all the notes of the accompaniment, it would have to be more exact in the designation of chords. The solution lay in the use of figures, which were more prevalent by far in the compositions of Peri, Caccini, and Cavalieri in the last years of the sixteenth century than they had been in Viadana's concertos. Cavalieri tried to put the middle parts in their correct register by using double digits from 10 to 18 to make the intervals in the accompaniment correspond exactly to those in the original voices. Thus, he revived the use of compound intervals. Whereas Tinctoris had dealt with every interval to the tridiapason (three octaves) in the middle of the fifteenth century, one century later Zarlino handled only the simple interval (an octave or less). Some forty years later, Cavalieri renewed interest in the compound interval to insure an accurate delineation of his music. For instance, to specify which part was to carry the 4–3 suspension, he wrote 4–3, 11–10, or 18–17. With the use of double digits, the accompanist could be guided toward reproducing the middle voices at the level of pitch conceived by the composer.[29]

[27] Schneider, op. cit., p. 7 f.   [28] Arnold, op. cit., p. 237.
[29] Emilio de' Cavalieri, La rappresentazione di anima, e di corpo (1600), in Prima fioriture del melodramma italiano (Rome, 1912).

After the extinction of double figures as a means for showing the position of compound intervals, the accompaniment could no longer duplicate the composer's intentions. Nevertheless, in an attempt to control the exact placement of notes within the chord, thorough-bass theorists described how the accompaniment should be distributed between the two hands. In 1628 Galeazzo Sabbatini indicated which intervals were to be played by the left hand and which were to be supplied by the right hand.[30] Wolfgang Ebner, in a treatise on the thorough bass, printed in 1653, also provided for dividing the harmony between the hands.[31] Soon the even distribution championed by Sabbatini and Ebner gave way to a practice whereby the left hand played the bass and the right supplied the chords. This method was far from Viadana's suggestion that the organist should prepare a tablature for his own use. Instead of trying to present the intervals of the chords as they would exist in a polyphonic composition, the accompaniment provided the harmonic background for the principal parts, three in number in the case of the trio sonata. The *basso continuo* had developed into an improvisational art in which the inner parts lost their melodic value and were woven into the harmonic fabric.

In the mid-eighteenth century, theorists were concerned with the parts supplied by the keyboard player, not as sovereign members of a polyphonic composition, but as a means of achieving a balanced keyboard style. From this point of view it was advantageous to look upon compound intervals as equivalent to simple intervals. There was no need for trying to place lines in exact registers, since the effect would be lost in the keyboard accompaniment. Saint-Lambert treated only the ninth differently from the second (1707).[32] Johann David Heinichen, speaking of quick notes in the bass, eradicated even this distinction (1728). "When a fast, virtually short note leaps a seventh, ninth, tenth, eleventh, etc., up or down (be it in slow or triple time), nothing new happens, but it is considered to be equivalent to the corresponding interval of a second, third, fourth, etc." [33]

Quantz, realizing that the high figures of Peri and Caccini were outmoded, modernized the rules for the planning of an accompaniment.

It has long been the rule that in the playing of a thorough bass the hands must not be spread too far apart, and consequently the right hand must not be played too high. This rule would be reasonable and good, were it only ob-

[30] Arnold, *op. cit.*, p. 110 ff.   [31] *Ibid.*, p. 132.

[32] Michel de Saint-Lambert, *Nouveau Traité de l'accompagnement du clavecin, de l'orgue, et des autres instruments* (Amsterdam, ca. 1710), p. 7.

[33] Johann David Heinichen, *Der General-Bass in der Composition* (Dresden, 1728), p. 366.

served constantly. For it creates a much better effect to play the accompanying harpsichord parts beneath the main part, than to play them with the upper part, let alone above it. When the old composers wanted the accompaniment an octave higher, instead of the third, fourth, fifth, etc., they set the tenth, eleventh and twelfth over the bass. Since there is no difference between these sets of numbers, just as there is no difference between the second and ninth, their idea is not completely unjustified. For reasons above mentioned, when a cellist plays solo, he is not accompanied in the same manner as a violinist. With the former, everything must be played in the right hand in the low register. If by experience the composer sets the bass too high and it rises over the main part, the bass should be played an octave lower, so that the fifths are not changed to fourths. In acompanying the violin, which has a wide compass of tones, the accompanist must observe whether the violinist plays mostly in the lowest register or the highest, so that he does not carry his right hand above the low tones of the violin; nor is he to remain at too great a distance when the violin ascends to extreme heights.[34]

A skillful accompanist could provide inner parts which, without being independent in a polyphonic sense, would restore a trio sonata to the status of a well-rounded composition.[35] Rules were formulated to show how the middle parts should be conducted to help the upper melody by imitation, introduction of new melodic figures, or supplementary movement in thirds and sixths with the principal parts. The effect of the composition was still to a great degree in the hands of the accompanist, but when the accompanist turned out to be J. S. Bach himself, there was no fear as to the outcome. Johann Friedrich Daube in his *General-Bass in drey Accorden* (1756) described Bach's skill in accompaniment.

Through him the upper part was bound to shine. He gave it life, when it had none, by means of his fundamentally skillful accompaniment. He knew how to imitate it so dexterously either with the right or left hand, or to bring in a counter-subject so unexpectedly, that the listener would swear it was composed thus with all diligence. At the same time the regular accompaniment [realization of the figures] was curtailed very little. In general, his accompaniment was always like a concerted part, worked out most diligently, and set next to the upper part; yet, the upper part was bound to shine at the right time. This privilege was also granted to the bass without disadvantage to the upper part. Enough! Whoever has not heard him, has missed very much.[36]

Diametrically opposed to the omission of parts was the method of converting a *canzone* into a trio sonata by absorption of parts. Within

---

[34] Johann Joachim Quantz, *Versuch einer Anweisung die Flöte traversiere zu spielen (1752)* (Leipzig, 1906), chap. xvii, sec. vi, par. 21.

[35] Carl Philipp Emanuel Bach, *Essay on the True Art of Playing Keyboard Instruments* [*Versuch über die wahre Art das Clavier zu spielen, 1759 and 1762*], trans. and ed. William J. Mitchell (New York, 1948), chap. vi, "Imitation," par. 7.

[36] Johann Friedrich Daube, *General-Bass in drey Accorden* (Leipzig, 1756), p. 204.

the category of trio sonatas for three active parts there is a subdivision in which with three parts the composer tried to give the illusion of four or five. Instead of merely omitting the inner parts in the hopes that the accompanist would improvise suitable melodic activity in the central register, the composer tried to incorporate the essential melodic activity of the middle parts into the three parts remaining in the trio sonata. This process did not involve tacking extra parts on to the basic ones by means of double stops. The absorption of parts under discussion was much more fundamental, reflecting techniques developed in the middle of the sixteenth century.

In their compositions for three and four voices the Netherlanders had discovered the art of camouflaging extra thematic entrances to induce the listener into hearing more voices in action than were actually present. Adrian Willaert reproduced this illusion in his *Fantasie o ricercari* (1549 and 1559).[37] In the *ricercari* for three parts, true to tradition, he exploited one motive or theme after another. After carrying a theme through the various parts, he sometimes introduced a fourth statement in a part which already had its turn. Using a motive or theme four times tended to square off the passage of the theme from voice to voice; coupling of the parts in a three-voice composition gave the effect of a greater quantity of parts. Specifically, in Willaert's ninth *ricercare* the middle part and treble state the theme successively at the interval of a fifth. Then when the bass and same middle part repeat this interval an octave lower, the listener has reason to believe he is hearing a fourth part entering the play. Actually, the middle part performs a dual role.[38]

In other compositions, although the interval of imitation or the order of entrance of the parts was different, the underlying scheme was frequently there. Jachet Buus, in a *ricercare* for four parts (1547) gave the theme successively to the treble, alto, bass, alto again, and then tenor, emphasizing the illusion of five parts by alternately beginning the entrances on either D or G. The alto has slyly presented a second statement of the theme before the tenor gives its first.[39]

In the three- and four-part compositions of the Netherlanders each voice was utilized to its fullest extent; in the four- and five-part compositions of the following generation of Italians and their disciples the potentialities of each voice were not exhausted with such determination. A measure of independence was sapped from the middle parts of an Italian *ricercare* or *canzone* when alto and tenor were allotted the

[37] J. W. v. Wasielewski, *Geschichte der Instrumentalmusik im XVI. Jahrhundert* (Berlin, 1878), p. 122.

[38] Adrian Willaert, *Ricercari a 3 voci*, ed. Hermann Zenck (Mainz and Leipzig, ca. 1933).   [39] Riemann, *op. cit.*, p. 70.

theme in the same register. Alto and then treble announce the theme in a *Ricercar a 4* by Annibale Padovano (1604).[40] After contrasting material has been introduced, the bass presents the theme. There is another intervening episode before the tenor finally enters with its statement. The tenor has been truly slighted, not only because it was ignored for so long, but because its statement is in the register already assigned to the alto at the very head of the composition. It was only a short step from this method of presentation to trio sonata style. After this sort of interruption in the order of imitative entrances, the tenor statement might be played by the alto instrument without discomforting the listener. Thus by enabling one melodic instrument to assume the work of two and by adding a thorough bass, this passage could easily be reorganized in a trio sonata instrumentation.

Biagio Marini's compositions are a pivotal point for the contraction of parts. First he wrote *canzoni*, Op. 8, which showed propensities toward being condensed into trio sonatas; [41] then he wrote trio sonatas which showed the effects of this condensation. The fact that he called a trio sonata with figured bass by the title *Canzone* (Op. 17, 1651), demonstrates how closely allied the sonata and *canzone* were. In the trio *canzone L'ara* there is the coupling of parts which Willaert used a century earlier to give the effect of more parts. The entrances of the theme are in pairs rather than by threes, as one might expect in a trio sonata.[42]

Giovanni Legrenzi in his trio sonata *Rosetta* (1671) [43] had four successive statements of the theme: by the first violin, then the second violin a fourth lower, then the bass in the original key, finally the bass again, this time in the contrasting key. Here the bass took care of a statement of the theme which would have been allotted to the tenor, had there been four parts. The procedure could be more daring than in Willaert's time because of the increase in range of the instrumental parts during the interim. By the middle of the seventeenth century one instrument was capable of covering more than one register in the restricted vocal sense of the sixteenth century.

There were even more striking methods for the absorption of parts than that of telescoping entrances of the theme to fewer voices. In sixteenth-century transcriptions of vocal music for keyboard instruments an instrumental part frequently governed material originally allotted to two or more vocal parts. Andrea Gabrieli based one of his

[40] *Ibid.*, p. 94.
[41] Dora J. Iselin, *Biagio Marini* (Hildburghausen, 1930), p. 6 of examples in back.
[42] Hugo Riemann, *Handbuch der Musikgeschichte* (Leipzig, 1920), II², 145.
[43] J. W. v. Wasielewski, *Instrumentalsätze vom Ende des XVI. bis Ende des XVII. Jahrhunderts* (Berlin, *ca.* 1874), p. 52.

keyboard compositions from the *Canzoni alla francese et ricercari ariosi; tabulate per sonar sopra istromenti da tasti* (1571, reprinted 1605), on Orlando Lasso's five-voice chanson, *Susanne un jour*. (Kinkeldey has greatly facilitated comparison by reprinting both vocal chanson and the keyboard transcription in juxtaposition.[44]) Certain obvious phenomena which occur when voices are transplanted to a keyboard instrument are confirmed here. From time to time one voice or another disappears. Since there is no way of doubling at the unison in a keyboard transcription, when two voices duplicate a note, one voice must be omitted. Similarly, not all the rests in the vocal lines are indicated in the instrumental transcription, because a rest disappears when a voice from another register occupies the space where the rest occurred. When the vocal bass rests, the lowest sounding instrumental part becomes the bass, regardless of which voice contained the notes originally. The bass here, as in the case of the early organ bass, is an accumulation of voices. If the vocal bass is silent it is most natural for the alto *(quinta pars)* and tenor to be contracted into the lowest line. Occasionally, but rarely, a higher voice is assimilated into the bass. The same kind of contraction occurs in the upper register. Where the original vocal soprano rests, in the keyboard transcription lower voices are incorporated upward into a treble line. The essence of the composition is absorbed into its outer limits. In this Gabrieli transcription with all the notes written out as they were intended to be heard, the lines of the middle voices tended to disappear. From here the invitation was extended to the thorough bass, in which the nonessential inner parts were improvised.

In general, an instrumental part in *Susanne un jour* is very often the combination of what were originally two or more vocal parts. The juncture usually comes where one part leaps up or down the interval of a third to pick up the line of another part. When adopted in eighteenth-century German composition, this procedure was called *Brechung*. Johann Mattheson introduced the subject as follows in his *Vollkommene Kapellmeister* (1739):

In today's melodic-harmonic art of setting or composition, even if, for the sake of clarity, fewer different instrumental parts are used than heretofore, still the harmony should retain its right. Therefore the method was introduced whereby three to four sounds are often heard consecutively in a single such part in full, yet broken, chords. For this, four parts would otherwise have been necessary, if they were to be heard on one beat. We call it *Brechen* [to break] when the sounds of a chord are not played at once, but successively.[45]

[44] Kinkeldey, *op. cit.*, pp. 264–274.
[45] Johann Mattheson, *Der vollkommene Kapellmeister* (Hamburg, 1739), p. 352.

Mattheson then discussed various aspects of *Brechung,* from two parts upward. First he showed how a two-part setting might be heard in a single part by means of broken chords. He connected the two parts either by means of a passing note from a note of one part to a note of the other a third away, or by a direct leap from one part to the other. At times, instead of merely alternating the notes of the two parts, he interlarded a slight embellishment. After demonstrating how to break upward from the lower part to the upper, he reversed the process and arpeggiated downward from the upper to the lower.[46]

ILLUSTRATION OF *Brechung* (FROM MATTHESON, *Der vollkommene Kapellmeister,* p. 353. *Corrected according to Mattheson's "Emendanda" in back of book.)

This is a description of the kind of technique that Gabrieli used in transcribing *Susanne un jour* when he contracted two voices into one. Mattheson, incidentally, permitted the quarter to be split, not only into eighths, but also into sixteenths and thirty-seconds. Yet, in spite of the further diminution, the principle of combining two parts remained the same. Next he presented a three-part phrase and gave five ways of contraction by means of broken chords: [47]

1. Bringing the two lower parts into one and leaving the upper part intact
2. Bringing the two upper parts into one and leaving the lower part intact
3. Not changing the middle part; the two others brought together into one
4. Two parts modified to incorporate the third part
5. All three parts incorporated into one

[46] *Ibid.,* p. 353.   [47] *Ibid.,* p. 354 f.

ILLUSTRATION OF *Brechung* (FROM MATTHESON, *Der vollkommene Kapellmeister*, p. 354)

He added that the fifth method, called the "harp way," and known as *arpeggio* in Italian, was widely used. In this sense *arpeggio* is a sub-division of *Brechung*. From three parts Mattheson proceeded to four given parts, which offered six ways of combination.

 1. Bringing the two upper parts into one; the two lower remain unchanged
 2. Three into two so that only the lowest part remains as it was
 3. All four parts broken into three
 4. The three upper into one, and the lower as it was
 5. All four parts into two
 6. All four into one [48]

Paralleling Mattheson's system, it is possible to build up a hypothetical case for the conversion of the four- and five-voice chanson, madrigal, or *canzone* into the three-part trio sonata. In the case of four vocal parts, the most obvious contraction is that of vocal tenor and bass into instrumental bass. For five voices, two transformations are likely. A vocal composition with two sopranos, an alto, a tenor, and a bass might be converted by combining the two soprano voices into the first violin part, transferring the alto intact to the second violin, and uniting the vocal tenor and bass in the instrumental bass. Or else a vocal work for two sopranos, two altos or tenors, and a bass might be turned into a trio sonata by allotting the two soprano lines to the two violins, and the vocal bass line to the instrumental bass. The two middle voices, whether they be altos or tenors, might be assimilated into the outer parts, as Mattheson provided under "method 4" of the rules for three parts, or "method 3" of the rules for four parts.

The reader must be warned that the above patterns have been reached by induction from the available material, which does not include five-part vocal pieces actually transcribed into three-part trio sonatas. The process is further complicated by the fact that the transcriptions of vocal works were made for keyboard instruments, not for a combination of strings. However, since the production of *canzoni* for the organ immediately preceded the composition of *canzoni* for a group of melodic instruments, in the light of the keyboard transcriptions the intervening step to the trio sonata may be implied. When the melodic lines were played by stringed or, at times, wood-wind instruments, the essential parts were brought to prominence, and the nonessential middle parts were left to the keyboard instrument of the thorough bass.

Trio sonatas, derived from the *canzonetta,* chanson, madrigal, and instrumental *canzone,* have been mentioned with and without melodic activity in the bass. In those cases arising from the three-voice *can-*

48 *Ibid.,* p. 355.

zonetta, the trio sonata was conceived without a part in the middle register. Where more voices were involved, either the middle parts were replaced by the improvising keyboard instrument, or they were absorbed into the three basic outer parts, in turn reinforced by the *continuo.* This classification is fortified by the types of composition which Salomone Rossi wrote prior to his trio sonatas. Amadino published Rossi's three-voice *canzonette* (Venice, 1589) and five-voice madrigals (1600, 1602, and 1603) before publishing his first trio sonatas (1607). Since Rossi was a pioneer in the field of the trio sonata, his own earlier works must have influenced him heavily. The title of the five-voice madrigals of 1600 specified that "some of the said madrigals [are] to be sung [to the accompaniment of] the chittarone, with its tablature placed under the soprano." [49] In the title of the second book of madrigals the term *basso continuo* was used rather than the name of the instrument on which it was to be played. The indication that the *continuo* was written under the cantus likewise appears. Thus, these compositions, really solo madrigals with accompaniment, reveal the fact that Rossi was strongly under the spell of the *continuo.* Transference of this preference to his instrumental works was natural.

The trio sonata has been considered as a contraction of voices; it may also be viewed as the result of an expansion of voices. Still another source for the distribution of parts in the trio sonata lies in the addition of parts to one or two given lines. The practice of building up a composition by adding voices to the already existing ones was affirmed by theorists of the sixteenth century, Pietro Aaron (1523), Lusitano (1553), Vicentino (1555), Zarlino (1558), Artusi (1586), Tigrini (1588), and Zacconi (1622). Zarlino in his *Istitutioni harmoniche* wrote a chapter on how to sing a third voice improvisationally to a duo, warning the singer to take notice, not only of one voice, but of both given voices when improvising the third, because various counterpoints might be written to one voice alone. For instance, if only the bass were taken into account, parallel octaves would result when the improviser sang in parallel thirds over the bass while the other given voice was in tenths with the bass. He took a two-voice movement from Josquin Després' six-voice motet, *Benedicta es coelorum regina,* and added two different third voices to the duo, once constructing the third voice between the given soprano and alto, the other time supplying a bass voice for them.[50]

---

[49] Robert Eitner, *Biographisch-bibliographisches Quellen-Lexikon* (Leipzig, 1898), VIII, 326.

[50] Gioseffo Zarlino, *Le istitutioni harmoniche* (Venice, 1558), Part III, chap. lxiv.

A century later, after the thorough bass had already taken hold, English theorists were still concerned with adding voices, a retrospective practice which may indicate that the addition of parts was an influential factor in the formation of the trio sonata. Christopher Simpson in his *Division Violist* (1659), corroborated this belief in his discussion of the two kinds of diminution or division to a "ground," or given bass line. The first type of diminution consists of improvisationally dividing the notes of the ground into notes of smaller value and supplying decorations to beautify the written bass.[51] The second species of diminution, descant diminution, has direct bearing on the subject at hand in that, by means of it a distinct, concordant part is added to the ground. Whereas in breaking the ground the improviser played the notes of the ground at the unison or the octave above or below, in descant diminution the improviser played only above the ground, at any concordant interval. In both types of diminution the performer intermingled discords at his own discretion.[52]

While discussing how two viols might improvise parts above a given bass, Simpson first gave rules on how to compose divisions for two bass viols on a ground, and then added that the rules were also applicable when constructing lines for two treble viols over a given bass:

If you make Division for Two Trebles; Both must be in the way of Descant to the Ground: and when they move in Quick Notes, Both Together; their most usuall passage will be in 3ds or 6ths to One Another; sometimes an intermixture with other Concords; but such, as must still have relation to the Ground. As for their answering One Another; their severall Motions, and Changes, in order to Variety; the same is understood as of the Former.[53]

Simpson's details of construction seem to review the method of expansion on a given voice which resulted in the trio sonata:

Of two Viols Playing together extempore to a Ground. First let the Ground be prick'd down in three several Papers; One for him who Plays upon the Organ or Harpsechord: The other two for them that Play upon the two Viols: which, for order and brevity, we will distinguish by three Letters; viz. A. for Organist, B. for the first Bass, and C. for the second.

Each of these having the same Ground before him, they may all three begin together; A. and B. Playing the Ground; and C. Descanting to it, in slow Notes, or such as may sute the beginning of the Musick: This done, let C. Play the Ground, and B. Descant to it, as the other had done before, but with some little variation. If the Ground consist of two Strains, the like may be done in the second: one Viol still Playing the Ground whilest the other Descants or Divides upon it.

[51] Chr. Simpson, *The Division-Violist; or, An Introduction to the Playing upon a Ground* (London, 1659), p. 21.
[52] *Ibid.*, p. 28.   [53] *Ibid.*, p. 48.

The Ground thus Play'd over, C. may begin again, and Play a Strain of quicker Division: which ended, let B. answer the same with another something like it, but of a little more lofty Ayre: for the better performance whereof, if there be any difference in the Hands or Inventions, I would have the better Invention lead, but the more able hand still follow, that the Musik may not seem to go less in performance but rather increase in the performance.[54]

So far as the addition of parts is concerned, the trio sonata was created by adding a bass line to two given upper parts,[55] or by constructing two upper parts over a given bass.

A subject that remains open for discussion in connection with the disposition of instruments in the trio sonata is the Italian composers' retention of two treble instruments. When the bass had no share in presenting the thematic material, if the composer wanted to have a means of introducing parts treated in fugato as they had appeared in the *canzonetta,* he had to have a second solo instrument to answer the first. He could achieve a greater spirit of contrapuntal homogeneity with two instruments in the same register, such as two violins, than with instruments in different registers, such as one violin and one viola. With regard to strings, the characteristics of the instruments themselves led to the use of two trebles. The violin, a treble instrument, had a broader range of tonal potentialities than the viola, a middle-register instrument for which the upper positions had not yet been developed. There was a drawback in choosing two identical treble instruments because they tended to blend. Nevertheless, contrast could be created by using different melodic or rhythmic material in the two parts. However, to the Italian originators of the trio sonata, preparation for abundant contrast was secondary to the consideration of whether or not they would be able to fuse the tone of the two instruments to achieve a smooth melodic-harmonic effect. They were not so concerned with the second treble's distinctiveness as with its ability to render fleeting passages brilliantly, with a tone superior to that of the viola, an instrument not constructed in direct proportion to its pitch. Violin range was sufficiently extensive so that usually the second violin could be placed in a slightly lower register than the first, despite constant crossing between the two. Besides, while writing duets for two sopranos the Italians had discovered such appealing qualities as the effect of fluid parallel thirds and sixths, which were likewise expressive when transferred to a matched pair of instruments. In contrast to Italian custom, the French did not always use two identical treble instruments.

[54] *Loc. cit.*   [55] See p. 42 f.

Abbé Raguenet observed in his *Comparison between the Italians and French with regard to Music and the Opera* (1702):

If we pass to pieces composed for several parts, what advantages do the Italians have over the French? I have hardly seen musicians in France who are not convinced that the Italians know how to turn and vary a trio better than the French. With us, the first treble ordinarily has enough beauty; but the second cannot maintain this quality in the low register into which they make it descend. In Italy they make the treble three or four tones higher than in France; so that the second trebles thus have a tone high enough to have as much beauty as our first trebles themselves.[56]

Raguenet here admitted the higher range of the Italians' second treble as well as its ability to compete and intermingle with the tone of the first treble. His challenge to the French disposition of parts was answered by Lecerf de la Viéville de Fresneuse. The latter's *Comparison of Italian Music and French Music* (1705) is in a series of dialogues, one of them between a chevalier and a count, Mr. du B., who dissect Raguenet's pamphlet line by line. To enlighten the inquisitive count, the chevalier asserts,

It is true . . . that [the Italian] second trebles are higher; whether they are more beautiful remains to be seen. I believe that they are more beautiful if performed separately. I do not agree that they are more beautiful in the trio itself. The first trebles of the Italians squeak because they are too high. Their second trebles have the fault of being too close to the first, and too far from the bass, which is the third part. These are two disagreements. I find it advantageous and profitable to make the second treble into a tenor, as we do—and not another treble as do the Italians—because the tenor occupies the distance between the bass and the treble and thus binds the chords of the trio. Instead, when the second treble is so high, it leaves too much of an interval and space between the first treble and the bass. So that, Mr. le Comte, it is not our fault that the second parts of our trios are only tenors. On the contrary, I maintain that the body of the trio is better off for it.[57]

The Italian usage of two treble instruments in the same register did not reign undisturbed. Both the French and the Germans challenged the Italian practice by replacing the second treble instrument with one in a different register, a procedure which eventually led to the dissolution of the trio sonata.

SOLO SONATA AND DUO

For clarity in classification the trio sonata has just been discussed apart from the solo sonata; but the two are bound together logically

[56] François Raguenet, *Parallèle des Italiens et des François en ce qui regarde la musique et les opéra* (Paris, 1702), p. 51 f.

[57] Lecerf de la Viéville, *Comparaison de la musique italienne et de la musique*

and historically. The trio sonata, comprising two equivalent upper melodic instruments over a thorough bass, emerged in 1607. A decade later the solo sonata appeared, retaining the *basso continuo* and reducing the two upper parts to one for a single melodic instrument, thus positing the ultimate ground upon which the problem of the unchallenged predominance of the outer parts would have to be solved. Just as Solomone Rossi is associated with the emergence of the trio sonata, so the appearance of the solo sonata is closely identified with Biagio Marini.

Obviously, the eighteenth century was inconsistent in its terminology. Although a trio sonata usually called for four players—and, at those times when both cello and bass viol were used together with the harpsichord, even five—the term "trio sonata" accounted for the two melodic instruments and only one bass. Accordingly, a composition for one melodic instrument and bass should have been called a "duo sonata," rather than a "solo sonata." Because the term "solo sonata" had a special meaning in the eighteenth century, compositions for one instrument alone have to be designated by other, more specific titles. It is convenient to name the single instrument precisely. In the case of a solo for a keyboard instrument, titles such as "harpsichord sonata" and "piano sonata" are in order, while in the case of a composition for a melodic instrument appearing alone, "unaccompanied violin solo" or "unaccompanied cello solo" are suitable.

Paralleling the trio sonata structure, there were some solo sonatas with, and others without melodic activity in the bass. Solo sonatas of the latter type, those with long sustained notes in the accompaniment, in relation to polyphonic instrumental works showed a simplification comparable to that of monodic vocal compositions after 1600 as against earlier Netherlandish and Italian vocal polyphony. Because of the inborn association of monody and cantata composition, in a cantata a vocal solo accompanied by an instrumental bass was called a "solo" in spite of the fact that there was more than one performer. In the case of a vocal solo and an instrumental accompaniment no one questioned the appellation "solo." By analogy, an instrumental solo with an instrumental accompaniment was likewise called a "solo." The designation "solo sonata" was logical only as long as the bass merely accompanied, but when the bass itself demanded attention the distribution of parts in the solo sonata was no longer the counterpart of the monodic vocal solo.

---

française, in Jacques Bonnet, *Histoire de la musique, et de ses effets, depuis son origine jusqu'à présent: & en quoi consiste sa beauté* (Amsterdam, 1725), II, 68–70.

Since the monodists prohibited artistic counterpoint, their compositions offer no clue to the origin of the solo sonata with an active bass. Counterpoint applied to monody merely in the broad sense that obvious errors such as parallel octaves and fifths were to be avoided. Otherwise, the only way to introduce counterpoint was *alla mente*, by improvisation. Exclusion of the bass from melodic activity fared better in the trio sonata than in the solo sonata. Even if the bass of the trio sonata remained purely harmonic, the two upper parts allowed opportunity for imitative effects and the interplay of parts taken over from the *canzonetta* and *canzone*. However, in a solo composition with accompaniment the thorough-bass instrument had to take part in exploiting the theme if there was to be any diversity in melodic presentation.

For one of the sources of the solo sonata Ortiz's combination of gamba and harpsichord must again be consulted, this time with concentration on the third type of collaboration, that in which the harpsichord played all the voices of a complete composition while the gamba played diminutions on one of them.[58] If the string player chose the treble for diminution, the effect was better when the harpsichord omitted that part. Alfred Einstein showed how this process led to the seventeenth-century solo sonata.[59] The material that Ortiz assigned to the harpsichord was contracted into the *basso continuo* of the solo sonata, while Ortiz's improvising string treble was accorded the role of a solo part.

Discant division on a bass was a source for the solo sonata as well as for the trio sonata.[60] For the English, Simpson codified the system of composition developing from divisions on a ground. Solo sonata instrumentation resulted when, in the division for a treble instrument and gamba over a bass, the treble instrumentalist devised a counterpoint against the bass while the gamba broke the bass line itself with diminutions. The chords of the *continuo,* performed on the clavier, were simultaneously reinforced and embellished by the bass gamba. In Simpson's words, "In Composing, for a Treble, and Basse, you are to consider the Nature, and Compasse of either Part; framing your Division according thereunto; which in the Higher Part, will be Descant; in the Lower, a more frequent Breaking of the Ground." [61]

A third source for the solo sonata was the trio sonata itself. By means of *Brechung* the three lines of the trio sonata were contracted into the two of the solo sonata. Either the two treble lines were condensed into

---

[58] See p. 17 f.
[60] See p. 36.

[59] Einstein, *op. cit.*, p. 17.
[61] Simpson, *op. cit.*, p. 49.

one, or the middle part was absorbed by the bass. With regard to the former possibility, the two upper parts of the trio sonata, when they were of an interlocking, imitative nature, could be reduced to one treble line which necessarily had many leaps in its construction. The latter possibility was related to the above-mentioned attempt at relieving the ills of the trio sonata. The cure killed the patient. Whereas the Italians kept two solo instruments in the treble register, manipulating them with an ear toward melodic and rhythmic variety, the French, Germans, and English often relegated the second treble to the middle register, where they lost it in the sweep of the thorough bass. The first violin predominated with solo brilliance while the second violin and bass accompanied. Mattheson in his *Vollkommene Kapellmeister* offered first-hand evidence of this step toward the disintegration of the trio sonata: [62]

In a trio where the bass struggles with the upper part for predominance, two work readily against one. That is to say, the two lower parts commonly go together and form a counterpoise to the upper, since the latter already rules sufficiently, and would become too strong for the bass if its power were doubled. For, since coarser sounds do not penetrate the ears nearly as sharply as finer, strengthening is better below than above. Everyone will understand that this has its basis in nature, i.e.,

PREDOMINANCE OF THE UPPER PART IN A TRIO (FROM MATTHESON, *Der vollkommene Kapellmeister*, p. 346)

When one upper part was thus singled out, the end of the trio sonata was in sight. Deprived of the essential equality between the two upper parts, trio sonata instrumentation ceased to exist.

Another line of development from trio sonata to solo sonata consisted in the transference of the second treble-instrument part in the trio sonata to the right hand of the clavier in the solo sonata. The basis

[62] Mattheson, *op. cit.*, p. 346.

for this procedure may have been the same as that which prompted Viadana to leave out voices. Here was an intermediary stage where the number of performers available may have been an influential factor in determining whether the work was to be performed as a solo sonata or as a trio sonata. With the necessity of providing for only one solo instrument, the trio sonata could be performed with fewer players at hand. Actual musical evidence for this phenomenon appeared in Biagio Marini's Op. 8 (1626), a violin sonata with the organ part written out.[63] Since the right hand of the organ part has the same material as the violin part, the organ plays the dual role of performing a solo part and furnishing the thorough-bass accompaniment. When there are extended rests in the right hand it may be assumed that the organ bass is to be treated as a thorough bass, with the accompanist playing simple chords. Marini said that a violin or a discant trombone could perform the treble melody of the organ. In that case the composition would be reconverted to a trio sonata.

The fact that the origin of the solo sonata may be traced to the trio sonata does not imply the immediate disappearance of the latter. For a while both existed side by side. In addition to the already noted advantages enjoyed by the trio sonata,[64] the lesser skill it demanded of the accompanist in comparison with the solo sonata was a further point in its favor. When only one solo instrument was involved, the keyboard player had not only to support, but often to complement it, balancing each nuance of its own principal line in the accompaniment against the line of the solo.[65] However, in a trio sonata, the additional melodic instrument lifted much if not all of this burden from the keyboard player. The solo sonata was apt to demand more polish, more refinement from an accompanist than did the trio sonata.

The already confused situation with regard to the designation of the solo sonata was not helped by the appearance of the term "duo" in instrumental as well as in vocal music. In the sixteenth century the Italians had composed pedagogical duos or duets which teacher and pupil performed together.[66] The compositions, intended to catch the pupil's fancy, were mostly in canon, based on vivid and lively motives of the *canzon francese*. In the seventeenth century composers took these duos for two melodic instruments, and added basses to them. This

[63] Arnold Schering, "Zur Geschichte der Solosonate in der ersten Hälfte des 17. Jahrhunderts," in *Riemann Festschrift* (Leipzig, 1909), quotes Marini's music, p. 320.
[64] See p. 37.
[65] C. P. E. Bach, *op. cit.*, chap. vi, "Performance," par. 2.
[66] Alfred Einstein, "Vincenzo Galilei and the Instructive Duo," *Music and Letters*, XVIII (1937), 360.

practice may have accounted for the persistence of the term "duo" at a time when the term "trio sonata" would have been more appropriate. Where a thorough bass was involved, the term "duo" wavered between application to the solo sonata and the trio sonata.

Several eighteenth-century theorists elucidated the status of the duo. According to Brossard, the duo "is a composition for two solo voices; or expressly, for two parts, of which one is sung and the other is played on some instrument. One also calls it a *Duo*, when two solo voices sing different parts although they are accompanied by a third part which is the thorough bass." [67] In keeping with the custom of the time, this definition may be applied to instrumental as well as vocal solists. When Brossard says that the duo is for two voices, the statement might seem to apply to the type of duo popular before the advent of the *basso continuo*. However, when he clarifies his thought, saying that one part is sung while the other is played on an instrument, he creates the impression of the solo sonata with solo and accompaniment. The next type of duo, with two soloists and a thorough bass, is equivalent to the trio sonata.

The duo became better codified in the hands of Bethizy. [68] Concerning the two-part duo, where both parts "sound in the manner of upper parts," he expressly declares that it may be written either for two voices or for two instruments. In reference to the type which approaches the solo sonata he writes, "the lowest part is a *basso continuo* or a bass which one may look upon as a *basso continuo* because it imitates the movements of one." There are duos of this species "composed for two voices, others for two instruments, others for a treble instrument and a voice which sings the bass, others finally for one voice and a *basso continuo*." Bethizy's third type of duo is a hybrid of the first two species since "each part is alternately an upper part and *basso continuo* or a quasi-*basso continuo* because it imitates the style of an upper line [or melody]." This type was composed for two tenor or bass instruments, specifically, for either two bass viols, or two cellos, or two bassoons. If one admits, along with the French, that a single melodic instrument may act as a thorough bass, a duo in which one of two melodic instruments has a solo and the other performs the *continuo* encroaches upon the territory of the solo sonata. However, when both melodic instruments are playing equivalent melodies, the composition may be classed as a bona fide duet.

[67] Sébastien de Brossard, *Dictionnaire de musique* (Paris, 1705), p. 22.
[68] M. de Bethizy, *Exposition de la théorie et de la pratique de la musique, suivant les nouvelles découvertes* (Paris, 1754), p. 249.

Bethizy did not account for the species of duo with thorough bass, which was equivalent to the trio sonata. But Rousseau, who supplied details about this type of duo, denied the thorough bass acknowledgment in the total count of the parts:

Duo. This name is generally given to all music in two parts. But today the sense is restrained to two reciting parts, vocal or instrumental, to the exclusion of simple accompaniments, which do not count. Thus, one calls a musical composition for two voices *duo,* although there is a third part for the thorough bass, and others for the symphony. In short, to constitute a duo two principal parts are necessary, between which the melody is equally distributed.[69]

This conception of calling a composition a duet to the exclusion of the thorough bass would be most logically applied to those trio sonatas in which the bass had a purely harmonic function and did not enter in the imitation. Georg Philipp Telemann (1681–1767) and Johann Friedrich Fasch (1688–1758) provide lucid examples of this type.[70] They wrote "trio sonatas" in which a canon between the two upper parts is supported by a harmonic bass not involved in the imitation. Although they could easily have called these compositions duets by discounting the *basso continuo,* the composers chose to call them trio sonatas.

So far as instrumental chamber music is concerned, it is possible to categorize the various combinations of participants. A rule outlining the instrumentation of the solo sonata, trio sonata, and duo may be devised on the basis of whether or not a thorough bass was included. The solo and trio sonatas had a thorough bass. If one deducts the stringed instrument in the *continuo,* the solo sonata had one melodic instrument and the trio sonata had two melodic instruments. On the other hand, the duo, without thorough bass, simply had two melodic instruments.

This use of the term "duo," established before the *continuo* came into existence, became the accepted one in the course of the eighteenth century, after the differences between the vocal and instrumental mediums had been ironed out. Marpurg defined the term "duet" within the instrumental medium in his *Handbuch bey dem Generalbasse* (1754). The real duo or duet "consists of two contrapuntal [*gearbeitete*] parts of equal standing and has no bass or other subsidiary part besides. There are very beautiful duets of this type for the flute by Capellmeister Telemann, for the violin by Leclair, and for the clavier by the late Capellmeister Bach." [71]

[69] Jean-Jacques Rousseau, *Dictionnaire de musique* (Paris, 1768), p. 179.

[70] *Collegium musicum,* ed. Hugo Riemann (Leipzig, 1934), Nos. 67, 68, 69.

[71] Friedrich Wilhelm Marpurg, *Handbuch bey dem Generalbasse* (Berlin, 1762), p. 223.

Marpurg called this type the "duo proper." Yet, at the time when he wrote, the solo sonata had not yet been completely disassociated from the term "duo." He felt constrained to list as a second type of two-part setting, "the flute or violin solo with accompaniment of a bass." Marpurg probed further, first detailing the specifications of the real duo. As he proceeded, he showed that the real duo needed no harpsichord accompaniment, whereas the solo sonata did:

Since the solo calls for the accompaniment of the harpsichord, it follows that the parts can be somewhat further apart from each other than in a real duetto. From this one sees how wrong those fiddlers or flutists are who by a laughable caprice have themselves accompanied by a cello alone, without the harpsichord. One can easily assume from this procedure that such players know nothing about composition. Those who imagine they are doing it better, have themselves accompanied by the viola. But here too, what a bad effect results! One does not know whether it really is a duo or a solo. And what false progressions result now and then when the viola rises above the violin! In a solo the accompaniment of the harpsichord must fill in the gaps between the two parts.[72]

It remained for Koch to crystallize this trend of thought. He associated the *continuo* only with the vocal duet; the instrumental duet had no further accompaniment.[73]

Although both the solo sonata and the instrumental duo each had two principal parts, the difference between them is easily summarized on the basis of the number of concerted parts in each. The term "concerted," indicating a part which stood out from the accompanying parts, may best be explained by a clarification of the terms "ad libitum," "obbligato," and *concertante*. The ad libitum part was optional, lending added fullness to the composition, but not absolutely essential for its rendition. Since ad libitum accompaniment was written down, it was one degree more independent than extemporaneous accompaniment in the thorough bass. Still further removed from the *continuo* and closer toward the solo style was the obbligato part, secondary in importance but occasionally carrying the melody for a few measures. An obbligato part could not be omitted without obviously weakening the composition. Finally, there was the *concertante* (concerted), reciting, or solo part which had, in addition to its distinct, independent line, a virtuoso flavor taken over from the concerto itself.

With this meaning of "concerted part" in mind, it may be said that an instrumental solo sonata had one, while a duet had two concerted parts. This distinction, in addition to the fact that the solo sonata had a thorough bass while the duo did not have chordal accompaniment, clearly identifies the constituents of each type.

[72] *Ibid.*, p. 226.
[73] Heinrich Christoph Koch, *Musikalisches Lexikon* (Frankfort on the Main, 1802), p. 497.

III: CHARACTERISTICS OF THE INSTRUMENTS

CHORDAL INSTRUMENTS

CHORDAL, or fundamental, instruments used for the thorough bass supplied the harmonic groundwork in early eighteenth-century chamber music. Harpsichord and clavichord affected chamber music directly; lute and organ entered the picture indirectly. The two latter instruments, although widely divergent in construction, played a similar role in the development of chamber style. Whereas each was an influential factor in the origin of the thorough bass, neither had standing as a *continuo* participant in chamber works.

When Mattheson wrote *Das neu-eröffnete Orchestre* (1713), the "smiling" lute, outstripped in versatility by the harpsichord and clavichord, had passed its prime as a thorough-bass instrument. "What one can present in chamber music with a thorough bass on the lute might possibly be good if one could only hear it." [1] In the orchestra the theorbo, an archlute with double pegbox and thirteen to fifteen strings, was still valued as a *continuo* instrument because of the depth with which its open drone strings reinforced the bass. However, such an instrument was unwieldy for chamber music.

As for the organ, in addition to the fact that it was located in the church, its sonority seemed more appropriate for church than for chamber music. Corelli specified the use of the organ in the thorough bass only for his *sonate da chiesa,* Op. 1 and 3 (1683 and 1684), in which the bass parts are entitled *Basso per l'organo.* For his *sonate da camera,* Op. 2 and 4 (1685 and 1694), he chose bass gamba and harpsichord. However, even the organ's position as a member of the *continuo* in the church aroused critical opposition. Mattheson could not understand why "they still retain the rattling, most disgusting regals in the church instead of the murmuring and whispering harmony of the harpsichord." [2]

In its capacity as solo instrument the organ had a greater influence on chamber music than it had as a member of the *continuo.* The organ *ricercare* and *canzone* furthered instrumental fugal techniques, while

[1] Johann Mattheson, *Das neu-eröffnete Orchestre* (Hamburg, 1713), p. 277 f.
[2] *Ibid.,* p. 263.

the style of the organ toccata with its extended arpeggios, liquid runs, and long pedal points seeped into chamber music. In Italy a composition was usually designated for a specific keyboard instrument. Domenico Scarlatti based his *Essercizi per gravicembalo* (1729) on harpsichord technique, as opposed to organ technique. On the contrary, in France organ music was not thus differentiated from music for other keyboard instruments. German composers sometimes failed to indicate whether a work was intended for the organ, harpsichord, or clavichord, contenting themselves merely with the specification "clavier"—a generic word covering all keyboard instruments—in the titles of their compositions. Often they were more explicit. J. S. Bach, for example, assigned the second part (1735) and the fourth part (1742) of his *Clavierübung* to a harpsichord and the third part (1739) to the organ.[3]

While the organ detached itself from the others and went its own independent way, the remaining keyboard instruments—harpsichord, clavichord, and piano—continued to be covered by the single term "clavier." The harpsichord with its brilliant, plucked tone had a more extensive usage in both accompaniment and solo music than the more delicate clavichord, whose strings were hit by tangents. Nevertheless, the clavichord, because of its greater sensitivity, appealed to the connoisseur. Despite its weaker tone, Carl Philipp Emanuel Bach believed that a good clavichord had all the advantages of the more recent piano and, in addition, could sustain the tone and produce a vibrato by motion of the finger on a key already struck.[4] He recommended that every keyboardist "own a good harpsichord and a good clavichord to enable him to play all things interchangeably. A good clavichordist makes an accomplished harpsichordist, but not the reverse. The clavichord is needed for the study of good performance, and the harpsichord to develop proper finger strength." [5]

The piano, the clavier instrument which was to supplant the harpsichord and clavichord, did not dominate the musical scene until its construction reached some degree of technical perfection. Only years after its invention (in the first decade of the eighteenth century) did musicians begin to accept the piano as an accompanying instrument, along with the harpsichord and clavichord. According to Quantz, "On a piano everything required [in an accompaniment] can be effected most easily; for this instrument, above all the others called clavier, has in itself most

---

[3] *Johann Sebastian Bach's Werke* (Leipzig, 1852–1926), Vol. III.
[4] Carl Philipp Emanuel Bach, *Essay on the True Art of Playing Keyboard Instruments* [*Versuch über die wahre Art das Clavier zu spielen*, 1759 and 1762], trans. and ed. William J. Mitchell (New York, 1948), Introduction to Part I, par. 11.
[5] *Ibid.*, par. 15.

of the qualities necessary for good accompaniment, depending only on the player and his judgment." [6]

With reference to chamber music, the clavier first gained importance in the thorough bass. In contrast to the French, the Germans insisted on the use of both keyboard and stringed instrument in the *continuo* accompaniment. Mattheson declared,

The harpsichord with its universality provides an almost indispensable accompanying bass for church, theatrical and chamber music. Among French musicians the clavier is not considered as absolutely necessary, and they usually are satisfied with a bass gamba or the like as bass; however, it sounds so naked and bare that a connoisseur is ashamed, and an uninitiated often cannot tell at all what is lacking. But it is to be hoped that the French, as has already happened in many musical things, will likewise change their resolution here and will dispense with such a useless caprice.[7]

Quantz affirmed the universality of the instrument with the remark, "I include the harpsichord in all music-making, whether it be small or big"; [8] and in giving the flutist pointers for performance, based his suggestions on the assumption that a harpsichord would ordinarily be in use. "Above all he must see to the correct tuning of his instrument. If there is a harpsichord for accompaniment, as there is ordinarily, he must tune the flute according to it." [9]

C. P. E. Bach was likewise of the opinion that "no piece can be well performed without some form of keyboard accompaniment," [10] and, more particularly, he held that the combination of a keyboard instrument and a cello was indisputably the most perfect support for a solo: [11]

Some soloists take only a viola or even a violin for accompaniment. This can be condoned only in cases of necessity, where good keyboardists are not available, even though it creates many discrepancies. If the bass is well constructed the solo becomes a duet; if it is not, how dull it sounds without harmony! A certain Italian master had therefore no reason to introduce this kind of accompaniment. What confusion when the parts cross! Or when the melody is distorted in order to avoid a crossing! As written by the composer both parts remain close to each other. How feeble the full chords of the principal part sound, unsupported by a real bass! All harmonic beauty is lost; and a great loss it is in *affetuoso* pieces.[12]

As late as 1779 Joseph Martin Kraus still considered keyboard support a necessity. He argued that even when the composer gave each part a melody of its own, there might be gaps in the parts taken as a whole.

---

[6] Johann Joachim Quantz, *Versuch einer Anweisung die Flöte traversiere zu spielen* (*1752*), reprint ed. A. Schering (Leipzig, 1906), chap. xvii, sec. vi, par. 17.

[7] Mattheson, *op. cit.*, p. 263 f.   [8] Quantz, *op. cit.*, chap. xvii, sec. 1, par. 16.

[9] *Ibid.*, chap. xvi, par. 2.   [10] Bach, *op. cit.*, Introduction to Part II, par. 7.

[11] *Ibid.*, par. 9.   [12] *Ibid.*, par. 8.

"Therefore in performance the most important thing is an instrument which fills in these holes. . . . Even the most beautiful solo, if it is performed without thorough bass is like words without thought. For the thorough bass, or the harmonizations of any piece are the thoughts themselves." [13]

The French, however, would not grant the clavier carte blanche. The thorough bass was subjected to severe cross-examination, especially on the question of doubling the bass line. Lecerf de la Viéville complained,

In general one hears in music only a *basso continuo*, always doubled, which often is a sort of battery of chords, and an arpeggiation which throws powder in the eyes of those who are not acquainted with it, and which, reduced to its simple form would approach our own. These thorough basses are good only for displaying the rapidity of the hand of those who accompany either on the harpsichord or the viol. Besides, to improve upon these basses, already too much doubled in themselves, they double them, and extol him who doubles the most. Therefore one does not hear the subject, which appears too bare in comparison with that great brilliance, and lives buried under a chaos of intricate and crackling sounds.[14]

This negation of arbitrary doubling of the bass was an advanced form of reasoning, for avoidance of mechanical doubling of any instrument was ultimately to become one of the tenets of the classical chamber style. Lecerf's sarcasm reached its height in his reproach to young harpsichordists for studying how to accompany instead of concentrating on how to play pieces.

Formerly people of quality left to musicians by birth and profession the business of accompanying. Today they make of it a supreme honor. To play pieces in order to amuse oneself agreeably or to divert one's mistress or friend is beneath them. But to be nailed three or four years to a harpsichord in order finally to achieve the glory of being a member of an ensemble, of being seated between two violins and a bass viol [*Basse de Violon*] of the opera, and to peck off, well or badly, a few chords which will not be heard by anybody—that is their noble ambition.[15]

Lecerf's scorn for accompaniment was counterbalanced by the views of the German theorist Heinichen, who saw nothing wrong in learning the accompaniment first and catching up on the pieces later. "Whoever wants to learn only the thorough bass on the clavier and not *Galanterie* at the same time, does not need to spend one or more years in the usual

[13] Joseph Martin Kraus, *Wahrheiten die Musik betreffend* (Frankfort on the Main, 1779), p. 29 f.
[14] Lecerf de la Viéville, *Comparaison de la musique italienne et de la musique française*, in Jacques Bonnet, *Histoire de la musique, et de ses effets* (Amsterdam, 1725), I, 297 f.
[15] *Ibid.*, III, 98.

way learning many suites and preludes; for these he can always retrieve or add later to better advantage." [16]

The harpsichord's role in the thorough bass attracted both amateur and professional. Simple accompaniments did not entail lifelong study and practice, although artistic accompaniments necessitated considerable skill. In the course of their exposition of the diverse ways of elaborating the thorough bass, the theorists came to the subject of ornaments, which they divided into two classes: fixed and variable. Fixed ornaments, such as the trill, grace note, slur, mordent, and *acciaccatura,* were more pertinent to solo clavier technique than to thorough-bass execution. In contrast, the variable ornaments, improvised to suit a given circumstance, were embellishments confined solely to the art of thorough bass. Passages, melodies, imitations, or arpeggios, when invented extemporaneously by the performer, functioned as an ornamentation of the written composition. Only when such contrivances were explicitly written out by the composer could they be regarded, not as ornaments, but as essential components of the composition.

"Passages"—fast notes progressing stepwise or by leap—were especially suitable in lively places. When such passages were embodied in the bass, the accompanist could improvise parts moving in thirds or sixths with the bass, instead of adhering to the notes indicated by the figures. Where the bass had no such runs or fast notes, the harpsichordist could introduce them into the right-hand part as ornaments.

Likewise, "melody" was viewed in two capacities. Heinichen considered the top line of the accompaniment as a real part, to the extent that he called it the "melody." [17] As an improvised line a "melody" was an embellishment, but as the top line of an obbligato clavier part the same melody was an inherent constituent of the composition.

Imitation too could be considered as an embellishment. At the start of a movement (if soloist and accompanist had agreed upon this prior to the performance) there might be a planned insertion of fugal entrances between the two. In the body of the work the keyboard player might improvise free or canonic imitations of phrases previously assigned to melodic instruments.

Arpeggiated chords also had significance in accompaniment, at first as an improvised ornament in the thorough bass and then as an element explicitly written into the composition. There was a method of improvising an arpeggiated accompaniment which, if incorporated into a composition, went under the title of the "Alberti bass." In his examples

---

[16] Johann David Heinichen, *Der General-Bass in der Composition* (Dresden, 1728), p. 95.   [17] *Ibid.,* p. 522.

Heinichen first presented simple chords, and then, having settled on a pattern of arpeggiation, broke the chords appropriately, treating one chord after another according to the given figuration. When dealing with chords in the left hand, he subjected a succession of three-part chords to the following preconceived figuration: lowest note of the chord, highest note, middle note, highest note. This particular pattern was later linked to the name of Domenico Alberti (*ca.* 1717–1740), a clavier player and minor composer. Heinichen considered that such arpeggios might be used if they did not hamper the concerted parts and the invention of the composer.[18]

Besides the "Alberti" figuration, another arpeggiation applicable to clavier technique was the broken octave, introduced in the bass to combat the monotonous effect of the "drum bass" with its long spans of repeated notes. Whereas fast repetitions on a single bass note were adaptable to stringed instruments, broken octaves were more suitable for the clavier. Alternation of the notes allowed twice as much time for the mechanism of the instrument to bring each key in readiness for the next stroke.[19]

Improvisation in the keyboard accompaniment had its hazards even when the bass was adequately figured, but when no figures were supplied, the perils were multiplied. The relationship of a bass note to what preceded and what followed was not enough to establish the harmony above that note. Where the composer modulated in an unconventional manner, it was impossible, without figures, even for a skilled harmonist to play the thorough bass correctly, unless he had the upper parts before him. Theorists had a great deal to say on behalf of the use of figures. Andreas Werckmeister remarked in his *Harmonologia musica* (1702) that it is foolish to deny the necessity of "signatures" (*Signaturen*), the collective figures, including numerals and sharp, flat and natural signs above the bass. Since there are various possibilities for progressing and for resolving dissonances, "it is clearly impossible for even an adept, who understands the natural course of harmony and composition, to play everything correctly in accordance with the idea of another." [20]

Heinichen, however, was faced with the existence of instrumental solos and duets "which ordinarily have no figures over the bass, but one must oneself derive them extempore from the score, indeed mostly from a single part above it, and must virtually guess the rest by art and ear." [21] Although skeptical of such unfigured basses, he made an attempt to help

---

[18] *Ibid.,* p. 565.   [19] *Ibid.,* p. 573.

[20] F. T. Arnold, *The Art of Accompaniment from a Thorough-Bass* (London, 1931), p. 66.   [21] Heinichen, *op. cit.,* p. 585.

the accompanist cope with them, dividing his findings under three head-ings.[22] Figures might be derived thus: (1) from vocal or instrumental voices written over the bass, which amounted to a partial or full score; (2) from a few easy general rules or noticeable intervals of the modes; [23] (3) from a few special rules, or from the ambitus of the modes themselves. Under this heading Heinichen gave special rules for major and minor.

C. P. E. Bach, after trying to evolve rules, soon decided that no method for unfigured basses could suffice:

We learned in the Introduction to Part Two that even when a bass is figured as it should be, a good accompaniment comprises many additional factors. This alone exposes the ridiculousness of the demand that accompaniments be real-ized from unfigured basses, and makes evident the impossibility of fashioning such an accompaniment to more than anyone's limited satisfaction. In recent times there has been a marked tendency to notate short, essential ornaments and signs that pertain to good performance. If only there were a corresponding decrease in unfigured basses! If only keyboardists were less willing to do every-thing demanded of them! Other ripienists can complain when they are given an incorrectly written part; but keyboardists must be satisfied with a part that is either unfigured or so sparsely figured that the signatures appear only over those notes whose chords are self evident.[24]

The fact that there was much discussion in the eighteenth century on the omission of figures in itself shows that use of the thorough bass was implied in cases where no figures appeared. To put it more directly, even when the writing was full voiced, and even if there was no part written out for a keyboard instrument, an improvised accompaniment on the keyboard was expected.

In addition to participating in the thorough bass, the clavier was also capable of playing obbligato parts. Fixed ornaments, nurtured in the solo clavier style, were also called into action in connection with obbli-gato clavier parts in chamber music. François Couperin le Grand attrib-uted the high degree of embellishment in music for harpsichord to the nature of the instrument. Instead of lamenting the fact that the harpsi-chord could not swell or sustain the tone in the manner of bowed in-struments, Couperin put its interrupted tone quality to good advantage in the direction of clearness, precision, and brilliance.[25] In the preface to the *Apothéose de Lulli* (1725), he admitted that grace notes and other

[22] *Ibid.*, p. 726 f.
[23] *Ibid.*, p. 734. The first rule under this category indicates how Heinichen made use of the successive intervals in the bass. He said, "if [the bass of] a chord in root position moves a semitone below or a major or minor third above, the latter note naturally has a 6."
[24] Bach, *op. cit.*, chap. vi, "The Need for Figured Basses," par. 1.
[25] *Oeuvres complètes de François Couperin*, ed. Maurice Cauchie (Paris, 1933), Vol. I, *L'Art de toucher le clavecin (1717)*.

fixed ornaments were induced by the harpsichord's short-breathed tone. "Bowed instruments sustain the sounds. On the other hand, since the harpsichord is not able to perpetuate them, it is most necessary to play the shakes or trills and the other ornaments for a very long time." [26] However, denying that the embellishments were merely pasted on to a given line, he insisted that they were an inherent component of the stylistic conception, and would have to be retained even if the compositions were transcribed for instruments which could sustain the sound better. Decorations served to animate the music by heightening the accentuation, connecting the tones, and providing the performer with opportunities for display. In the preface to his third book of *Pièces de clavecin* (1722), Couperin wrote,

I am always surprised (after the care which I have given to mark the ornaments suitable for my pieces, which I have elsewhere explained clearly enough in a special study, known under the title of *L'Art de toucher le clavecin*), to hear the people who play them without mastering them. It is a negligence which is not pardonable, because one may not arbitrarily use any ornaments that one pleases. I declare that my pieces must be performed as I have marked them and that they never would make a definite impression on people who have true taste unless one observes to the letter all that I have marked, without augmentation or diminution.[27]

Judging by the difficulties which harass the modern musician who attempts to translate the signs for the ornaments into living notes, one would assume that there was a large chance for misinterpretation in the eighteenth century, even if the performer had the best of intentions. Johann Sebastian Bach met with severe opposition because he circumvented the hazards of ornamentation by writing out the notes rather than using symbols. The mind of the eighteenth-century musician had been so conditioned to seeing ornaments in their compact abbreviated signs that when the ornaments were written out the music became confusing. The *Critischer Musikus*, edited by Johann Adolph Scheibe, contained in 1737 a tirade against J. S. Bach in the form of a letter from a traveling musician.[28] Scheibe is suspect, although he denied authorship, and while the letter did not mention Bach by name, Scheibe, later on, was at too obvious pains to point to this ambiguity and to suggest that perhaps neither Bach nor Leipzig was intended.[29] In any case, the passage contains the following:

This great man would be the wonder of whole nations, if he had more charm, if he did not deprive his pieces of naturalness by making them bombastic and

26 *Ibid.*, X, 51.   27 *Ibid.*, IV, 6.
28 Johann Adolph Scheibe, *Critischer Musikus* (Leipzig, 1745), I, 46 f.
29 *Ibid.*, p. 833.

diffuse, and if he did not obscure their beauty by much too much dexterity. Since he judges according to his own fingers, his compositions are exceedingly difficult to play; for he demands that singers and instrumentalists be able to produce by means of their throats and instruments what he can play on the clavier. But this is impossible. All the ornaments, all the little grace notes, and everything which goes into the manner of playing, he writes out with real notes. That not only deprives his pieces of the beauty of their harmony, but it also makes the melody unintelligible.[30]

Ornaments were of such importance that it was desirable to have them visible as well as audible. Although the harpsichord ornamentation of chamber style was derived from the decorative techniques of the solo clavier sonata, compositions for solo clavier lie outside the bounds of chamber music. Handel gave opus numbers only to his instrumental ensemble compositions with thorough bass, excluding vocal works and those for solo keyboard; an indication that he considered solo sonatas for melodic instrument and bass to be in a class apart from clavier sonatas. Scheibe made this distinction in his writings:

Now I must say something about sonatas written for one instrument alone. These so-called solos are usually accompanied by a bass and generally have a great similarity to cantatas which are set for only one voice without further accompaniment other than the bass, as one observes in arias. Such solos are now set for all sorts of instruments. The most common are for violin, transverse flute, oboe and bassoon. But what concerns lute and clavier solos cannot be counted among these. These instruments need not be accompanied by a special lower part, since they themselves can supply the bass to their accompaniment. Also, real clavier and lute solos are either similar to real concertos, or they receive an altogether distinct arrangement from so-called suites.[31]

In separating the category of the solo sonata from sonatas for fundamental instruments, Scheibe confirmed the inclusion of the solo sonata in chamber music and the exclusion of the lute and clavier sonata. According to this line of thought, the conclusion may be drawn that chamber style requires at least one special instrument to play the bass, regardless of whether the bass be played by a combination of stringed and keyboard instruments, keyboard alone, or string alone. Chamber style encourages participation in performance rather than skilled technical display for its own sake. Therefore, because chordal instruments can play the bass in spite of intricate activity in the rest of the melodic terrain, and because the chordal instrument in a solo capacity may take on a concerto flavor, solos for chordal instruments are apart from chamber style.

[30] *Ibid.*, p. 46.   [31] *Ibid.*, p. 681.

MELODIC INSTRUMENTS

Treble.—The change of preference from treble viol to violin matured in time for the violin to become an established contemporary of the harpsichord and clavichord.[32] Toward the 1580s the Italians began to distinguish between two classes of stringed melodic instruments, the viola da gamba (leg viol) and the viola da braccio (arm viol). Within each of these categories there developed a family of instruments from the treble down to the bass. By 1616, when Bartholomäus Praetorius wrote five-part pavanes and galliards for all musical instruments, but "particularly for *viole di gamba* and *viole di braccia*," the Germans had also acknowledged the two groups. Although the names originally referred to the position in which the instruments were held during performance, the families were subsequently distinguished by their construction. The gamba's flat back, its frets and numerous strings soon rendered the family obsolete. Whereas the viola da braccio produced the modern string family of violin, viola, cello, and bass, the viola da gamba family did not survive past the eighteenth century.

First of the braccio instruments to displace its gamba counterpart was the violin, appearing in Italy in the middle of the sixteenth century. The violin, which had no difficulty in taking precedence over the treble viol in Italy, met with opposition in England and France. Devoted to their smooth, pale ensembles of viols, the English found the sound of the violin too penetrating and overpowering. They relegated the "coarse" violin to dance tunes played by common fiddlers, and for their art music preferred viols of various sizes. The French too were reticent about forsaking the viol, especially in dance music. Pierre Trichet observed in his *Traité des instruments de musique* (1650) that for "a well-rounded and harmonious ensemble of viols, four at least, of different size and dimension according to their range, are necessary." [33]

In Italy, however, a treble instrument capable of dominating over all else was compatible with the spirit of composition. The gamba had been of use to the Italians as an instrument on which extemporization was extremely effective. But after the improvisatory types had developed into the more concrete solo sonata and trio sonata, Italian composers relinquished the gamba for the richer sound of the violin. In accordance with Italian leadership in the field of bowed instruments, the violin dis-

[32] The piano achieved prominence among chordal instruments too late to be a determining factor in the period of chamber music under discussion.

[33] J. Ecorcheville, *Vingt Suites d'orchestre du XVIIe siècle français 1640–1670* (Paris, 1906), I, 89.

placed the treble viol by the beginning of the seventeenth century. Even pieces designated for viols in the title were performed with violins in the treble and alto parts.[34]

Remnants of the treble viol lingered longest in France. As late as 1740 Hubert le Blanc berated violin music from every angle in an effort to raise the status of the viol. His outlook was limited because he based his conclusions on the compositions of Corelli, Geminiani, Somis, and Leclair, works which rarely went beyond the fifth position.[35] In *Sonates à deux violons ou dessus de viole sans basse* (Op. 2, *ca.* 1751) by Jean-Marie Leclair the second (1703–1777),[36] allowance for treble viols as substitutes for the two violins shows that agitation on behalf of the gamba instrument had some effect.

Nevertheless, Frenchmen abreast of the times had to admit that the feminine charm of the treble viol could not compete with the masculine powers of the violin. The resources of the violin reached beyond the chamber, to orchestra and opera in particular, and caused repercussions which were to bring new wonders to chamber music. Raguenet observed,

When it comes to instruments and instrumentalists, the Italians again have the same advantage that they have over us with regard to the voice and singers. Their violins are mounted with strings thicker than ours, they have much longer bows, and they know how to draw twice as much sound from their instruments as we do. The first time that I heard our opera orchestra on my return from Italy, the memory of the Italian sonority made our violins seem so feeble that I thought they all had mutes.[37]

Ostensibly at odds with Raguenet, Lecerf de la Viéville concerned himself with praising the violin in general, not with praising a particular country's use of the violin. He pondered the question of why the treble viol could not convey emotions other than tenderness with the facility of the violin:

Does [the treble viol] likewise express sadness, fury? Does it play fast airs, airs of movement? Is it also masculine? No. I beg you to notice that with its four or five strings the violin makes you feel certain passions to perfection, and expresses all of them in an admissible and correct manner. That quality belongs to it alone. Besides, it matters very little whether it has four strings, or five. The Italians tune their five strings in fourths; we tune our four strings in fifths; it amounts to the same thing. The violin, tuned in these two diverse

[34] Alfred Einstein, "Zur deutschen Literatur für Viola da Gamba," *Publikationen der Internationalen Musikgesellschaft, Beihefte, Zweite Folge,* I, 12.

[35] Andreas Moser, *Geschichte des Violinspiels* (Berlin, 1923), p. 166.

[36] Lionel de la Laurencie, *L'École française de violon de Lully à Viotti* (Paris, 1922), I, 346.

[37] François Raguenet, *Parallèle des Italiens et des François en ce qui regarde la musique et les opéra* (Paris, 1702), p. 65.

fashions, is always both the epitomy and perfection of music. First of all the diminutions, those charming diminutions without which art could scarcely go to the heart, are better on the violin than anywhere else. . . . Since its finger-board has no frets, it divides the tones as it pleases. It diminishes them to the limit, without losing anything, and passes from one to the other while diminishing imperceptibly, with the same capacity for softness, and penetration, as a beautiful voice would have.[38]

The violin was in France to stay. Italian sonatas and their French counterparts were so much a part of French musical life that the violin was indispensable. The violin sonatas and concertos of Corelli, Vivaldi, and Geminiani, well received in France, could be performed on no other instrument.[39]

England's resistance likewise gave way. Thomas Mace in 1676, seeing the intruder coming, prepared accordingly. He declared that one may add to the ensemble "A Pair of Violins, to be in Readiness for any Extraordinary Jolly, or Jocund Consort-Occasion; But never use Them, but with This Proviso, viz. Be sure you make an Equal Provision for Them, by the Addition, and Strength of Basses; so that They may not out-cry the Rest of the Musick, (the Basses especially)." [40]

John Jenkins (1592–1678) formed a connecting link in the change from viol to violin in that he composed for both the old and the new. His *Fancies* for viols appeared only in manuscript, whereas his more up-to-date sonatas for two violins and bass were published in 1660. Burney considered that "These were professedly in imitation of the Italian style, and the first of the kind which had ever been produced by an Englishman. It was at this time an instance of great condescension for a musician of *character* to write expressly for so ribald and vulgar an instrument, as the *violin* was accounted by the lovers of lutes, guitars, and all the *fretful* tribe." [41]

Theory books confirmed the acceptance of the violin and codified the techniques associated with it. In spite of Italy's astounding development in violin technique, there was a significant lack of theoretical writings on the violin in Italian. Francesco Geminiani, an Italian by birth, re-wrote his method for the violin in three languages: in English (published in the 1740s), French (published in 1752), and German (edited after his death).[42] Even though Geminiani migrated from Italy to England in 1714, his native country could have claimed his work if it had so

38 Jacques Bonnet, *Histoire de la musique* (Amsterdam, 1725), III, 105 f.

39 Michel Brenet, *Les Concerts en France sous l'ancien régime* (Paris, 1900), p. 109.

40 Thomas Mace, *Musick's Monument* (London, 1676), p. 246.

41 Charles Burney, *A General History of Music* (London, 1776–1789), III, 408.

42 Karl Gerhartz, "Die Violinschule in ihre musikgeschichtlichen Entwicklung bis Leopold Mozart," *Zeitschrift für Musikwissenschaft*, VII (1925), 561 f.

desired; yet there was no Italian publication of his study. In Italy the practice of the violin was so much alive that it was customary for the student to go directly to the master, instead of consulting a written digest of his theories. Corelli, Vivaldi, Veracini, and Nardini did not record their methods; Tartini left but a single letter of instruction, that to his pupil Maddalena Lombardini. He wrote the theoretical study sometime near the 1760s, after Maddalena Lombardini, a former student at the *Conservatorio degli Mendicanti* in Venice, had married Ludovico Syrmen, a composer of lesser magnitude.[43] Shortly after Tartini's death, the letter was printed in French in *Europe littéraire* (1770). Burney translated it into English (1771) and Hiller into German (1784). In cosmopolitan circulation this letter eventually outrivaled the Geminiani treatise.

Tartini stated the fundamentals of bowing with such clarity that a beginner may still find it profitable reading:

Your principal practice and study should, at present, be confined to the use and power of the bow, in order to make yourself entirely mistress in the execution and expression of whatever can be played or sung, within the compass and ability of your instrument. Your first study, therefore, should be the true manner of holding, balancing, and pressing the bow lightly, but steadily upon the strings; in such manner as that it shall seem to breathe the first tone it gives, which must proceed from the friction of the string, and not from percussion, as by a blow given with a hammer upon it. This depends upon laying the bow lightly upon the strings, at the first contact, and on gently pressing it afterwards; which, if done gradually, can scarce have too much force given to it, because, if the tone is begun with delicacy, there is little danger of rendering it afterwards either coarse or harsh.[44]

Tartini taught, not by means of exercises devised for special purposes, but by direct application to living music. The teaching material mentioned in the letter is drawn from Corelli's solo violin sonatas, Op. 5, a work that was, and still is, standard in the field. This letter was written some time between the first two editions of Leopold Mozart's *Violinschule*, appearing in 1756 and 1769. According to Schubart, in the *Violinschule* L. Mozart ". . . bends toward the Tartini school, but allows the student more freedom in the management of the bow than the latter." [45]

[43] Marion Scott, "Maddalena Lombardini, Madame Syrmen," *Music and Letters*, XIV (1933), 149–163.

[44] *A Letter from the Late Signor Tartini to Signora Maddalena Lombardini (Now Signora Sirmen)*, trans. Charles Burney (London, 1779; reprinted 1913), p. 11.

[45] Christ. Fried. Dan. Schubart, *Ideen zu einer Ästhetik der Tonkunst* (Vienna, 1806), p. 157 f.

Despite the fact that the Germans made such a specialty of double stops and chordal playing on the violin that the effect is particularly associated with them, as in all innovations in the field of music for strings, the Italians participated from the start. This time an Italian on German soil did the honors, thus providing ground for nationalistic debate as to which country deserves the credit. Biagio Marini, in his Op. 8, *Sonate, symphoniae, canzoni* (1626), wrote an imitative *canzone* called *Capriccio che due violini sonano quattro parti* (Capriccio in Which Two Violins Play Four Parts). The first violin performs both the treble, entering on the fifth of the scale with the customary *canzone* rhythmic pattern (♩♩♩), and the alto, starting a measure later on the tonic. Double entrances on two violins launch a four-part *canzone*. Marini even went beyond double stopping. In the same collection there is a *Capriccio per sonare il violino solo con tre corde a modo di lira* (Capriccio for One Violin Playing on Three Strings in the Manner of a Lira), a composition devoted to three-part chordal harmony, but making no attempt at contrapuntal imitation.[46] Since the musical content of both these capriccios was thoroughly compatible with what had been going on in Italian composition in the early seventeenth century, their historical interest lies in the consistent use of a melodic instrument for the purpose of playing several parts simultaneously.

In the eighteenth century the ability to play double stops was essential equipment for a rounded violin technique. It was while trying to find an aid toward playing double stops in tune that Tartini (before 1720) made his famous discovery of the existence of the differential or combination tone, a third sound which is induced as a bass to the two notes played. Tartini adequately tested the effect of double stops in the *Devil's Trill Sonata,* which according to legend was conceived in a dream when he was twenty-one years old.[47] From the point of view of technical display, any listener who might have remained unimpressed by the full-bodied sound in the first movement, must have been awe-stricken by the last movement where the upper part maintains a continuous trill during stretches of concentrated chordal manipulation.

Among the many complaints expressed against the use of double stops on the violin was Charles Avison's trenchant observation: "Even the Use of double Stops on this Instrument, may, in my Opinion, be considered as one of the Abuses of it; since, in the Hands of the greatest Masters, they only deaden the Tone, spoil the Expression, and

---

[46] Hugo Riemahh, *Handbuch der Musikgeschichte* (Leipzig, 1920), II², 101 f.

[47] George Dubourg, *The Violin: being an account of that Leading Instrument and its Most Eminent Professors, from its earliest date to the Present Time.* Third Ed., (London, 1850), p. 57 f.

obstruct the Execution. In a Word, they baffle the Performer's Art, and bring down *one good* Instrument to the State of *two indifferent ones.*" [48]

Le Blanc took a different approach in condemning chordal playing on the violin. He argued that a melodic instrument, trespassing upon the territory of a chordal instrument, could not even steal properly because there were so few chords that an instrument like the violin could actually play. Keyboard players were annoyed when they saw the violin trying to take over their work:

The harpsichord openly revolts against the violin, complaining that the violin trespasses on its chordal territory, and what is more, that the violin pretends to triumph in this style, for which its small number of chords renders it so unsuitable. The violin's chords, confined within such small limits, can only be meager. The diminished fifth and (of more value) the third which prepares it, along with some arpeggios in which the chords make use of open strings, make a great deal of noise through the force of the strings, so strongly compressed. Compared to the violin, an instrument deprived of the effect of chordal filling, the harpsichord sounds like an enormous sea, a vast ocean. [49]

In spite of attacks on the violin for trying to play chords, musicians continued to press the search for greater ease in multiple stopping. The composer might even prescribe an altered tuning of the strings to facilitate the playing of a particular composition. Nonstandard tuning predetermined by the composer was referred to as *scordatura,* if the music was notated according to the finger positions on a violin with normal tuning. The lute had already been subjected to tunings which enabled the player to perform arpeggios otherwise not feasible. In the case of the modern violin, Biagio Marini was among the first to suit the tuning to the occasion. In order to make possible a passage in thirds, he gave directions to lower one of the strings for a few measures, notating the measures as they sounded. Perhaps the first composer to treat the violin as a transposing instrument was the German, Johann Heinrich Schmelzer, in his second sonata for violin solo (1664). [50] Schmelzer's pupil, Heinrich Biber, in the 1670s composed a set of sonatas which were to become the touchstone of *scordatura* writing. [51] Biber carefully noted the appropriate *scordatura* before each of the twelve sonatas, so that the violinist could tune his instrument and play the notes just as if he were setting his fingers on the customary violin fingerboard. The performer had to adjust his mental image of the music to compensate for the tones which

[48] Charles Avison, *An Essay on Musical Expression* (London, 1752), p. 92.

[49] Hubert le Blanc, "Défense de la basse de viole contre les entreprises du violon et les prétentions du violoncel," *La Revue musicale,* IX[1] (1927), 138.

[50] Michelangelo Abbado, "La 'scordatura' negli strumenti ad arco e Nicolò Paganini," *La rassegna musicale,* XIII (1940), 214.

[51] *Denkmäler der Tonkunst in Österreich,* Vol. XII[2].

ensued. If he misinterpreted the *scordatura,* the number of wrong notes might be disastrous. In front of the eleventh sonata Biber wrote the following *scordatura:*

in place of the normal tuning:

BIBER'S *Scordatura* FOR SONATA XI

Usually Biber was able to list the strings from top to bottom, but here, instead of the d' string being in its customary place, the normal a' string was retuned down to d'. In other words, the retuned strings were not placed on the violin in the order of their pitch. To represent his intention in a way corresponding to his usual procedure, Biber would have had to write on two staves.

Scordatura   **Normal Tuning**

d"   e"
d'   a'

g'   d'
g   g

RECONSTRUCTION OF BIBER'S *Scordatura*
FOR SONATA XI

Instead he took a short cut which misled some twentieth-century experts into reading a series of parallel fifths.[52] They were duly corrected.[53]

Although the *scordatura* had its advantages, wholesale application was fruitless. If the composer made double stops easy to play, he often made running passages difficult. By 1752 Quantz spoke of the *scordatura* as already a thing of the past: "On the violin [the Germans] played more harmonically than melodically. They composed many pieces for which

---

[52] *Ibid.,* p. 55.

[53] Max Schneider, "Zu Biber's Violinsonaten," *Zeitschrift der Internationalen Musikgesellschaft,* VIII (1907), 471–474; Guido Adler, "Zu Biber's Violinsonaten," *Z.I.M.G.,* IX (1907), 29 f.

the violins had to be retuned. The strings, according to the indication of the composer, were tuned in seconds, thirds, or fourths, instead of in fifths, in order to facilitate chords. But this, on the other hand, caused no small difficulty in the passages." [54]

Besides its facilitation of double stopping, *scordatura* was of use to those interested in having the violin accompany itself with its own bass. In 1738 Michel Corrette wrote *L'Ecole d'Orphée,* a "Method for easily learning how to play the violin in the French and Italian style; with some principles of music and many lessons for one and two violins; a work useful for beginners and for those who wish to succeed in performing sonatas, concertos, pieces in the usual tuning [*pièces par accords*] and pieces with lowered strings [*pièces à cordes ravallées*]." [55] With the improvement in technique the range of the violin was constantly increasing in the upper regions, but in the normal tuning the lowest note was fixed at g. Corrette wanted to amplify the bass as well.

A *Sonate énigmatique* attributed to Pietro Nardini (1722–1793), pupil of Tartini, had a *scordatura* which enabled the solo violinist to play both the melody and the accompaniment. The composer wrote next to the *scordatura,* "By means of this tuning the bass is played." [56] Nardini constructed the violin part on two staves, both of which the violinist was supposed to read at once.

The desire to compel the violin to play both melody and bass may be regarded as an attempt to put the violin solo in a class with the lute and clavier solo. The outer limit of this possibility would be the purely speculative consideration of the violin as a chordal instrument. With or without *scordatura,* unaccompanied violin and cello solos are an uneasy incursion into the realm of chamber music. In spite of the amount of music written for those instruments without accompaniment, very little has survived in the modern repertoire; and with good reason. Although composers tried to achieve the feats possible in a clavier or lute solo, a pure melodic instrument by its very nature negates such a procedure. The violin demands companionship in performance, as does the cello. Only a composer like Bach—to whom apparently all things were possible—could produce enduring results while compelling an instrument into atypical and uncongenial procedures.

Although *scordatura* was fundamentally concerned with facilitating the playing of chords, a by-product of its use was a few more lower notes on the violin. In contrast, activity toward the extension of the upper

---

[54] Quantz, *op. cit.,* chap. xviii, par. 81.   [55] Gerhartz, *op. cit.,* p. 560.
[56] J. B. Cartier, *L'Art du violon ou division des écoles choisies dans les sonates italliens, françoise et allemande* (Paris, 1803), p. 320.

range of the violin beyond the point where position shifts are efficacious was dependent, not on altering the usual method of tuning, but on the introduction of harmonics. At the end of the seventeenth century most composers did not make demands beyond the third position. As higher notes were introduced on the e″ string, the violinist did not make use of the corresponding higher positions on the other strings. Positions beyond the third were employed as a means of extending the range of the instrument upward, and not for the tonal effect produced through the use of higher positions on the lower strings. Corrette embodied this advance in technique in his *Ecole d'Orphée* by advocating the use of the fourth position on all four strings, and the seventh position, a‴, on the highest string.[57] Leopold Mozart also provided for the shift to the seventh position on the e″ string. He distinguished between two kinds of positions, the "whole positions," corresponding to what are now the odd-numbered positions, and the "half positions," now even numbered. It was not until the early 1790's, in Adam Hiller's *Anweisung zum Violinspielen,* that positions ran in the order of consecutive numbers, as is customary now.[58]

So far as extending the upper range of the violin is concerned, shifting was supplemented by the introduction of harmonics, a technique which has enjoyed a permanent place in the practice of the violin. In the preface to *Les Sons harmoniques, sonates à violon seul, avec la basse continue,* Op. 4 *(ca.* 1738), Jean-Joseph Cassanéa de Mondonville wrote:

> The work which I am presenting may at first seem difficult to many people for a reason which often discourages most of our pupils. They are afraid of the positions because they do not understand them completely. Those which are encountered in the course of these sonatas need not be forbidding. In order to dispel all difficulty, one only has to apply oneself to my new method of playing.
> The distant intervals are not the most difficult when the ear shows us how to grasp certain harmonious sounds. The most gratifying are those which come from the harmonic progression. They are so very natural in the trumpet, in the French horn, etc., that it is impossible for these instruments to form others besides the third, fifth and octave, unless they digress twenty-two intervals from the fundamental, after which they can vary their sounds diatonically. These same progressions are found on all sorts of instruments except that some are more responsive than others. Why should we not find that same sensitiveness in the violin which, according to general opinion is the most perfect instrument.[59]

Mondonville then indicated where the string should be touched lightly in order to achieve the desired sound. He went through the divi-

[57] Gerhartz, *op. cit.,* 560.

[58] Johann Adam Hiller, *Anweisung zum Violinspielen.* Leipzig: Breitkopf, [1792]; Grätz: C.F. Trötscher, 1795.

[59] La Laurencie, *op. cit.,* I, 426.

sions of the string all the way up to that producing the third octave above the sound of the open string. From there on he conjectured that it is possible to proceed diatonically. Mondonville observed that the division of the string may be made either on the upper or lower portion, except in the case of the octave which is produced by dividing the string exactly in half.

La Laurencie maintains that there was no violin method before 1740 which mentioned how to play harmonics by touching the finger lightly on the string. He goes so far as to say that no German, French, or Italian composer used harmonics on the violin before Mondonville's Op. 4.[60] There was, however, a medieval stringed instrument called the *trum-scheit* or *trompette-marine* on which only harmonics were played. In 1636 Mersenne discussed the subject, as did the physicist Sauveur, in 1701. Mondonville's contribution, therefore, was to adapt the already existing practice of playing harmonics to the violin.[61]

In addition to harmonics, pizzicato, use of mutes, unison on two strings, and various bowings, all were part of the growing violin technique. Quantz said that pizzicato could be played on the violin with the thumb, or better, with the point of the first finger. About pizzicato in chamber music specifically, he asserted, "In a small musical performance in the chamber the strings should not be plucked too strongly if one does not want it to sound disagreeable." [62] On the use of mutes he said, "In some pieces they put mutes on the violin, viola and cello to express the sentiments of love, tenderness, flattery, sadness." [63]

Quantz devoted his celebrated *Essay* to the flute. Yet, he saw the importance of understanding the violin and the clavier because, "seldom is any music performed without the aforementioned instruments." [64] In eighteenth-century chamber music the transverse flute, recorder, and oboe were sometimes used as substitute instruments for the violin. Paralleling the relation of the viol to the violin, the recorder and the transverse flute were used side by side before the latter won out. Bach and Handel made use of both instruments throughout their careers. Handel wrote four sonatas for the recorder, Nos. 2, 4, 7, and 11 of the *XV Solos for a German Flute, Hoboy or Violin with a Thorough Bass for the Harpsichord or a Bass Violin*, Op. 1.[65] Within the collection he indi-

---

[60] *Ibid.*, I, 428.

[61] Frédéric Hellouin, *Feuillets d'histoire musicale française* (Paris, 1903), p. 49.

[62] Quantz, *op. cit.*, chap. xvii, sec. ii, par. 31.

[63] *Ibid.*, chap. xvii, sec. ii, par. 29.   [64] *Ibid.*, chap. x, par. 20.

[65] Despite the number "fifteen" in this title, the first three editions of Op. 1 contained only twelve numbers. Although the original publication by Witvogel in Amsterdam (1724) was copied intact by John Walsh in London (1733), Samuel

cated which of the eight flute sonatas were for the transverse flute (*Traversa solo*) and which for the recorder (*Flauto solo*). The four sonatas for recorder were for the alto instrument in F, the only active member of a once extensive family. Comparison of the recorder sonatas in this collection with those for the transverse flute reveals that the latter have more frequent passage work and leaps, features with which the recorder often cannot cope, since its range of leaps is limited, and in certain keys passage work is very awkward to execute with rapidity and ease.

For his *Brandenburg Concertos* J. S. Bach used the recorder in Nos. 2 and 4, and the tranverse flute in No. 5. However, for his chamber music —suites, trios, unaccompanied and accompanied flute sonatas—Bach designated the *Flauto traverso*. In comparison with the recorder, the transverse flute offers the performer greater opportunity to show his sensitivity and to color his playing.

Telemann juxtaposed the two types of instrument in the D minor Quartet for recorder (or bassoon, or cello), two transverse flutes, and harpsichord with cello, from his *Tafelmusik,* II, No. 2 (1733).[66] Since the recorder part is to be transposed down two octaves when the recorder is replaced by the bassoon or cello, the piece is a feat of double counterpoint.[67] Telemann at times distinguishes between the timbre of the recorder and that of the two flutes by giving the recorder solo material while the flutes have accompanying intervals. At other times he mingles the sound of the three treble instruments, leaving the differentiation to the discernment of the listener.

The French have claimed honors for the victory of the transverse flute over the recorder. Jacques Hotteterre (d. 1761), in a work dealing with the three important wind instruments, *Principes de la flûte traversière, ou flûte d'Allemagne, de la flûte à bec ou flûte douce, et du hautbois, divisés par traités par le sieur Hotteterre-le-Romain, ordinaire de la musique du Roy (ca.* 1707), produced the earliest known instructions for the transverse flute.[68] Some years later Charles de Lusse (b. 1720), in his *Six Sonates pour la flûte traversière avec une tablature des sons harmoni-*

Arnold in the third edition (1786) replaced two of the sonatas with substitutes. Eventually, the number was increased to fifteen, at variance with Handel's original intention. *Georg Friedrich Händel's Werke,* ed. Friedrich Chrysander (Leipzig, 1879), Vol. XXVII.

[66] *Collegium musicum,* No. 59; *Denkmäler deutscher Tonkunst,* LXII, 118.

[67] Max Seiffert, "G. Ph. Telemann's 'Musique de table' als Quelle für Händel," *Bulletin de la Société Union Musicologique,* IV (1924), 18.

[68] Ernest Thoinan, *Les Hotteterre et les Chédeville* (Paris, 1894), p. 38. Hotteterre may have been nicknamed "le-Romain" because of a possible journey to Italy and residence in Rome.

ques, gave an exposition of playing harmonics on the flute comparable to that of Mondonville for the violin.[69]

Although there are eighteenth-century compositions for transverse flute written in keys containing three flats or even four sharps, composers found it best to consider the instrument for a composition in a key with no more than two sharps or flats and to confine its part to a range of two octaves. The flutist had trouble enough playing even a simple composition in tune, for his instrument was in a crude state of construction, with the holes often misplaced. He had much greater odds to overcome than the string player whose violin was perfect. It is well known that modern stringed instrument makers are continually trying to reproduce eighteenth-century instruments as exactly as possible.

Because of the technical limitations of the flute, Charles Avison advised adherence to scalewise passages:

In Compositions for the *German* Flute, is required the same Method of proceeding by *conjoint Degrees,* or such other natural Intervals, as, with the Nature of its Tone, will best express the languishing, or melancholy Style. With both these Instruments [flute and oboe], the running into *extreme Keys,* the Use of the *Staccato,* or distinct Separation of Notes; and all irregular Leaps, or broken and uneven Intervals must be avoided; for which Reason alone, these Instruments ought never to be employ'd in the *Ripieno Parts* of Concertos for Violins, but in such Pieces only as are composed for them.[70]

A major in the regiment of Louis XV by the name of Ancelet, in his *Observations sur la musique* (1757), confirmed the right of the flute to a place in sonata literature in spite of its limited range of passions. While excluding the flute from music dealing with demonic, violent, or warlike subjects, Ancelet asserted that the instrument would be more appropriate "in tender and pathetic pieces and the accompaniments of the little airs and *brunettes* [71] in the sonatas and concertos written by the best masters, who themselves, however, should not overdo it." [72]

Hubert le Blanc, champion of the viol, also favored the flute, especially as played by a flutist like Michel Blavet. The latter was so popular that there were requests at the *Concerts Spirituel* to have him appear in every concert.[73] Le Blanc felt that the flute, as well as the viol, was being undermined by the violin.

---

[69] La Laurencie, *op. cit.,* I, 430.   [70] Avison, *op. cit.,* p. 95 f.

[71] The *brunette,* a short composition on a rustic, tender, or lively subject, was written for a solo voice with or without instrumental accompaniment. Derived from the bergerette and villanella of the preceding period, the *brunette* was popular at the end of the seventeenth and beginning of the eighteenth centuries.

[72] Louis Fleury, "Flute and Flutists," *Musical Quarterly,* IX (1923), 522.

[73] Brenet, *op. cit.,* p. 129.

The flute can declaim better than the violin and is more of a mistress of swelling [the tone] or of making diminutions. At the end of the concert people were of the opinion that the flute, played by a Blavet, is preferable to the first violin, when it is a question of imitating the voice, which cannot, as everyone knows, sing several tones at once.

The violin, wishing to dominate at any price whatever, and to annihilate the flute as well as the viol, if it could, made astonishing efforts in that direction. They went so far as to compose chords which are unplayable on the flute and tiring beyond imagination for the viol, because these chords are in connection with the open D and G strings on the violin. The viol necessarily needs more strings since it is tuned in *fourths* and *thirds,* in comparison with compositions made for an instrument tuned in *fifths.*[74]

Further proof of the flute's acceptability lies in the frequent provision made for substituting the flute for the violin. Jean-Philippe Rameau in the introduction to his *Pièces de clavecin, en concerts, avec un violon ou une flute et une viole ou un deuxième violon* (1741), gave careful directions for performing a violin part on the flute:

Where there are chords, one should choose the note which forms the most beautiful melody, and this note is ordinarily the highest.

With regard to the notes which exceed the lower range of the flute, I have been obliged to use various signs to take their place, without confusing the music.

An 8, for example, shows that the music from that 8 to the letter *U,* which stands for *unison,* must be played an octave higher.

In a rapid passage of several notes, it suffices to substitute adjacent notes which are in the same harmony for those which descend too low, or to repeat those which one considers suitable; except in cases where one finds small noteheads on the stems, almost like specks, which indicate exactly what should be played by the flute.[75]

Ways of bringing a violin part within reach of the flute were contrived because compositions for the violin were usually more complicated than those for the flute. Jean-Marie Leclair l'aîné (1697–1764) tried to prove the simplicity of his violin sonatas by showing that they could also be played on the flute. The preface preceding Leclair's second book of violin sonatas (*ca.* 1728) reads,

The benevolence which the public bestowed on my first book made me hope that it would not receive this one less favorably, and, in order to merit the good fortune of pleasing it more generally, I have taken care to compose sonatas for the capacity of people more or less skilled, since most may be played on the German flute. Those which may be too difficult are not without their

[74] Le Blanc, *op. cit.,* IX[1], 138.
[75] Jean-Philippe Rameau, *Oeuvres complètes* (Paris, 1896), II, xxi.

merit when they are well executed, and may serve as exercise for those who are in need of it.[76]

Quantz's personal ventures with playing the violin, oboe, and flute may be regarded as a symbol for the interchangeability of the three instruments. Before 1713 Quantz practiced the violin as his main instrument. According to J. A. Hiller, Quantz studied the "solos" of Biber, Walther, Albicastro, Corelli, and Telemann.[77] In 1719 at Dresden came the next step in Quantz's career.

The violin, which until then had been his main instrument, was to be exchanged for the oboe. But on both instruments his comrades who were in the service longer thwarted him from distinguishing himself, a desire very close to his heart. The displeasure over it caused him to study seriously the transverse flute, which he had already practiced to some extent, since on this instrument he did not have to fear any great opponent in the company which he kept. For the erstwhile flutist Friese, whose leading passion was not music, willingly surrendered to him the first place at the flute. In order to achieve his aim more securely, at this time he took lessons in Dresden from the famous Büffardin,[78] from whom he really learned only mechanical perfection and swiftness in passages, techniques which constituted the outstanding skill of his master. He did not pursue these lessons longer than four months.[79]

Familiarity with both the violin and the oboe revealed to Quantz the possibilities inherent in the flute, and he directed his attention toward writing compositions specifically for the flute. Hiller's explanation of how Quantz came to devote his creative talents to this instrument is an almost exact translation of Burney, who wrote, "The scarcity of pieces, composed expressly for the German flute, was such, at this period, that the performers upon the instrument were obliged to adopt those of the hautbois, or violin, and by altering or transposing, accommodate them to their purpose, as well as they could. This stimulated Quantz to compose for himself." [80]

Quantz wrote several hundred flute compositions during his thirty-year service with Frederick the Great. The latter, duly appreciative of his composer-teacher, gave Quantz a palace at Potsdam in which to live. Although Quantz was well paid for his compositions, the king would

---

[76] M. Leclair l'aîné, *Second Livre de sonates pour le violon et pour la flûte traversière avec la basse continue*, Op. 2 (Paris, ca. 1728).

[77] J. A. Hiller, *Lebensbeschreibungen berühmter Musikgelehrten und Tonkünstler neuerer Zeit* (Leipzig, 1784), p. 204.

[78] Pietro Gabriel Büffardin, first flutist in the electoral chapel in Dresden from 1716 to 1749.

[79] Hiller, *op. cit.*, p. 211 f.

[80] Charles Burney, *The Present State of Music in Germany, the Netherlands and United Provinces* (London, 1773), II, 171.

not consent to their publication, and most of them remained in manuscript in the library at Potsdam.

Composition for the "evenly-speaking oboe" [81] was likewise of a conservative texture, without daring leaps. Because oboe parts had a more restricted range and smaller intervals in the figuration than parts for the violin, Avison maintained that "the *Hautboy* will best express the *Cantabile,* or singing Style, and may be used in all Movements whatever under this Denomination, especially those Movements which tend to the *Gay* and *Chearful.*" [82] This quotation sounds like an echo of Scheibe who said, "In a solo for the violin, a composer . . . can digress as far as the nature of this instrument will permit. But a solo for the oboe must always be more cantabile, since this instrument greatly resembles the human voice." [83]

The love for wind instruments was a typically German preference. In an autobiography written for Marpurg's *Historisch-kritische Beyträge zur Aufnahme der Musik* Quantz told an anecdote which neatly summed up the Italian outlook on wind instruments. The incident occurred in 1725 when Quantz went to Naples. There he met his countryman Hasse, who at that time was studying with Alessandro Scarlatti.

I begged Herr Hasse to introduce me to his master, the old Scarlatti, which he was quite willing to do. However, he received the anwser: "My son," (so Scarlatti used to call him), "you know that I cannot bear wind instruments because they all blow falsely." Disregarding the refusal Herr Hasse did not stop urging the old man until he finally gained permission to take me there. Scarlatti played for me on the harpsichord, which he knew how to play in a skilled way, although he did not possess as much perfection of performance as his son. Then he accompanied me in a solo. I had the fortune to win his favor to such an extent that he composed a few flute solos for me.[84]

If Quantz had not eventually won Scarlatti over to the side of the flute, the story, which shows the Italian distaste for wind instruments, probably would never have been told. Scarlatti could have been satisfied only by a skilled performer like Quantz, able to manipulate his instrument so that it sounded in tune.

When an Italian achieved fame for his playing of a wind instrument, it was often on foreign soil. Giuseppe San Martini of Milan excelled on the oboe in England. According to Hawkins,

He was a performer on the hautboy, an instrument invented by the French, and of small account, till by his exquisite performance, and a tone which he

[81] Mattheson, *op. cit.*, p. 268.   [82] Avison, *op. cit.*, p. 95.

[83] Scheibe, *op. cit.*, I, 682.

[84] Friedrich Wilhelm Marpurg, *Historisch-kritische Beyträge zur Aufnahme der Musik* (Berlin, 1754), I, 228.

had the art of giving it, he brought it into reputation. Martini arrived in England about the year 1729, and was favoured by Bononcini, Greene, and others of that party, as also by Frederic, prince of Wales, who was his great patron. When Greene went to Cambridge to take his degree Martini attended him, and performed in the exercise for it; and had there a concert for his benefit, which produced him a considerable sum. He was an admirable composer; and, for instrumental music, may, without injury to either, be classed with Corelli and Geminiani. His first compositions were Sonatas for two flutes, and others for German flutes: These are scarcely known, but the greatness of his talents is manifested in six Concertos and twelve Sonatas, published by himself, the latter dedicated to the late princess of Wales.[85]

Likewise, the Italian Besozzi brothers, Alessandro (1700–1775), excelling on the oboe, and Antonio (*ca.* 1707–1781) on the bassoon, won recognition at the Dresden court chapel. In *Wahrheiten der Musik betreffend* Kraus mentions Besozzi the oboist:

Wind instruments are less capable of acrobatics, and for this reason one always hears more melody on these instruments than on the violins of our day. Besides, one can achieve the greatest dexterity on them without falling into buffoonery. . . . The men: Besozzi in Dresden, Fischer in London,[86] Lebrun in Mannheim,[87] whom I had the pleasure of hearing, have achieved the utmost skill on the oboe, without supplanting true melody thereby.[88]

Schubart stressed the fact that wind instruments were more cultivated in Germany than in Italy, saying that since the time of Emperor Charles VI,

Vienna had totally thrown off the Italian chain and had achieved its own characteristics in church, theater, mimic, chamber, and folk styles, which the foreigner admired with quiet envy. Profundity without pedantry, gracefulness throughout and in each part besides, always pleasant color, great understanding of the wind instruments, perhaps somewhat too much comic salt, are the characteristics of the Vienna school.[89]

In the introduction to their dictionary, Choron and Fayolle stressed the German desire for color by means of wind instruments.

In many respects the Germans are in music what the Flemish are in painting; less scrupulous in design, they seek effect in color. That is to say, they like chords which are the most sonorous, such as are produced by wind instruments; a fact which made them pass for preeminent harmonists in contrast to people who confuse *sonority* with harmony. That skill, which consists in the simultaneous use of sounds, is the same all over Europe. It is perhaps the part of art on which all musical nations agree most definitely, in spite of the diversity of

[85] John Hawkins, *A General History of the Science and Practice of Music* (London, 1776), V, 369.
[86] Johann Christian Fischer (d. 1800), born in Freiburg, was oboist in the court chapel in Dresden (1764–1771), and went to London (1768).
[87] Ludwig Lebrun (1746–1790) was oboist in the Mannheim court chapel (1764).
[88] Kraus, *op. cit.,* p. 74.   [89] Schubart, *op. cit.,* p. 77.

CHARACTERISTICS OF THE INSTRUMENTS

language; but the choice of instruments, and consequently the effects, differ in each nation. Thus the Italians love pure harmony, the Germans brilliant harmony, and the French, who wrongly derive their authority from the example of the latter, are generally accused of loving noise somewhat.[90]

The Germans, French, and English often mixed wind and stringed instruments in the same composition. Shy of the wind instruments, the Italians adhered to two violins in the trio sonata. But the Germans, desiring the element of contrast lacking in Italian trio sonata literature, introduced wind instruments in place of the violins and also provided for a mixture of winds and strings. According to Scheibe,

The so-called *Trio* consists of three special parts, of which two are upper parts, and the third constitutes the lower part or bass to them. For the former one sometimes takes flutes, oboes, violins or lutes alone; or two types of instrument, like a transverse flute and a violin, or an oboe and a bassoon; or else one may write for other instruments, combining them according to one's own choice.[91]

Compositions with two upper melodic parts performed by a wind and a stringed instrument favored the wind instrument for the first melodic line and the stringed instrument for the second. Unless the flute or oboe of a chamber work was displayed to advantage, its resources were wasted. On the other hand, the violin could be of use in accompanying as well as in solo passages. In the type of trio sonata where the two parts were no longer equivalent in musical content, range, or instrumental capacity, it was natural to allot the upper sustained melodic part to the flute or oboe and to give the second line, at times melodic, at times accompanying, to the violin. Johann Gottlieb Graun, in the first movement of a trio for oboe, violin and bass, set up a steadily moving triplet figure of broken chords in the violin part before introducing the melody in the oboe part.[92] In the last movement of the same work, in $\frac{6}{8}$ time, he discretely confined the groups of three notes in the oboe part to the range of an octave, whereas he sometimes encompassed a tenth in corresponding figures in the violin part. If a violinist were to play the oboe line, a possibility for which Graun provided, he would have found nothing amiss, although the part would no doubt have appeared rather simple to him.

When wind instruments were used in combination with stringed instruments, the composer had to compensate for the latter's greater versatility. If he wrote two simultaneous lines for the violin, such as a melody plus a simple accompaniment, and wanted the flute or oboe to imitate the passage, he had to supplement the wind part with an accompani-

90 Al. Choron and F. Fayolle, *Dictionnaire historique des musiciens* (Paris, 1817), p. lxxiij.
91 Scheibe, *op. cit.*, p. 676. 92 *Collegium musicum*, No. 24.

ment on a second instrument. For instance, in a *Conversation galante et amusante entre une flûte, un violon, une basse de viole et basse continue,* Op. 12, No. 1,[93] a composition for three melodic instruments besides a simple functional bass, L. G. Guillemain (1705–1770) combined two parts, the melodic line and a drone accompaniment, for the violin. The result amounted to a series of broken intervals, alternating between melody note and drone note. When he gave the same snatch of melody to the flute an octave higher, he had to provide an additional instrument for the drone, in this case the gamba.

EXCERPT FROM A *Conversation galante et amusante,*
Op. 12, No. 1, 1st Movt., by Guillemain

Guillemain also used another technique for allotting two lines to the violin. Instead of *Brechung,* he gives the violin double stops in thirds. When the flute imitates the same passage, the gamba again underlines it. Below is a quotation from the second movement where the violin enters with double stops, which, beginning at measure five, are divided between the two other melodic instruments.

This passage contains a combination of both methods for giving two lines to the violin. In imitation of a flute line accompanied by *Brechung* in the gamba (measure 3), the violin alone carries all three lines by means of double stops combined with *Brechung* (measure 7). It is a striking attempt at making the violin equivalent to both the flute and gamba.

[93] *Ibid.,* No. 58, p. 3.

EXCERPT FROM A *Conversation galante et amusante,*
Op. 12, No. 1, 2d Movt., by Guillemain

Bass.—When Stefano Landi designated the cello for the *continuo* in
the introductory symphony of his opera *San Alessio* (1634), the cello had
already displaced the bass gamba in Italy.[94] So far as the choice of
a melodic instrument in the bass register was concerned, Germany kept
pace with Italy. With the admission of the thorough bass into German
instrumental music about 1620, the cello appeared as the bass melodic
instrument.[95] Yet, while the rest of Europe maintained a *continuo* style
with a keyboard instrument doubled by the cello, the French held that
a single gamba was sufficient foundation in a musical composition.

The French had taken the bass gamba unto themselves, just as the
Italians favored the violin, the Germans the flute, and the English the
harpsichord. Le Blanc considered this equitable distribution the gift of
Divine Intelligence.[96] Be that as it may, the *basse de viole,* with six
strings tuned D, G, c, e, a, d', was especially esteemed in France. This
sole surviving member of the gamba family had in its favor a range of
three full octaves from D to d", a propensity toward blending in ensemble, and a capacity for figuration rich enough to compensate for the
omission of a keyboard instrument.

[94] Hugo Goldschmidt, *Studien zur Geschichte der italienischen Oper im 17.
Jahrhundert* (Leipzig, 1901), p. 33.
[95] Einstein, *op. cit.,* p. 12.   [96] Le Blanc, *op. cit.,* p. 44.

Since its extended range enabled the gamba to participate in the middle register as well as in the bass, it proved a more difficult instrument to replace than the more limited treble gamba. Two members of the braccio family were required to pry it loose from its double stronghold: the cello to supplant it in the *continuo,* and the viola to assume its duties in the middle register.

In France in the first half of the seventeenth century the gamba had often been used for the bass without the support of a keyboard. Publications at that time contained only one printed bass part, usually with figures. When there was no filling-in chordal instrument, the figures were probably used for performance on the many-stringed gamba.[97] Mattheson, skeptical of this procedure, remarked in *Das neu-eröffnete Orchestre,* "Some pretend that they perform the thorough bass on the gamba, complete proof of which I have not had the fortune of seeing to date." [98]

Virtuosity in accompaniment meant to a Frenchman virtuosity on the part of the gamba player. Ancelet, while discussing Jean Baptiste Senallié (1687–1730), said,

Senallié, a man of taste and of rather weak performance, has trained a great number of pupils. He has composed several books of sonatas which are in general favor because of the beauty of their melody. And as it was absolutely necessary that he reconcile himself to the bass gamba which was in fashion at that time, in order to display it well, Senallié composed elaborate basses, full of arpeggios and difficulties. The accompanists' conceit revelled in this, because it was understood that he who produced the greatest quantity of notes was the most brilliant and the cleverest. Therefore Senallié's sonatas had a prodigious sale, through which he profited in order to support and establish his family. A fine example for musicians.[99]

Senallié's efforts were criticized by Blainville who observed that his "simple and naive sonatas would perhaps be more valuable if he had sought less to elaborate their basses." [100]

Many Frenchmen were consistently opposed to a *continuo* keyboard instrument. Although they wanted to write duos for stringed instruments, they realized that compositions for violin and cello could scarcely hold together without chordal padding. One solution—the use of two parallel bass gambas—was thought attractive because of the instrument's adaptability in ensemble. According to Le Blanc,

For perfectly performing the treble and bass, nothing in the world is equivalent to two parallel bass gambas, as in the hands of Père Marais playing his pieces accompanied by M. de Saint-Félix; and Forcroi le Père playing sonatas accompanied by M. de Bellemont.[101]

[97] A. Moser, *op. cit.,* p. 64.   [98] Mattheson, *op. cit.,* p. 283.
[99] La Laurencie, *op. cit.,* I, 172 (Ancelet, p. 13).
[100] C. H. Blainville, *L'Esprit de l'art musical* (Geneva, 1754), p. 88.
[101] Forcroi le Père refers to Antoine Forqueray (1671–1745), who dedicated one of

This parallelism is superior to any other union of paired instruments; for the violin and the cello are too much impeded by the distance of their tones at the double octave. The bass accompaniment on a tenor gamba is all the more charming and attractive; it results in a sweetness of harmony without equal. The violin, in the midst of the harpsichord and cello, has the effect of the small octave on the harpsichord, which many people deprecate and proscribe in spite of its flute-like quality, the reason for its existence.[102]

By the time this was written, the gamba was the exception rather than the rule in countries other than France. It had already become normal procedure to use a cello for reinforcing the keyboard bass in a chordal accompaniment. Although the cello had appeared in Italy toward the end of the sixteenth century,[103] a few decades elapsed before gamba players could adjust themselves to the cello's unfretted fingerboard. Some gamba characteristics were, however, carried over. In Brossard's *Dictionnaire* and Mattheson's *Neu-eröffnete Orchestre,* the cello was described as having five or six strings like the gamba. Mattheson's remarks are valuable because they shed light on the transitional stage of the string basses:

The prominent cello, the *bassa viola* and *viola da spalla,* are comparatively small bass-fiddles, with five and possibly six strings, on which one can perform all sorts of fast passages, variations and embellishments with less work than on larger instruments. Especially the *viola da spalla,* or shoulder viol, has a great effect in accompaniment, because it can penetrate strongly and express the tones clearly. A bass can never be brought out more distinctly and clearly than on this instrument. It is fastened with a ribbon on the breast and is, so to speak, slung on the right shoulder. This has not in the least stopped or hindered the fine resonance.[104]

The viola da spalla, shallower than the usual cello, was a boon to itinerant musicians because of the method of carrying it on the shoulder. However, it was not long before the modern cello won out over these transitional instruments. The four-stringed cello must have been well established for Leopold Mozart to write, "Formerly it had five strings; now it is played only with four. It is the most common instrument on which to play the bass. They were built in varying sizes. The difference was not perceptible in the quality and strength of their sound." [105]

In the second half of the seventeenth century the cello started on its

---

his compositions to M. de Bellemont. Marin Marais (1656–1728) and Forqueray were the two most famous virtuosos on the viola da gamba.

[102] Le Blanc, *op. cit.,* IX², 141.

[103] J. W. v. Wasielewski, *Das Violoncell und seine Geschichte* (Leipzig, 1925), p. 44.

[104] Mattheson, *op. cit.,* p. 285.

[105] Leopold Mozart, *Versuch einer gründlichen Violinschule (1756)* (Vienna, 1922), p. 3.

rise from the perfunctory role of emphasizing a simple harmonic bass to the status of a solo instrument. The establishment of the cello as a solo instrument not only enhanced its role in solo composition, but also assured its place as a full-bodied member of the chamber ensemble. Because the nature of the *basso continuo* inhibited a solo handling of the bass instrument, the development of virtuoso cello playing was slow. The first composer whose work is linked to the cello as a solo instrument is Domenico Gabrielli (1659–1690), called "Minghino dal violoncello" in Bologna, his native city, due to the distinction of his cello sonatas.[106] Attilio Ariosti (1666–1740) and Giovanni Battista Bononcini (1672–1750), both of whom had ties with Bologna and Berlin, transmitted an artistic handling of the cello to the Germans. Italian influence reached Paris through Johann Baptist Stuck (*ca.* 1680–1755), a composer who, born in Florence of German parents, went to Paris as a cellist in the service of Louis XIV. Yet, by the middle of the eighteenth century, neither Italy, France, nor Germany had produced on the cello a specialist of Corelli's magnitude on the violin. It is evidence of the tardy acceptance of the cello that Evaristo Felice dall'Abaco (1675–1742) did not write solo compositions for the instrument.[107] Dall'Abaco is a logical composer to cite as witness, for, after spending his youth in Italy, his native land, he became court cellist in Munich in 1704. Quantz summarized the standing of the cello neatly: "Solo-playing on this instrument is not such an easy matter." [108]

As was the case in the early stages of violin performance, fledgling cellists were loath to leave the lower part of the fingerboard. In emulation of the violin, musicians tried to adapt the pattern of violin positions to the cello, but the cellist could not blindly follow in the wake of the violinist, even though both played instruments from the same family. Disregard of the differences in fingerboard dimensions of the two instruments created a stumbling block which was overcome in time. It became obvious that the cellist would have to disturb the position of his hand more often than the violinist because the fingers could not span so large a compass on the cello. As compensation, the cellist's fingers had fewer notes to command in each position. Just as shifting could not be transferred verbatim from the violin to the cello, so chordal playing, *scordatura*, and harmonics had to be reworked in terms of the lower instrument's own requirements. J. S. Bach's unaccompanied cello sonatas re-

---

[106] *Cello-Bibliothek klassischer Sonaten* (Mainz, 1930). Sonatas by Domenico Gabrielli, ed. Ludwig Landshoff, Nos. 76, 77.

[107] A. von Dommer, *Handbuch der Musikgeschichte*, ed. A. Schering (Leipzig, 1923), p. 583.   [108] Quantz, *op. cit.*, chap. xvii, sec. iv, par. 12.

quire far less chordal playing than his violin sonatas; the former avoid even simple two-part polyphony. So far as *scordatura* is concerned, Bach's fifth suite for cello solo, in C minor, makes use of it by lowering the a string to g.[109] The fact that in his sixth suite Bach uses a five-stringed instrument, tuned C, G, d, a, and e', shows that the transitional bass instruments were still current about 1720.[110]

When Forkel and Gerber mentioned an instrument which Bach "invented," possibly they meant nothing more than this five-stringed cello. According to Gerber,

The stiff manner in which the cello was handled in his time impelled Bach toward the invention of what he called the viola pomposa for the lively basses in his works. It was somewhat longer and higher than a viola. To the depth and four strings of the cello a fifth, e', was added, and it was held on the arm. This convenient instrument gave the player the opportunity to execute the higher and faster passages more easily.[111]

These descriptions do not fit the actual viola pomposa used by other composers (Telemann, Graun, and Lidarti),[112] but seem rather to refer to the transitional five-stringed cello-like instrument used by J. S. Bach. The arguments justifying the viola pomposa sound very much like those Le Blanc used on behalf of the gamba when he emphasized its capacity to blend in ensemble. There was too great a risk in omitting keyboard support unless the instrument playing the bass could climb to the middle register.

In view of French agitation for the gamba, it is surprising that France was first in the field with an instruction book on the cello. Michel Corrette, already cited as a violin theorist, wrote about the cello in 1741.[113] It did not take long for the cello to overtake the gamba's compass. Once the thumb positions were exploited and harmonics were introduced, the cello could handle all the mobility required of a bass instrument. Jacopo Bassevi (1682–1783), called Cervetto, wrote cello sonatas which were in the style of Tartini's violin sonatas, with scales and double stops. Yet Cervetto rarely went into the treble clef. But further discussion of cello virtuosity (which was not actually achieved until the end of the eighteenth century, when Luigi Boccherini came upon the scene) is irrelevant to an investigation of the emergence of chamber style. More to the point is an examination of the place of the cello as the bass of a trio or quartet. When the gamba was found too weak to hold its own in ensemble play-

[109] *Johann Sebastian Bach's Werke*, XXVII, 81.   [110] *Ibid.*, p. 87.
[111] Ernst Ludwig Gerber, *Historisch-biographisches Lexicon der Tonkünstler* (Leipzig, 1790), I, 90.
[112] Curt Sachs, *The History of Musical Instruments* (New York, 1940), p. 367.
[113] Wasielewski, *op. cit.*, p. 64.

ing in relation to the violin, the cello stepped in as the bass instrument able to counterbalance the violin.

By 1650 the set of parts printed for an ensemble piece included two bass parts, one for the keyboard instrument and one for the stringed. These two basses were often identical except for the inclusion of figures for the keyboard player. However, deviations began to creep into the cello part. Instead of merely doubling the clavier, the cello often had diminutions on the basic part. Although not completely independent, the cello part broke up long notes into groups of shorter ones, or played short passages an octave higher for greater emphasis. Sometimes a special string effect appeared in the bass part. It was then the clavierist's turn to rest and let the cello take the spotlight.

Freer handling of the cello already had its roots in seventeenth-century ensemble music. Biagio Marini wrote a *Sonata a 4* for two violins, viola, and unfigured bass in which the bass was divided.[114] A solo bass instrument was sometimes permitted to render the theme, or variations on it, while the thorough bass remained silent. At times the dissociation of bass parts was made apparent in the title as well as in the music, e.g., Torelli's *Sonata for Violin Solo, Cello Obbligato, and Harpsichord.*[115] Here both violin and cello execute technical feats, arpeggios, and fast runs, while the harpsichord supplies the background with sustained organ points reminiscent of the sixteenth-century organ toccata. However, although the violin tackles double and triple stops, the cello does not. The violin is designated "solo," while the cello, confined mainly to diminutions on the figured harpsichord bass, is called "obbligato."

Henry Purcell also allowed the cello some independence from the keyboard bass in his *Sonatas of 3 Parts* (1683),[116] as well as his *Sonatas in 4 Parts* (1697); [117] works which, incidentally, exemplify the inconsistencies of seventeenth- and eighteenth-century chamber music terminology. Both sets have the same trio sonata instrumentation: two violins and bass. Yet, in the largo of the fifth composition in the *Sonatas of 3 Parts,* when the cello does not double the keyboard bass but has a line of its own, there are often four parts by virtue of the division of the bass. Conversely, in the *Sonatas in 4 Parts* the two violins account for two of the parts, while the third and fourth parts cannot be considered as separate entities. There are likewise *Sonates en trio* by Jean François Dan-

---

[114] L. Torchi, *L'arte musicale in Italia* (Milan, 1897–1900), VII, 76.

[115] J. W. v. Wasielewski, *Instrumentalsätze vom Ende des XVI. bis Ende des XVII. Jahrhunderts* (Berlin), No. 35, p. 64.

[116] *The Works of Henry Purcell* (London, 1893), Vol. V.   [117] *Ibid.,* Vol. VII.

drieu (1682–1738) which at times have a doubled bass, and at times have a divided bass resulting in four parts.[118]

In his *Tafelmusik* Telemann attempted a precise distinction between the trio and quartet by naming the compositions according to the number of melodic parts, not the number of melodic instruments. There are three melodic lines in his trios and an effort toward four melodic lines in his quartets, regardless of the instrumentation. Whereas the trios consistently have two treble instruments, and a thorough bass including both string and keyboard, the quartets are varied in the number of melodic instruments designated. The Quatuor for violin, flute, cello, and *continuo,* in E minor,[119] could be considered as a trio sonata in which the cello tends to break away from the *continuo* to become a concerted instrument. Sometimes the cello is allowed to present thematic material without reinforcement by the *continuo;* otherwise, either the cello and thorough bass are identical, or the cello elaborates a diminution of the bass line. Telemann, consciously striving to free the cello from the keyboard bass, must have regarded this Quatuor in E minor more as a composition with four parts than with three, even though he specified only three melodic instruments. In the same collection there appeared a Quatuor with four melodic instruments: flute, oboe, violin, and cello, besides the *fondamento* or figured bass.[120] Because the latter composition had an identical line in the cello and *continuo,* there was no question but that it was a quartet and not a quintet.

When ornamenting a given line, the cello's role corresponded to that of the melodic instruments in the sixteenth and early seventeenth centuries. However, in the eighteenth century the performer did not extemporize the diminution, as formerly, but was expected to play what the composer planned for him. Quantz warned that

A cellist must be careful not to embroider the bass with decorations, as was formerly the bad custom among some great cellists, and must not try to show his skill at the wrong time. For when a cellist, if he does not understand the art of composition, wishes to bring arbitrary decorations into the bass, he does still more harm than a violinist in the accompanying part; especially if the cello part is a bass over which the main part is constantly occupied in decorating the simple melody with ornaments. It is not always possible for one to divine the thought of the other, even when they both have equal knowledge. Besides, it is absurd to make the bass, which should support and render harmonious the ornaments of the other parts, into a sort of upper part, and to rob it of its serious pace, thereby hindering or obscuring the necessary decorations of the upper part. It cannot be denied that melodic and concerted basses in a solo

[118] La Laurencie, *op. cit.,* I, 158.
[119] *Denkmäler deutscher Tonkunst,* LXI/LXII, 196.   [120] *Ibid.,* p. 27.

sometimes suffer from too much embellishment. If only the performer of the bass has enough insight and knows the proper place for it, and if at such an opportunity he adds some ornaments in a skillful manner, the piece becomes more perfect.[121]

Quantz showed foresight by desiring the cellist to play the notes specified, rather than hazard an improvisation which might clash with what the other players were doing. However, instead of preparing the way for a bass line which was to be a melody-bearer in its own right, he expected the bass to remain subordinate and to adhere to an expression of the harmonic implications of the composition without venturing into elaborate ornamentation. The compositions with divided bass lines were transitional pieces. Composers were soon to find out that a single bass part could carry both a fundamental harmonic line to support the composition, and a melodic interest of its own. In the mid-eighteenth century composers were still undecided whether the melodic bass belonged to the harmonic bass or whether the two really had to be considered apart. They were reluctant to allow the bass parts independent existence, and yet they did not realize that the two functions could be consolidated into one part. Hence the confusion in terminology which resulted from sometimes counting the bass as one part and sometimes as two. By the time the solo development in cello virtuosity was carried over to the ensemble, the thorough bass was near extinction. Anton Filtz (1733–1760) went to an extreme in cello consciousness when he named the cello first in the title of his sonatas now known as Op. 6. By specifying that these six sonatas were for *violoncello obligato, flauto traverso o violino e basso,* he made the inclusion of the cello obligatory while the upper register was left to a choice between flute or violin.[122]

In chamber music the status of the "proud bassoon," [123] a possible substitute for the cello, was not of great importance. As a solo instrument it had a rating only in wind ensembles. About the middle of the eighteenth century bassoon sonatas could be played on the cello (*peuvent s'exécuter sur le violoncelle*), and sometimes vice versa. Carlo Graziani, one of La Pouplinière's musicians, published six sonatas for cello and harpsichord (*ca.* 1760). In the fourth sonata the bassoon replaced the cello and finished the movement.[124] Just as there were titles with obbligato cello, there were those admitting an obbligato bassoon, e.g., the *Six Symphonies à quatre parties avec un basson ou violoncelle obligés,* Op. 3 (1755) by Papavoine, head of the second violin section in the or-

[121] Quantz, *op. cit.,* chap. xvii, sec. iv, par. 3.
[122] *Denkmäler der Tonkunst in Bayern,* XVI, xvi.
[123] Mattheson, *op. cit.,* p. 269.
[124] Georges Cucuel, *Etudes sur un orchestre au XVIIIme siècle* (Paris, 1913), p. 12.

chestra of the *Comédie-Italienne* at Paris (1760).[125] Like the other winds, the bassoon was usually an alternative whose part could be played by a stringed instrument. Sometimes after carefully specifying wind and string mixtures, the composer would negate his taste in instrumental color and variety by adding that it could all be managed by strings— thus, the *Six Quartets: Three for the Flute, a Bassoon, a Violin, and a Cello, and Three for an Oboe, a Violin, a Bassoon, and a Cello; They May Be Played by Two Violins and Two Cellos, or a Viola, a Cello, and Two Violins, Op. 3,* by Adrien Leemans (organist at St. Donatien in Bruges).[126] Even as late as 1767 the instrumentation was variable.

Occasionally, an outstanding composer-performer composed for the bassoon and then brought the part to life in performance. Ernst Eichner (1740–1777) was one such musician, over whom Junker waxed enthusiastic. "To hear a duet performed both by Abel and Eichner—Abel's sensitive gamba [127] accompanied by the equally expressive bassoon of Eichner—with the fullest strength, and with the same variation of power, and of coloring—to hear?—Ha! to hear that!" [128] Not every solo bassoonist could hold his own in a duet with a stringed instrument. "It was Eichner's lot to procure for the bassoon admission to the realm of song-like instruments, to which it was entitled by nature. Its tone is full, round, manly, without being empty, without being coarse,—tenor voice; but also tenor song. The singable, the pleasant is also the final aim of his instrument." [129]

Schubart added to the picture of Eichner:

This favorite of the graces played the bassoon with uncommon charm. He commanded its rolling, mocking tone completely, and raised its pitch to the finest tenor, and to the loveliest contralto. His performance, as well as the style of his compositions, were full of pleasing charm and dissolving sweetness. Only he crowds too much confection into his compositions, and thereby destroys the unity of the setting. Thus his style often becomes spotty and many a piece seems to have more than one motive. Frederick the Great used to say that he was only dessert: on the other hand the Crown Prince enjoyed him as hearty nourishment.[130]

[125] La Laurencie, *op. cit.,* II, 266.

[126] Adrien Leemans, *Six Quatuor: trois pour la flute, un basson, un violon, et un violoncelle, et trois pour un haubois, un violon, un basson, et un violoncelle; on peut les executer à deux violons et deux violoncelles, ou un alto, un violoncelle, et deux violons, Oeuvre IIIe* (Paris, *ca.* 1770).

[127] Karl Friedrich Abel (1725–1787) was the last of the great gamba virtuosos. Burney lamented "that he had not in youth attached himself to an instrument more worthy of his genius, taste, and learning. . . . The place of gambist seems now as totally suppressed in the chapels of German princes, as that of lutenist." (Burney, *A General History of Music,* IV, 679.)

[128] Carl Ludwig Junker, *Zwanzig Componisten* (Bern, 1776), p. 4.

[129] *Ibid.,* p. 41.   [130] Schubart, *op. cit.,* p. 92.

In less distinguished hands the bassoon did not always fare well as a solo instrument. Since there was no uniformity in the construction of wind instruments in the eighteenth century, Avison offered the following recommendation:

As to Wind-Instruments, these are all so different in their Tone, and in their Progressions through the various Keys, from those of the stringed Kind, besides the irremediable Disagreement of their rising in their Pitch, while the others are probably falling, that they should neither be continued too long in Use, nor employed but in such Pieces as are expressly adapted to them; so that in the general Work of Concertos for Violins, &c. they are almost always improper; unless we admit of the *Bassoon,* which, if performed by an expert Hand, in a soft and ready Tone, and only in those Passages that are natural to it, may then be of singular Use, and add Fullness to the Harmony.[131]

This would imply that if a bassoon were to be used in chamber music, the work would have to be written with its specific needs in mind. Chamber music must constantly interweave the instruments at its disposal, because it has so few available. Whereas the orchestra, rich in players, could allow the wind instruments to be silent during the middle movement because a full complement of stringed instruments remained at hand, in a chamber composition the composer could scarcely spare one instrument out of three or four for an extended period without weakening the basic ensemble. If the bassoon were chosen for a work, it had to carry its melodic line on an equal footing with the other melodic instruments. In instances where the musical content rendered this impossible, another instrument would clearly have been preferable. The only time that the bassoon did not have full melodic responsibility was when it was a component of the thorough bass. Again, in orchestral music a bassoon might be efficiently utilized as a reinforcement of the bass; but in chamber music where every instrument counted, the melodic *continuo* instrument very often had the added duty of breaking away from the keyboard instrument to introduce melodic diminutions on the harmonic line. The nature of the bassoon was not conducive toward its being the only melodic instrument in the thorough bass; a string bass was required to help carry the line. Avison warned, "The *Bassoon* should also have those gradual Movements which naturally glide in their Divisions, and have the easiest Transitions from one Key to another; and may be admitted as a *Principal* in the *Solo,* or *Rinforzo* in the *Chorus,* but never in the latter without a sufficient Number of other Basses to qualify and support it." [132]

When lost in a sea of string and keyboard bass doublings, the bassoon

131 Avison, *op. cit.,* p. 114.   132 *Ibid.,* p. 97.

could not be considered a chamber music instrument. However, it could be so regarded either when it formed part of a small ensemble of wind instruments or when it was capable of handling a part with melodic interest. Merely as a doubling instrument it could scarcely be entitled to the same privileges as the cello.

Middle Register.—Since four-part writing did not completely disappear with the rapid rise of the trio and solo sonatas, chamber music continued to require the services of a melodic instrument in the middle register. The *canzone,* sinfonia, and sonata, formerly written for an ensemble of gamba instruments, were allotted, toward the middle of the seventeenth century, to instruments of the *braccio* family. Now and then an unwary historian, finding a *canzone* in which each instrument carries an independent melodic line, has been misled into thinking that he has discovered "the first string quartet." In reality, the middle parts of the *canzone* were indicated exactly, not because the composition heralded the classical string quartet, but because the composer chose to include the middle parts in spite of the fact that the *continuo* was already in use in contemporary compositions.

Locating the prototype of the classical string quartet by arithmetically computing the number of instruments involved is a useless pastime. There are factors other than the presence of four solo instruments involved in the classical string quartet. Eaglefield Hull is not convincing when he calls Gregorio Allegri's *Symphonia* for two violins, alto, and bass viol (1650) "the earliest known string-quartet." [133] Hull bases his contention on Allegri's statement that his composition had an absolute number of instruments (*numeris absolutissima*), fortified by Kircher's deduction that the art in this composition was so exact that nothing might be added or subtracted.[134] Actually, the Allegri piece, with its four equivalent parts in the old style, is no different in construction from the organ *canzoni* of the time.[135] Allegri's affirmation that the composition is definitely for four instruments, far from establishing its modernity, confirms its obsolete nature. He wanted to make sure that his *Symphonia* would be performed in the old fashion, as it was written. A new fashion, in which the middle parts might be omitted, was already in sight. The Italians, in rejecting polyphonic composition, soon made provision for performing full-bodied works in the *basso continuo* fash-

133 Eaglefield Hull, "The Earliest Known String-Quartet," *Musical Quarterly,* XV (1929), 72–76.
134 Athanasius Kircher, *Musurgia universalis sive ars magna consoni et dissoni* (Rome, 1650), I, 487–494.
135 Cf. G. Frescobaldi, organ works in *Collectio musices organicae,* ed. Fr. X. Haberl (Leipzig, 1889).

ion. Massimiliano Neri wrote four-part *canzone* for two violins, viola, and bass (1644) in which each movement was conceived polyphonically and no part was slighted.[136] Neri, however, was aware of modern developments, for appended to his *Sonate e Canzone a 4* were *correnti* "really to be played by four, but also by three and two when the middle parts are omitted." He knew that the thorough bass would be on hand to round out the harmonies, and he consequently felt free to sanction the omission of the inner parts. The *continuo*, therefore, was expected to compensate for the missing performers, a duty already demanded of it by Viadana several decades earlier.

Similar instructions appeared in German and French compositions. The trend toward three parts is clear in the *Studentenmusik* of Johann Rosenmüller (1654), where the reduction from five parts to three graphically re-enacted the theoretical origin of the trio sonata. Even in France, where opposition to the *continuo* was strongest, provision was made for leaving out the middle parts. Charles Desmazures, for example, in the preface to his *Symphonic Pieces in Four Parts for Violins, Flutes and Oboes* (1702) observed that,

One will have great ease in playing them since each of the parts is bound separately, with the exception of the second treble which is together with the contratenor. I did this so as not to have a fifth volume and for the convenience of those who do not have a great number of instruments. As the treble instruments and the basses manage everything well enough, one can play them even without the tenor or contratenor.[137]

This example differed from the polyphonic instrumental *canzone* in that the writing was really for two trebles and a bass; the two middle parts, though written out, were conceived with the idea that they would probably be omitted.

Melodic instruments in the middle register might have slipped even further into oblivion, if not for the German unwillingness to abandon polyphonic writing. As an alternate to the Italian trio sonatas for two treble instruments and a bass, German composers wrote works for one treble instrument, gamba and independent *basso continuo*. The gamba, with its broad range linking the treble to the bass, was able to bring to compositions with mixed setting a cohesion impossible in the trio sonata without a middle register melodic instrument. The Germans realized that the compass of the gamba made feasible fugal entrances on different pitches, thus assuring the inclusion of a preconstructed middle line

---

[136] J. W. v. Wasielewski, *Instrumentalsätze vom Ende des XVI. bis Ende des XVII. Jahrhunderts*, p. 32.
[137] Lionel de la Laurencie, "Un Émule de Lully: Pierre Gautier de Marseille," *Sammelbände der Internationalen Musikgesellschaft*, XIII (1911), 54.

and limiting the amount of dependence on the thorough bass. Trios with gamba were a specialty of German composers in the second half of the seventeenth century, as evidenced by the work of Dietrich Buxtehude (1637–1707), Johann Philipp Krieger (1649–1725), Johann Heinrich Schmelzer (1623–1680), Philipp Heinrich Erlebach (1657–1714), and Dietrich Becker (composed 1668).

In trio sonatas for violin, viola da gamba, and thorough bass, the gamba part, when it constituted a diminution of the thorough-bass line, was in the bass register. However, when the gamba and the *continuo* had separate lines the gamba was in the middle register. The gamba's diversity in registration was exemplified in Buxtehude's sonatas, where its fugal entrances were either in unison with that of the violin, a fourth or fifth below, or as much as a twelfth or two octaves below. In Buxtehude's Sonata in D major from his Op. 2 (*ca.* 1696), the gamba range is a full three octaves, from D to d".[138] The *arietta*, which is constructed on a ground bass, demonstrates the dual role of the gamba both as a bass and a middle register instrument. During the original statement of the ground bass, the gamba and harpsichord lines are similar, since Buxtehude wanted to emphasize the ground bass to insure its recognition throughout the movement. For this initial statement, therefore, the doubled bass line and the violin line together constitute only two melodic parts. During later repetitions of the bass, the viola da gamba often goes its own way, making for three melodic parts. In the last statement of the ground, the gamba again duplicates the harpsichord line, drawing the threads together and establishing a firm conclusion.

In Telemann's Sonata in F major for violin, viola da gamba and harpsichord (between 1712 and 1721) the gamba acts as a middle register instrument, independent of the *continuo* bass, which has a harmonic function and rarely enters in the imitation.[139] However, the lower limit of Telemann's gamba is B♭, in contrast to Buxtehude's D, a minor sixth below. In the first and third movements of the Telemann work the gamba enters an octave below the violin, while in the second and fourth movements it is a twelfth lower. Telemann really saw the gamba as a contrasting melodic instrument to the violin, and demonstrated its range in this capacity.

Besides the sonata for one treble instrument, gamba and *continuo*, the Germans nurtured a combination for two treble instruments, gamba and *continuo*. As in the mixed sonata with one violin, the *continuo* at times presented the bass line in a fashion suitable for a keyboard instru-

138 *Denkmäler deutscher Tonkunst,* XI, 90.
139 *Nagels Musik-Archiv* (Hannover, 1927–1940), No. 151.

ment, while the gamba varied it in a string manner; at other times gamba and *continuo* were identical. The quartet combination was equivalent to trio sonata instrumentation with the addition of a gamba. Not only did the gamba increase the opportunity for fugal entrances, but it acted as a solo instrument set off against the basic trio sonata instrumentation. Besides Krieger and Buxtehude,[140] Johann Kasper Kerll (1627–1693) also wrote for two violins, viola da gamba, and thorough bass. In the introductory adagio of his Sonata in G minor Kerll utilized three melodic instruments for fugal entrances, contrasting the gamba to the violins throughout the movement, but not actually setting the gamba off by itself.[141] On the other hand, in the second allegro, after the thorough bass states the theme, the gamba, entering with a diminution on the theme in the same register, remains a soloist for the first half of the movement while the two upper parts are silent. The substance of the gamba's solo play consists of an abundance of sequences. At long last the second violin enters with the theme in its undecorated form an octave higher than its original statement in the *continuo*. Next the first violin enters with the theme at a fifth, followed by the gamba, likewise with the basic theme, in the original register. The gamba is again a member of the ensemble. Its previous solo lapse into toccatalike fantasy shows that the gamba even in a composed role could not forget its heritage as a solo improviser. Kerll's plan for this movement was archaic in other respects also. No sooner did he complete the fugal statements of his first theme, than he discarded it and fugally introduced another which he pursued until the end of the movement. This use of disjointed themes, each with its own set of entrances, recalled the motetlike construction of the *ricercare* and *canzone*.

While the gamba was reluctant to surrender its position as a bass instrument in chamber works, it was even more reluctant to give up the middle register. As late as 1745 Scheibe prescribed the viola da gamba for the third concerted part in the "quatuor" or "quadro." [142] He was interested in the gamba as a color contrast to the other two melodic instruments, preferably flute and violin. Mattheson, however, was modern enough to insist upon the viola, the only member of the quartet that had not yet been well established in other instrumental combinations.

The bass moves along very respectably, so that it furnishes a good, serious fundamental part. Above it one constructs first the upper part with a suitable melody, either for the transverse flute, or the violin, or the like. For the second

140 *Denkmäler deutscher Tonkunst*, XI, 164.
141 *Denkmäler der Tonkunst in Bayern*, II², 159.
142 Scheibe, *op. cit.*, II, 679.

part perhaps one chooses an oboe with diminished notes, *diminutis notulis* (in common parlance a variation), and finally an arm viol, viola di braccio, an alto or tenor violin for the usual accompaniment.[143]

The modern viola, an instrument of the braccio family, arose from the miscellany of instruments answering to the name of viol. Just as the viola da gamba referred only to the bass gamba, so the term "viola da braccio" came to mean only the alto violin or viola. Mattheson contrasted the "affable and penetrating violin" with "the filling-in viola, violetta, viola da braccio or brazzo." [144] The latter "serves for middle parts of all sorts, like *viola prima* (as in high or real alto parts), *viola secunda* (like the tenor), etc., and is one of the most useful components of a harmonious concert; for when the middle parts are missing the harmony goes astray, and where they are badly set everything else becomes dissonant. At times a virtuoso also plays a braccio solo." [145]

At the height of the thorough-bass era in the eighteenth century, even in compositions where the viola had to maintain its thematic entrances with the same assurance as the violin, musicians could not be expected to treat a middle register instrument with the same devotion as a treble or bass. The role of the viola, in music inherently conditioned by the thorough bass, was necessarily limited. As champion of the tenor's share it did not have much to defend. Jean-Jacques Rousseau's concise account reveals the viola's relationship to the trio sonata disposition for two trebles and bass: "Instrumental music is also divided into four parts, which correspond to those of vocal music, and are called treble, fifth, tenor, and bass, but ordinarily the treble is divided into two, and the fifth is united with the tenor, under the common name of *viola*." [146]

Occasionally, the viola stepped out of its role as an instrument of reinforcement. Limits enclosing the middle register were no more rigid than boundaries for the treble and bass; even a middle register instrument was not exclusively confined to its own territory. Leopold Mozart indicated that, aside from playing the alto or tenor part, the viola could perform the bass to a high upper part.[147] Quantz went so far as to give the violist directions for those occasions when no cellist was on hand.

When, in want of a cello, the violist accompanies a trio or a solo, he must, as often as possible, play an octave lower, unless he goes in unison with the bass, and must take good care that he does not go above the upper part, so that the fifths with the fundamental part are not changed to fourths. He would also do well if he, in a solo, would always keep an eye on the upper part, so that when

[143] Johann Mattheson, *Der vollkommene Kapellmeister* (Hamburg, 1739), p. 358.
[144] Mattheson, *Das neu-eröffnete Orchestre*, p. 281.   [145] *Ibid.*, p. 283.
[146] Jean-Jacques Rousseau, *Dictionnaire de musique* (Paris, 1768), p. 363.
[147] L. Mozart, *op. cit.*, p. 2.

it plays in the lower register he can act accordingly. E.g., given that the upper part has a' and the bass its highest d [d']: if the violist wants to take it on the highest string, the fifth which the parts make together would become a fourth, and this would not create the same effect.[148]

A FAULTY SUBSTITUTION OF THE VIOLA FOR THE CELLO

Despite the fact that the viola's main duty was that of an accompanying instrument in the middle register, neglect of this central range continued into the mid-eighteenth century. At that time, although composers again began to feed the tenor some musical sustenance, the part was still undernourished because no good performer cared to choose the viola as his instrument. Advice to the performer to work hard on the viola was based on the ulterior motive that he could use the instrument as a steppingstone to the violin. Quantz was aware that the viola was neglected by superior musicians:

One commonly regards the viola as something of little importance in music. The reason may perhaps be that it is often played by people who are still beginners in music or who have no special talent to distinguish themselves on the violin; or also because this instrument brings all-too-little advantage to its player. For this latter reason skilled people do not like to play it. I believe, nevertheless, that a violist must be just as skilled as a second violinist, to prevent the whole accompaniment from being defective.[149]

Although Quantz was referring here specifically to a violist playing in the *tutti* of a concerto or accompanying a vocal soloist, he indicated that his remarks could also be applied to the viola player as a soloist. He urged the violist to be more diligent in an effort to make his technique equal to that of the violinist, declaring that "A good violist must also be capable of playing a concerted part as well as a violinist: for example, in a concerted trio or quartet. Unlike in older days, this beautiful sort of music is no longer fashionable; probably because very few violists apply themselves to their instrument as much as they ought to." [150]

What Quantz had to say with specific reference to the viola in a trio or quartet is the most pertinent part of his discussion:

If the violist is requested to play a trio or a quartet, he must observe carefully what kind of instruments play with him, so that he can regulate the strength and weakness of his tone accordingly. Against a violin he can play with almost

---

[148] Quantz, *op. cit.*, chap. xvii, sec. iii, par. 16.
[149] *Ibid.*, chap. xvii, sec. iii, par. 1.   [150] *Ibid.*, chap. xvii, sec. iii, par. 5.

the same strength, against a cello or bassoon, with the same strength, and against an oboe somewhat weaker, because the tone is thinner than that of the viola. But against a flute, especially when it plays in the low register, he must play the weakest.[151]

This advice may be profitably applied to a composition such as Johann Gottlieb Janitsch's *Echo* in D major, a chamber sonata for transverse flute, oboe, viola da braccio, and thorough bass (1757).[152] To insure equality among the three concerted instruments, the violist must play with a weak tone. Janitsch, impartial toward his feature instruments, wrote for three active parts supported by a drum bass. The viola opens the first movement with a statement of the theme. Somewhat later the oboe takes the theme a fifth higher than the first statement. Then toward the middle of the movement the flute presents it an octave above the viola. In the second movement Janitsch reverses the order of thematic presentation. Flute, then oboe, and viola, present the theme in the same relative ranges as in the previous movement. To balance the succession of instruments equitably, in the third movement the oboe is the first to state the theme.

Janitsch conformed to contemporary custom by allowing for substitute instruments. In the parts, he indicated that the oboe could be replaced by a violin or a second flute, and the viola da braccio by the viola da gamba. Although the mid-eighteenth-century composer did not always feel that a particular part could be played by one instrument and by no other, he was aware that the performance had to be consistent with the instrumentation selected. Once the performer had made his choice between the violin, oboe, or flute, viola or gamba, cello or bassoon, he had to act accordingly. Quantz clarified this concept by grading the relative intensities involved when a particular instrument is utilized in various combinations.

The tendency of the time toward observing the qualities of each instrument is marked. Avison, for example, observed,

Let every Composer, whether for the Church, the Theatre, or Chamber, thoroughly consider the Nature and Compass of the Voices or Instruments, that are employ'd in his Work; and, by that Means, he will the more easily avoid the common Error of not sufficiently distinguishing what Stile or Manner is proper for Execution, and what for Expression.

He should also minutely observe the different Qualities of the Instruments themselves. For, as vocal Music requires one Kind of Expression, and instrumental another; so different Instruments have also a different Expression peculiar to them.[153]

---

[151] *Ibid.*, chap. xvii, sec. iii, par. 14.   [152] *Collegium musicum,* No. 68.
[153] Avison, *op. cit.,* p. 94.

Scheibe, with reference to the quartet in particular, remarked that "above all the nature and the true individualities of the instruments which one uses must be taken into consideration and observed most closely." [154] In this respect he considered Telemann the outstanding quartet composer. Telemann was upheld as a model composer again and again. The most complete contemporary description of the *quadro*, the one in which Quantz sums up instrumentation, style and pattern, concludes with a reference to Telemann.

A quatuor or a sonata for three concerted instruments and a bass part is really the touchstone of a true contrapuntalist, but also an occasion on which those who are not yet well established in their science may come to grief. The performance of quartets has not yet become fashionable, and consequently cannot be so well known to all. It is to be feared that in the end this sort of music must suffer the fate of the lost arts. A good quatuor demands: 1) A pure four-part setting, 2) A good harmonious melody, 3) Correct and short imitations, 4) A combination of concerted instruments chosen with much discernment, 5) A really bass-like fundamental part, 6) Ideas which one may invert, so that one may build above as well as below; meanwhile the middle parts must retain at least a tolerable and not displeasing melody, 7) One must not be able to notice which of the parts has the preference, 8) Each part, after it has rested, must re-enter, not as a middle part, but as a main part, with an agreeable melody; yet this refers not to the fundamental part, but only to the three concerted upper parts, 9) When a fugue appears, it must be worked out with all four parts, according to all rules, masterfully, but yet tastefully.

A certain group of six quatuors for different instruments, mostly flute, oboe and violin, which Mr. Telemann already composed some time ago, but which has not yet been engraved, may serve as an extremely beautiful model for this sort of music.[155]

Except where entrances were concerned, the middle parts of the average *quadro* movement were acceptable solely by virtue of their being unobjectionable. However, if a movement was fugal, all four parts had to be given equal importance in a more positive way. To clarify the two species of movement, the strict and the free, one must consider the compositional patterns of the seventeenth and eighteenth centuries.

[154] Scheibe, *op. cit.*, II, 679 f.   [155] Quantz, *op. cit.*, chap. xviii, par. 44.

IV: FASHION OF COMPOSITION

Da Chiesa AND Da Camera STYLES

*S*HORTLY after the advent of the trio sonata in the seventeenth century, as a result of the application of thorough-bass methods to the *canzone* and suite respectively, two basic types unfolded: the *sonata da chiesa* (church sonata) and the *sonata da camera* (chamber sonata). The consolidation of the vague contours of the *canzone* into an ordered series with fewer, more-extended movements, created the four characteristic movements of the *sonata da chiesa* with the tempo succession slow, fast, slow, fast, and with the third movement often set in a contrasting key. In theory, the movements of the *sonata da chiesa* bore no relation to dance types, while the *sonata da camera* comprised a series of alternate walking and hopping dances, contrasted in time, but unified in key. The works of Tarquinio Merula (1637) provided early examples of the substitution of the term *sonata da chiesa* for *canzone*, although Merula did not discard the older title entirely. As an early specimen of the *sonata da camera,* Johann Vierdanck's *Newer Pavanen, Gagliarden, Balleten und Corrente, mit 2 Violinen und einem Violon, nebst dem Basso continuo* (Rostock, 1641) may be cited.[1]

The partial coördination of the two species may be found in Biagio Marini's Op. 22, *Different Types of Sonatas, da chiesa and da camera, for All Sorts of Musical Instruments, for Two, Three and Four Parts* (1655).[2] The collection has works marked balleto, sarabande, corrente, sinfonia, and sonata. Although none of the individual compositions was described as either *da chiesa* or *da camera*, it is evident that the *sonate da chiesa* are the six compositions called "Sonata." Since the number of movements varied from one sonata to another, it is not feasible to coördinate the patterns of construction on this basis. However, in general one may say that the movements of the sonatas in *da chiesa* style were juxtaposed with a discriminating ear toward contrast of tempo and meter. On the other hand, the *da camera* movements remain as individual dances (sarabande, corrente, and balletto), except in the first and second balletti where the dances are grouped into larger units.

---

[1] *Organum* (Leipzig, 1930), *Dritte Reihe: Kammermusik,* No. 4.
[2] Dora J. Iselin, *Biagio Marini, sein Leben und seine Instrumentalwerke* (Hildburghausen, 1930), p. 34; Luigi Torchi, *L'arte musicale in Italia* (Milan, 1897–1900), VII, 19.

The first balletto, really a set of variations rather than a sonata, divides into four sections on the same bass, plus a fifth section which, although true to the established harmonic frame, abandons the previous meter. Closer to the nature of the *sonata da camera* is the second balletto, with its entrata grave, balletto, gagliarda, corrente, and retirata. Opus 22 is striking in its contrast of *da chiesa* and *da camera* style within one set of compositions. Marini was a leader, along with Giovanni Battista Fontana (fl. 1600–1630), Marco Uccellini (b. *ca.* 1615), and Giovanni Legrenzi (1626–1690), in organizing the sonata into well-defined successions of movements.

Eventually characteristics of *da chiesa* and *da camera* patterns were intermingled. So far as the *sonata da chiesa* was concerned, the first three movements usually remained true to the original conception. An introductory first movement, often ending on the dominant, led directly to a fast movement in fugal style, which in turn preceded a melodic movement, sometimes conceived polyphonically. It was in the fourth movement that the dance element was frequently introduced, via the gigue, with or without its dance name.

On the other hand, in the *sonata da camera* it was the first movement which showed a *da chiesa* influence. The *sonata da camera,* like its predecessor, the older instrumental suite, had at first a loose organization. Instead of combining an array of dances into a unified composition, Italian composers left to the performer the task of linking together movements chosen from each of several species of dances. German composers, however, preferred to order the dances in a given succession. Johann Rosenmüller, who migrated to Venice after thirty-five years in Germany, published there his *Sonate da camera* (1667), suites coördinated in the German manner. Rosenmüller's contribution consisted in opening the suite with an introductory movement not of dance character. His first movement, in two or three sections with a reprise, is an expression of round, full harmony devised to establish the tonal center of the composition. Set in so sober a fashion the first movement of the *sonata da camera* was endowed with a flavor almost identical with that of the *sonata da chiesa.*

Among the first to enrich the *sonata da camera* with more expansive, freely founded movements in the style of the *sonata da chiesa,* Giovanni Battista Vitali (1644–1692) deserves especially to be noted for the spontaneity and cogency of his music. Giuseppe Torelli (1650–1708) omitted the dance titles in his *sonate da camera,* while Giovanni Battista Bassani (1637–1716) ignored the dance characteristics to such an extent that he wrote prestissimo sarabandes (1677).

The terminology soon became, in a strict sense, incongruous, for the *sonata da chiesa* readily absorbed *da camera* influences, and, conversely, works performed outside the church, and without the use of the organ, continued to display a *da chiesa* pattern of movements. But the terms, however incongruous, persisted, and it remains only to note that as general or fundamental types (or styles) they divided the field of chamber music between them.

Assimilation of *da chiesa* and *da camera* elements is particularly easy to observe in Corelli's trio sonatas, which are divided by opus numbers into groups of church sonatas and chamber sonatas. The difference in instrumentation between the two types has already been described.[3] Of course, Corelli did not adhere blindly to the theoretical patterns any more than Haydn did to what was later called the "sonata form." The interrelationship between Corelli's chamber and church sonatas becomes evident upon comparison of their opening movements; the *da camera* preludio is equivalent to the *da chiesa* largo. In both he pays homage to a homophonic, or a pseudo-imitative style. If homophonic, the three melodic instruments enter together on the tonic triad. Cello, second violin and first violin play the root, third and fifth of the chord respectively, often in a stereotyped 𝅘𝅥. 𝅘𝅥𝅮𝅘𝅥𝅘𝅥 rhythm. If pseudo-imitative, the first violin, accompanied by the bass, opens on the tonic note. After a lapse of a beat or more, the second violin comes in on the tonic also. Although these spaced entrances invite the listener to expect an imitation, the two violins merely indulge in a series of suspensions against each other while the bass is occupied with a downward-moving scale. After bringing the first phrase to a cadence, there is a general rest. Then the first phrase is repeated in a contrasting key—dominant, or relative major if the sonata is in minor. Such similarity of detail makes analogous movements from the two species of sonata virtually indistinguishable.

The voice leading of one Corelli preludio in particular (the first movement of the eleventh *sonata da camera* of Op. 4) intensely disturbed Lecerf de la Viéville, who found in its twenty-four measures "all the bad progressions imaginable." [4] Several years later theorists, among them Saint-Lambert,[5] were still wary of the melodic leap of an augmented second or an augmented fourth, decried by Lecerf. The latter is more convincing in his complaint about several tedious measures, full of repe-

---

[3] See p. 46.

[4] Jacques Bonnet, *Histoire de la musique* (Amsterdam, 1725), IV, 202 f.

[5] Michel de Saint-Lambert, *Nouveau Traité de l'accompagnement du clavecin, de l'orgue, et des autres instruments* (Amsterdam, *ca.* 1710), chap. vi, rule 17.

titious imitation, toward the end of the movement. "A true chime of
death in the seventeenth, eighteenth, nineteenth, and twentieth measures; many repetitions everywhere; and what is worse in my opinion, a
first treble which is completely lacking in inspiration, and which only
has the scum of melody." [6]

Critics were constantly reproaching Corelli for one progression or another in his sonatas. Another movement which attracted attention was
the first allemande of the third sonata of Op. 2. Burney reported an

ALTERNATIVE "BASES" FOR EXCERPT FROM CORELLI'S SONATA, OP. 2, NO. 3
(FROM BURNEY, *A General History of Music*, P. 53)

argument started in 1685 by Giovanni Paolo Colonna, master of the
chapel of San Petronio of Bologna, who objected to a passage which he
thought sounded like consecutive fifths: "Every lover of Music will be
sorry that the charge against Corelli should be well-founded; but it must
be owned that the base is indefensible in the passage which has been
condemned by Colonna, and was not likely to have passed uncensured,
even in an age much more licentious than that of Corelli." The "better
bases" (a and b in the following example), suggested by Burney because
they "were easy to find without altering his design or destroying the

[6] Bonnet, *op. cit.*, IV, 203.

effect of his trebles," certainly circumvent the straightforward line which
Corelli sought.[7]

Now it would generally be acknowledged that in Corelli's bass the
notes imagined through the succeeding rests form a series of suspensions.

When Corelli wrote a slow prelude for a *sonata da camera* of four
movements with tempi alternating between slow and fast, the over-all
pattern was equivalent to a *sonata da chiesa*. Among both species of
sonata he included four-movement compositions in a major key with the
third movement in the relative minor. As opposed to the old suite in one
key, restriction of tonality was not self-evident in the *sonata da camera*
when the third movement was not a dance movement. The movement
in contrasting key, usually ending on the dominant, was either a
freely invented adagio or a grave which often amounted to no more
than a modulatory chordal phrase bridging the span from the second
movement to the fourth. Four-movement sonatas in minor normally remained in one tonality throughout.

In general, Corelli laid emphasis on incorporating the flavor of the
dance into both genres without calling attention to specific dance distinctions. When a movement of a *sonata da chiesa* resembled a dance
form the dance name was usually withheld in spite of the nature of the
movement. Conversely, when a movement of a *sonata da camera* assumed the expression of the corresponding *da chiesa* movement, the
dance name was retained although the movement became a character
piece. For example, the title *Allemande* covered a wide range of tempi.
Although most of the allemandes were allegro, some were presto, largo,
vivace, or adagio. By the time Corelli was through exploiting the allemande, nothing specifically dancelike remained.

For both chamber and church sonatas Corelli wrote movements divided into many sections with changes of tempo and meter, usually with
repetition of a section or sections within the movement. Often an arpeggiated allegro alternated with a sustained adagio section. In some of
these *canzone*like movements the influence of the original *da chiesa* keyboard instrument was apparent. Not all of the distinctions between the
styles of the church and chamber sonata were being annulled. In the
church sonata the effect of the organ was recognizable in passages where
the keyboard instrument had a prolonged pedal point while the violins
gambol above with lengthy chains of arpeggios on one chord—a style
reminiscent of the old toccata.

There are other respects in which the two species of writing continued
to differ. Dances in the *sonata da chiesa* were distinguishable from those

---

[7] Charles Burney, *A General History of Music* (London, 1776–1789), IV, 53.

in the *sonata da camera,* in that there were three active melodic parts in the former and only two in the latter. The church sonata conscientiously made thematic use of the cello as well as the violins, whereas the chamber sonata allowed the cello to lapse into *continuo* placidity. In the chamber sonatas there were fewer polyphonic movements in which the bass entered the imitation, whereas in every allegro movement of the church sonatas the bass took part in the imitative exposition of the theme. On this point hinges a conclusion that was implicit in the second chapter.[8] The first type of trio sonata mentioned there, in which the bass did not engage in the melodic activity, is the *sonata da camera* in its purest form. The second type, in which there were three active melodic parts, is the epitome of the *sonata da chiesa.* Dance movements, because of their melodic periodicity and rhythmic clarity, may be created with a purely harmonic bass, but polyphonic movements, built up in horizontal layers, require that the bass join the imitative play. Corelli modified this distinction by allowing the bass melodic entries in *da camera* dance movements, compensating for them by suppressing the theme in the second violin part. Without a complementary exploration of compositional patterns, instrumentation alone cannot reveal the clue for investigating the trio sonata. The distinguishing factor between the church and chamber sonatas was the first allegro movement. The introductory movement as well as the middle slow movement was often identical in both cases. Although the last movement was usually polyphonic in the church sonata, this movement too could be couched in dance terms. The only *da chiesa* movement which was characteriscally polyphonic in all three parts and which was conceived without obvious reference to dance types was the second.

The title *da chiesa* rarely appeared over a solo sonata.[9] Corelli's solo sonatas, Op. 5 (*ca.* 1700) were not divided under the heading of *sonata da chiesa* and *sonata da camera,* as were his trio sonatas. Perhaps Corelli thought it presumptuous to imply in his title that a solo sonata was capable of the elaborate part writing that was a prerequisite for a *da chiesa* style. Nevertheless, a parallel distinction is inherent in Op. 5, whereby Nos. 1 through 6 may be construed as church sonatas, and Nos. 7 through 12 as chamber sonatas. This assumption is easily substantiated on the basis of the criteria just established. First of all, sonata No. 1 contains a *canzone*like movement featuring arpeggiated sections on a single chord, such as are characteristic in the trio sonata of the *da chiesa* type. Secondly, the first group of sonatas (church sonatas) in Op. 5 utilizes double

[8] See p. 21.

[9] An exception is Tommaso Albinoni (1674–1745), *Sonate da chiesa a violino solo e violoncello e continuo,* Op. 4 (Robert Eitner, I, 90).

stops in an effort to retain the *da chiesa* practice of contrapuntal voice leading, while the second group (chamber sonatas) does not. In order to reproduce with only one violin the part writing of the *da chiesa* trio sonata, Corelli had to contract the two upper parts into one, which he did notably in the fugal allegro movements. The violin not only must make the initial statement of the theme, but also the customary fugal answer, an obligation which can be fulfilled only through double stopping. As in the trio sonata, the third entrance of the theme was left to the *continuo*. Despite Corelli's skill in condensing the two violins of the trio sonata into one in the solo sonata, it is plain that a rigid adherence to fugal writing would have hampered the future of the solo sonata. Even Corelli, after the exposition of the theme, employed fugal texture only incidentally or not at all. The advance of the solo sonata almost of necessity impeded the development of the *sonata da chiesa*.

The twelfth sonata of Op. 5, differing from any pattern of *sonata da camera* mentioned so far, was based on a theme called *La Folia*. Chronologically speaking, composition based on the art of varying a given theme antedates the *sonata da camera*. The chamber sonata emerged from the suite, which in turn had originated in the variation. The precedent for variations using trio and solo sonata instrumentation was well established by the time Corelli came on the scene. Especially dear to the Germans, the variation principle flourished in the works of Johann Jacob Walther (1688) [10] and Heinrich Biber (1681),[11] both of whom preferred the melody in the upper part, the violin line abundantly embellished, and the bass unadorned. In Biber's first sonata the same bass is repeated almost sixty times. Although Corelli likewise allotted the *Folia* melody to the treble, he gave more consideration to the bass. During the statement of the *Folia* theme the bass remains purely functional, but in the ensuing sections, while the harmony remains the same, the bass as well as the theme is varied. The bass often shares in pursuing a motive which is interlocked with the progression of the upper part, or it occasionally has a distinctive figuration itself. Since a variation design appears elsewhere in Corelli's Op. 5, in a sonata designated as a *da chiesa* type,[12] it would seem arbitrary to regard the variation principle as an attribute primarily of the *sonata da camera,* unless one remembers that, just as dance movements were carried over from the chamber to the church sonata, so variations on dances were similarly transferred.

Other composers likewise combined *da chiesa* and *da camera* styles within a single work, e.g., Nos. 4 and 5 of Evaristo Felice dall'Abaco's

10 *Organum,* III, No. 28.   11 *Denkmäler der Tonkunst in Österreich,* V[2].
12 Sonata No. 5, fourth movement.

Op. 3, XII *Sonate a tre* (1715).[13] Although both compositions are *sonate da chiesa* with the slow, fast, slow, fast alternation of tempi, sonata 5 is a "normal" church sonata, while sonata 4 defies convention with a second movement that is clearly a gigue, even though the dance designation is not mentioned in the superscription. The conversion of the first allegro of a *sonata da chiesa* into a dance movement was a step toward the final amalgamation of the two sonata types. With Corelli it was only the finale of the *sonata da chiesa* which could become dancelike. With dall'Abaco even the second movement, ordinarily the bulwark of the church sonata, succumbed to dance influence. However, in the second movement of sonata 4, despite its dancelike *da camera* nature, there is still a trace of one important *da chiesa* characteristic. The finale of No. 9, a *sonata da camera* in the same opus,[14] serves well for comparison, since the gigue rhythm assures similarity of motive with the second movement of No. 4. The difference between the two gigues lies in the extent to which the bass participates contrapuntally. In sonata 4 the bass formally states the theme in its entirety, while in sonata 9 the bass has no thematic independence whatsoever. Although the dance style invaded the first fast movement, the very core of the church sonata, vestiges of *da chiesa* style nevertheless lingered to the extent that the bass still continued to play a melodic part in the movement.

Since Italy showed the greatest constructive interest in the sonata, composers from other countries who wished to explore further had to build on the Italian foundation. Germany, England and France all looked directly to Italy for guidance. Among the German visitors to Italy perhaps the most important in this connection were: Nicolaus Adam Strungk (1640–1700) who, while spending several years there with the Duke of Hanover, met Corelli in Rome; [15] Johann Adam Birckenstock (1687–1733), who, after studying in Italy for five years, turned out German sonatas modeled upon Corelli; and Johann Georg Pisendel (1687–1755) who studied with both Torelli and Vivaldi.

England, too, tried to copy the Italian masters. Many English composers went to Italy to study, while others, like Henry Purcell, openly admitted their indebtedness. In the preface to his *Twelve Sonatas of Three Parts* (1683) Purcell put the matter plainly:

I shall say but a very few things by way of Preface, concerning the following Book, and its Author: for its Author, he has faithfully endeavour'd a just imitation of the most fam'd Italian Masters; principally, to bring the Seriousness

---

[13] *Collegium musicum*, Nos. 41 and 42.   [14] *Ibid.*, No. 43.
[15] Trio sonata for two violins, viola da gamba, and organ in *Organum*, III, No. 18.

and gravity of that Sort of Musick into vogue, and reputation among our Country-Men, whose humor, 'tis time now, should begin to loath the levity, and balladry of our neighbors.[16]

The sonatas of the Italian masters who influenced Purcell must have antedated those of Corelli. According to Burney,

It does not appear that at this time any of the works of Corelli had been published even in Italy. And though, a few years before Purcell's death, they may have been brought hither and circulated in manuscript, yet they were not published at any of our Music-shops, in print, till 1710. So that Purcell had no better Italian Music for violins to imitate than that of Bassani, Torelli, or others inferior to them; and though his sonatas discover no great knowledge of the bow, or genius of the instrument, they are infinitely superior in fancy, modulation, design, and contrivance, to all the Music of that kind, anterior to the works of Corelli.[17]

Purcell's sonatas, although contemporary with those of Corelli, could not be similar in content. In 1680 Purcell was still writing fantasias with from three to seven contrapuntal parts for a chest of viols. Since no publisher would undertake these outmoded compositions, he succumbed to fashion three years later by producing trio sonatas. His first set of sonatas is closer in texture to his fantasias than the second set (published posthumously in 1697). The later group shows Italian influence much more clearly than the first set; the writing is less forced contrapuntally, and the dissonances formed by passing chords are not so abrupt as in the earlier works. In both sets, the fugal movements, which give the sonatas their *da chiesa* character, are usually labeled *Canzona*, indicating a conscious demarcation both from the homophonic and from the lighter contrapuntal movements. The *Canzona* appeared usually as the second movement of the sonata, the same central position which a polyphonic movement of this kind had occupied in the *sonata da chiesa*.

Purcell concentrated on *da chiesa* patterns, and his works, in consequence, could not bear so directly upon the general trend of sonata development as compositions more amenable to *da camera* influence. In France, however, the pendulum swung in the other direction. To the French, who had long reveled in the clarity and simplicity of dance types, the Italian *da camera* style was much more readily acceptable than the *da chiesa* style. In 1692 François Couperin le Grand, seeking a judicious union of Italian and French art, developed, with the daring of a pioneer, a sonata in the vein of the Italian *sonata da chiesa*, with slow and fast movements alternating. However, since the French would not tolerate purely instrumental work unrelated to a dance or a literary idea

16 H. Purcell, *Complete Works* (London, 1878–1928), Vol. V; see p. 78 above.
17 Burney, *op. cit.*, III, 502.

unless they could blame it on an Italian, Couperin presented these sonatas under an Italian alias. When the time came to publish them for
French consumption, he tempered his youthful ardor for the Italian
style by appending a long series of dances to the end of each sonata. He
felt compelled to satisfy the French craving for dance forms by adding,
for example, an allemande, two courantes, a sarabande, gigue, chaconne,
gavotte, and a minuet. His, however, was a mechanical solution. Absolute instrumental movements occupied the first half of the sonata and
dance movements the second half. The sonatas eventually appeared under the title *Les Nations, sonades et suites de simphonies en trio en
quatre livres séparées* (1726), with a preface in which Couperin disclosed
his hoax:

Several years have already passed since some of these trios were composed.
Several manuscripts thereof, which I distrust because of the negligence of the
copyists, have been circulated in the world. From time to time I have increased
their number, and I believe that those who value the truth will be satisfied
with them. The first sonata in this collection was also the first that I composed;
it may have been the first composed in France. Its history is curious. Charmed
by those of Signor Corelli, whose works I love, on my life, in the same way as
the French works of M. Lulli, I ventured to compose one which I performed in
the concert where I had heard those of Corelli. Knowing the eagerness of the
French for foreign novelties above all, and distrusting my own powers, I did
myself a very good turn with a little white lie. I pretended that a relative of
mine actually in the entourage of the King of Sardinia had sent me a sonata
by a new Italian author. I arranged the letters of my name so as to form an
Italian name which I put in its place. The sonata was devoured with avidity,
and I refrained from apology. Feeling encouraged, however, I wrote others,
and my Italianized name won great applause for me in disguise. My sonatas,
fortunately, invited enough favor so that the ambiguity did not make me blush.
I compared these first sonatas with those which I have composed since and did
not change or augment anything of importance. I have only added some long
suites of pieces to which the sonatas only serve as preludes, or a sort of introduction.[18]

This juxtaposition of *da chiesa* and *da camera* movements did not
prevent Couperin from permeating the "abstract" movements with the
French love of the dance. The *chiesa* style, borrowed from the Italians,
and the *camera* style, synonymous with the French suite style, were consolidating their forces.

The hybrid of *da chiesa* and *da camera* styles, expressed in Couperin's
Les Nations, was echoed several years later in Handel's trio sonatas of
Op. 5 (London, 1739). In his first set of trio sonatas, Op. 2 (London,
1733) Handel adhered to the *da chiesa* type: slow, fast, slow, fast, with a

[18] *Œuvres complètes de François Couperin*, ed. Maurice Cauchie (Paris, 1933),
IX, 7 f.

polyphonic allegro as a second movement and often also as a fourth. But in his Op. 5 the *da chiesa* type underwent decided changes which resulted in an intensified union of styles. The initial sonata in this opus, a pattern for the rest, at first follows the regular *da chiesa* design: slow, fast, slow, fast with the third movement in the relative minor key. The fourth movement, "Polonoise, Allegro," in spite of its fugal entrances has a dance character. This movement, acting as a pivot between the *da chiesa* and *da camera* styles, leads to the "Gavotte," a dance tacked on as the fifth movement. Although the number and choice of dances at the end of the other Op. 5 sonatas vary, in all but sonata 4 (which opens with an allegro) the *da chiesa* pattern is followed by one or more *da camera* movements.

Each of the sonatas in the opus has a polyphonic second movement, while several also have contrapuntal fourth movements. In No. 5, the second movement is entitled *Come alla breve,* a parody on the strict contrapuntal style with numerous suspensions and rigid neighboring-note embellishments. Among the intervening movements of Op. 5 there are dances such as passacailles, operatic airs, or polyphonic movements. All the sonatas end with a dance movement, the gavotte and the minuet each used upon three occasions and the bourrée represented once.

Handel sought an internal coördination of styles in Op. 5: a conclusion confirmed by comparing Op. 2, No. 3, in the conventional four-movement *da chiesa* pattern, with Op. 5, No. 6. For the latter sonata Handel reworked the first three movements of Op. 2, No. 3, substituted a different allegro for the fourth movement, and then added a dance movement at the end, thus demonstrating for posterity the process of conversion which took place when a *sonata da chiesa* absorbed the influence of the *sonata da camera*. Not only did he alter the pattern of movements, but he changed the very essence of the whole work, amplifying the motives in the upper parts, making the bass line flow, constructing the musical bridges from the motives of the theme itself instead of from irrelevant connective material, and, finally, maneuvering so that the total effect was harmonically more sound and linearly less clashing. Some of the improvements were the kind which appear when a competent composer revises his own work. However, the fact that in the revision Handel did not adhere to the original number of movements in itself shows that he was not merely house cleaning. His intention was to remodel according to the fashion of the times.

Complete dissolution of the distinction between *sonata da chiesa* and *sonata da camera* came with the adoption of character titles. To designate the particular quality of a movement, the eighteenth-century musician used a term which, in a literal sense, indicated only the tempo at which the movement should be performed. The movements of the *sonata da chiesa*, being free of nonmusical obligations, were naturally receptive toward identification by tempo. However, since the position of a movement in the sonata was also a relevant and important consideration, the tempo alone could not satisfactorily reveal the movement's character. In the usual *da chiesa* four-movement pattern, the two slow movements, first and third, and likewise the two fast movements, second and fourth, were of contrasting character. The first movement might begin with all three parts at once, while the third movement might rely upon only one upper part, accompanied by the bass, to introduce the main theme, followed later by the second upper part with a countertheme. It was in good taste to use the first-movement pattern for the third movement, providing that the two were contrasted in some way. If the first movement was in duple time, then the third was preferably in triple time; or if both were in the same meter, then it was advantageous to compose one of the slow movements in a tempo faster or slower than the other.[19] In the case of the fast movements, one was usually fugal while the other was either strict or free. The speed of the fugal movement was so closely associated with the term "allegro" that the tempo became synonymous with the nature of the movement over which it appeared. Leclair, in the preface to his Op. 13 (1753), emphasized the close relationship between tempo and character by equating the tempo "allegro" with the character "gay." [20] To Leclair "gay" meant a speed which was fast, but not *very* fast. When the performer played an allegro fugue at a very fast speed, he denied the character of the movement and rendered it trivial.

The use of tempo-character titles in *da camera* movements was not so immediate. Through the first two decades of the eighteenth century it was customary in trio sonatas of the *da camera* type to write both the title (dance, introductory, or vocal) and the tempo indication above the movement. For example, the movements of Dall'Abaco's *sonata da camera* Op. 3, No. 9, were designated: largo, entrata; allemanda, allegro; aria, largo (sarabanda); and giga, allegro. Over the opening movement, although the composer wrote "largo" first, he felt constrained to add the introductory title "entrata." From the second and fourth movements it is evident that the same tempo could be attached to different dances. When the dance titles were omitted, "allegro" often indicated either the character of an allemande, a corrente, or a gigue, depending upon the

[19] Johann Adolph Scheibe, *Critischer Musikus* (Leipzig, 1745), p. 678.
[20] M. Leclair l'aîné, *Ouvertures et sonates en trio*, Op. 13 (Paris, *ca.* 1753).

time signature: $\frac{4}{4}$ in the case of the allemande, $\frac{3}{4}$ for the corrente, and $\frac{6}{8}$ or $\frac{12}{8}$ for the gigue. Since the performer knew the character of the dance corresponding to each of these time signatures, he could easily establish the tempo of the movements without the name of the dance. Purcell in his *Lessons* (1696), began his explanation of tempo in the old-fashioned way by describing the duration of a semibreve as the time it would take to say "one, two, three, four," etc. But he changed his procedure when it came to describing $\frac{6}{8}$ time. He realized that if he associated this meter with the gigue and passepieds, familiar to all, the speed would be easily grasped.[21] In other words, the character of a piece was often sufficient to determine its tempo.

The gavotte and minuet retained their names, while the other dance names were often omitted and only the corresponding tempo indications given. Marpurg, reviewing this trend in his *Clavierstücke mit einem practischem Unterricht für Anfänger und Geübtere* (1762), declared that sonata titles like "allegro," "adagio," "presto," and others could be applied to movements which approach the character of allemandes, courantes, and gigues.[22] Giorgio Antoniotto, in 1760, grouped dances of a similar character under one tempo heading, saying specifically that "adagio" was a substitute title for sicilienne or sarabande, while allegro gratioso referred to the minuet.[23]

Character titles did not evolve solely in the realm of chamber music. Appellations which referred originally to opera arias were later transferred to instrumental music. Characteristic aria types developed within the various tempi. The smooth-flowing, lyrical andante aria, for example, was more caressing than the decisive, rhythmically angular largo aria. Eventually, the types were stylized to the extent that the tempo indication denoted the character of the piece.

Crosscurrents among *da chiesa, da camera,* and operatic styles created a confusion in titles. All would have been clear if the *da chiesa* allegro had stayed in the *sonata da chiesa* and the operatic largo had been content to remain at the opera. However, when the *da chiesa* allegro penetrated the *sonata da camera,* it had to share its tempo name with certain dances also called allegro. Likewise, the operatic largo had to divide the honors with the dance sarabande. The connections between tempo titles and character were scarcely solidified. A good case in point is Tartini's Sonata in B♭ major, in the usual four-movement sequence with tempo

21 Purcell, *op. cit.,* VI, (v).
22 J. Loisel, "Les Origines de la sonate classique," *Le Courrier musical,* X (1907), 524.
23 Giorgio Antoniotto, *L'arte armonica; or, A Treatise on the Composition of Musick* (London, 1760), p. 104.

titles: largo, allegro, largo, allegro.[24] Although two movements have the same title, their character is different in each case. The opening largo, in C time, displays the intricate rhythmical subdivisions with many dotted notes associated with the operatic largo; while the third movement largo, in $\frac{3}{4}$ time, is in sarabande style. The two allegros, although both in duple time and dancelike, are differentiated by a smooth motion in the first in contrast to a dotted, marchlike rhythm in the second. Even where there were counterinfluences between the mediums, differences in tempo remained. The largo at times may have had a sarabande character both in opera and in chamber music, but its tempo was not necessarily the same in the two genres. Avison's report bears witness to the variation of tempo terminology in diverse fields:

It is also by the Efficacy of musical Expression, that a good Ear doth ascertain the various Terms which are generally made use of to direct the Performer. For Instance, the Words *Andante, Presto, Allegro,* &c. are differently apply'd in the different Kinds of Music above-mentioned: For, the same Terms which denote *Lively* and *Gay,* in the Opera, or Concert Style, may be understood in the Practice of Church-Music, as, *Chearful* and *Serene,* or, if the Reader pleases, less lively and gay: Wherefore, the *Allegro,* &c. in this Kind of Composition, should always be performed somewhat slower than is usual in Concertos or Operas.

With regard to the Instrumental Kind; the *Style* and *Air* of the *Movement* must chiefly determine the exact *Time* or *Manner,* in which it ought to be performed: And unless we strictly attend to this Distinction, the most excellent Compositions may be greatly injured, especially when the Composer is not present, either to lead, or give the *Air* of his Piece.[25]

Aside from the confusion in tempo designation due to the interchange of mediums, there was further cause for bewilderment within the dances themselves. Established dances were often slowed down to the point where their original character and rhythm were scarcely recognizable. Handel wrote largos (e.g., in the violin sonatas in F major, No. 12, and A major, No. 14) which, in spite of the slow tempo, actually were based on the old rhythm of the courante. Likewise, the Belgian musician Jean-Baptiste Loeillet (1680–1730) opened a trio sonata in G major with a lento affettuoso which is actually in $\frac{6}{8}$ gigue style.[26]

Some of Leclair's solo sonatas were transitional pieces in which movements without dance titles appeared, as well as movements clinging to the older method of designation. For example, in his four-movement solo sonata in E minor, the opening adagio is actually a chaconne, due

[24] *Alte Meistersonaten für Geige und Klavier,* ed. K. Geiringer (Vienna, *ca.* 1937), pp. 13–21.
[25] Charles Avison, *An Essay on Musical Expression* (London, 1752), p. 107 f.
[26] Ed. A. Béon (Paris, 1911).

to the constant repetition of the ground bass; the allegro ma poco, a movement in $\frac{3}{4}$ time, is in reality a courante; [27] while the closing movement, a gavotte in $\frac{2}{4}$ time, is merely labeled "allegro." In these movements Leclair refrained from referring to dance titles. But in the third movement, which alone retained its dance name, he reverted to old-fashioned terminology, writing "sarabanda, largo," in the usual order of dance title followed by tempo. To cite another example among many, in the sonata, *Le Tombeau,* where the movements are called "grave"; "allegro ma non troppo"; "gavotte, allegretto grazioso"; "allegro," only the third movement retained its dance title.[28]

While the merger of *da chiesa* and *da camera* elements and the codification of character titles were in process, the trio sonata was being displaced inexorably by the solo sonata. Although both Scheibe and Quantz discussed the trio sonata with reference to the old four-movement *da chiesa* pattern, Scheibe admitted that when three- and four-part sonatas were worked out in concerto style, "one may now and then omit the first slow movement, and immediately begin with the lively movement." [29] Corelli had used the three-movement pattern in his *da chiesa* trio sonata Op. 3, No. 6, fast, slow, fast (1689). However, the three-movement pattern in *da camera* style received a much greater impetus from the solo sonata than from the trio sonata. When it came to characterizing the movements in the threefold adagio, allegro, allegro pattern, Scheibe and Quantz shifted their attention to the solo sonata. The character of the adagio, the first movement, was well formulated, and Quantz's rules, covering operatic, *da camera,* and *da chiesa* styles, may be taken as standard:

In order for a solo to do honor to the composer and performer: 1) The adagio in itself must be cantabile and expressive. 2) The performer must have the opportunity to show his judgment, invention and insight. 3) Delicacy must be mixed here and there with something spiritual. 4) One must create a natural bass on which it is easy to build. 5) A thought must not be repeated too many times either on the same tone or in transposition; for that will not only tire the player, but will also have a sickening effect upon the listener. 6) The natural melody must at times be interrupted by some dissonances, to excite passions in the listener. 7) The adagio must not be too long.[30]

Whereas the second and third movements of the solo sonata were both called "allegro," the meaning of the term varied according to the posi-

27 *Alte Meistersonaten,* pp. 3–12.

28 *Die hohe Schule des Violinspiels,* ed. F. David (Leipzig, *ca.* 1880), p. 44.

29 Scheibe, *op. cit.,* II, 675.

30 Johann Joachim Quantz, *Versuch einer Anweisung die Flöte traversiere zu spielen* (1752), reprint ed. A. Schering (Leipzig, 1906), chap. xviii, par. 48.

tion of the allegro movement in the sonata. Quantz's prescription follows:

The first allegro demands: 1) a fleeting melody, coherent and somewhat serious; 2) a good connection of the thoughts; 3) brilliant passages well united to the melody; 4) a good arrangement in repetition of the thoughts; 5) beautiful, well-chosen passages at the end of the first part, which must be adjustable so that one can close the last part with them in transposition. 6) The first part must be a little shorter than the last. 7) The most brilliant passages must be used in the last part. 8) The bass must be composed naturally and must always move in a lively manner.[31]

Scheibe added to this that the first allegro could be, "fuguelike or with free imitation; yet one must make sure that the modulation is clear and adequate for the instrument and that it displays the instrument at its best. A cantabile, original, clear, and agreeable phrase would be most suitable for the main subject. After this follow divers variations and vigorous and extensive passages, yet the main subject must predominate noticeably." [32]

In discussing the second allegro Quantz completely dissociated the term "allegro" from tempo: "The second *allegro* can be either very gay and fast, or moderate and arioso. One must regulate it according to the first [allegro]. If the first is serious, the second may be gay. But if the first is lively and fast, the second must be moderate and arioso." [33]

One may well wonder how possible it is to derive a single tempo from an allegro designation which one can interpret as "either very gay and fast, or moderate and arioso." Giorgio Antoniotto also disregarded tempo implication in the title "allegro." He warned that people understood the term to refer to a quick and lively movement, when actually "this term allegro regards the manner of expressing the notes, but not to the measure of the time." [34]

Even when tempo designations were regarded as a guide to expression rather than to speed, they were not ignored as long as the time signatures retained their function of determining relative units of time in various compositions. Movements with eighth notes as the basis of the speed were to be played faster than movements based upon quarter note measurements. If the implications of the time signature were carried out in composition, a glance at the graphic aspect of a page of music gave the performer a convincing idea of the tempo. J. S. Bach was so meticulous in his use of meter signatures that in the *Well-tempered Clavier* he relied on the meter alone to determine the speed of most of the pieces. The use of a high fraction in a meter signature occasionally appeared also in Bach's

31 *Ibid.,* chap. xviii, par. 49.   32 Scheibe, *op. cit.,* p. 682.
33 Quantz, *op. cit.,* chap. xviii, par. 50.   34 Antoniotto, *op. cit.,* p. 104.

chamber works, as the $\frac{12}{16}$ time in the allegro of his first flute sonata.[35] However, in his chamber music Bach did not rely solely on exact designation of the meter, but also included titles.

A clear proof that the careful statement of the meter in the time signature freed the title (andante, allegro, etc.) from responsibility in determining tempo may be found in Handel's Op. 5, No. 6. Here he offered a choice of two alternate fifth movements, an andante in $\frac{6}{8}$ time or a menuett, allegro moderato in $\frac{3}{8}$. The style of the movements is so similar that their tempi must be identical in spite of the fact that one is marked "andante" and the other "allegro moderato." In a modern edition, Max Seiffert gave each movement the same metronome marking ($\quad = 120$), thereby indicating his belief that the unit of time has the same speed in both cases. In determining the tempo of an eighteenth-century composition the graphic aspect must be considered along with the superscription. Where the basic note values are the same, the tempi are equivalent, despite the implications of the verbal titles.

In accordance with the principles along which character titles evolved, there could be no such absurdity as a movement with a largo character and a very fast tempo. There were certain limits of tempo within which a given character title had meaning. As the tempo indication took on character significance, it still continued to indicate speed in the broad sense of denoting whether a movement was relatively fast or slow. Because pieces of similar character had like tempo and quality of sound, Leclair, in the preface to his fourth book of violin sonatas (1738), could instruct performers to group the movements according to their character:

All those who wish to succeed in performing this work in the taste of the author ought to strive to find the character of each piece, as well as the real tempo and quality of sound which suit the different pieces. An important point—which one cannot stress too much—is to avoid that confusion of notes which are added to vocal pieces and that confusion of expression; they serve only to distort the compositions. It is not less ridiculous to change the tempi in two successive rondeaux, and to play the major faster than the minor; it is all right to enliven the major by the fashion of playing it, but that may be done without accelerating the tempo.[36]

Since the tempo was determined by the character of the piece, the rondo, whether in major or minor, had one definite speed.

With the metamorphosis of dance titles into character titles, the identity of the *sonata da camera* dissolved; with the conversion of the trio sonata to the solo sonata, the strict polyphony of the *sonata da chiesa*

---

[35] *Johann Sebastian Bach's Werke* (Leipzig, 1852–1926), IX, 18.
[36] M. Leclair l'aîné, *Quatrième Livre de sonates à violon seul*, Op. 9 (Paris, *ca.* 1738).

gave way to a freer style. As the *sonata da chiesa* and the *sonata da camera* amalgamated into a sonata type containing contrast within itself, adherents of the French and Italian styles were reconciled to some extent. The inclusion of the dance flavor, even without the dance title, satisfied the French love for the dance and allayed French suspicion of pure instrumental music; while the omission of the dance title satisfied the Italian desire to write pure instrumental music.

Style Galant AND LEARNED STYLE

Following upon the union of *da chiesa* and *da camera* styles, the fashion of chamber composition turned in the mid-eighteenth century to the *style galant (ungebunden, frey Styl)*. Italian terms succumbed as the new musical style became identified with the luxury, frivolity, and grace of the pleasure-loving French court. The Germans, anxious to emulate French conduct and thought, willingly joined the rest of Europe in adopting French terms which were soon to become conventional. Mattheson addressed the *homme galant,* before the style associated with that name was fully synthesized, in the title of *Das neu-eröffnete Orchestre* (1713): "The Newly-Inaugurated Orchestra, or Universal and Basic Introduction on How an *Homme Galant* May Acquire a Perfect Understanding of the Loftiness and Majesty of Noble Music, Form His Taste Accordingly, Understand the *Technical Terms* and Argue Cleverly about This Admirable Science." [37] For his convenience, the *homme galant* was promptly instructed as to what concerned him and what did not. The old contrapuntal divisions into the simple and diminished or florid styles, into the serious and luxuriant styles, into ancient and modern styles, were all superfluous. What Mattheson considered pertinent and sufficient is interesting. "The greatest difference exists between church, theater and chamber music, and that is enough for an *homme galant*." [38]

These differences each had a definite bearing on the *style galant*. The core of the style was chamber music, actually called *Galenterie-Music* by Meinrado Spiess. [39] When to the chamber style the flavor of the theater style was added, and the resultant combination was contrasted with the church style, the *style galant*—fanciful, personal, and elegant—reached the stage of crystallization. Although devotees of the *style galant* denounced counterpoint in a strict sense, they considered "counterpoint," in the limited sense of music for several parts, as the basis of composition. According to Blainville,

[37] Johann Mattheson, *Das neu-eröffnete Orchestre* (Hamburg, 1713).
[38] *Ibid.,* p. 113.
[39] R. P. Meinrado Spiess, *Tractatus musicus compositorio-practicus* (Augsburg, 1745), p. 161.

Counterpoint is like painting on glass. It is a lost art for which one seeks the rules in vain, without being able to find them. It is however to the genius of counterpoint that we owe our musical foundation: the art of composing for several parts, a system very different from, and therefore superior to that of the ancient and modern Greeks, and all the other people of the east.

Little by little the dawn of good taste is beginning to appear, to eclipse that Gothic, not to say grotesque style.[40]

On the contrary, counterpoint as practiced in the learned style had more rigid connotations. The learned style (*style travaillé; gearbeitet, gebunden,* or *gelehrt*), characterized as severe, pithy, and objective in consequence of its penchant for fugal entrances, imitation, and canon, was the mid-eighteenth-century version of the church style. Quantz recognized the opposition between the learned style and the *style galant.* "Trios are either, as they say, worked or *galant.* It is the same with the solo." [41] About the learned style in particular he remarked,

It seems that the so-called learned music, and especially the fugues of the time [of Telemann] are outlawed as pedantry by most musicians and amateurs, perhaps because only a few recognize their worth and use. But he who wants to learn must not allow himself to be frightened away by prejudice; rather he can be reassured that his effort will be most amply rewarded. For no reasonable musician will deny that the good so-called learned music is one of the principal means of paving the way both for an insight into harmony and for the knowledge of how to perform a good, natural melody, and even to embellish it.[42]

As examples of well-worked-out compositions with fugues, Quantz recommended some of Telemann's trios. The latter's familiarity with the learned style enhanced the value of his works in the *style galant.* Telemann, a contemporary of Bach and Handel, saw the taste of his time swerving irrevocably toward the more decorative, less severe style, and he tailored some of his chamber music accordingly. In place of strict polyphonic part writing he employed such devices of the *style galant* as presenting a theme in stark unison and contrasting this exposition with the introduction of small motives slipping from part to part, or ending each section of a movement with several measures of broad unison. Indeed, when so inclined, he imbued himself in the *style galant* to the point of inviting censure. Schubart found fault with Telemann's chamber works because, "although he wrote them all with the utmost thoroughness, yet products of this kind are too subservient to fashion to last long." [43]

[40] C. H. Blainville, *L'Esprit de l'art musical* (Geneva, 1754), p. 96 f.
[41] Quantz, *op. cit.,* chap. xviii, par. 29.
[42] *Ibid.,* chap. x, par. 14.
[43] Christ. Fried. Dan. Schubart, *Ideen zu einer Ästhetik der Tonkunst* (Vienna, 1806), p. 166.

Considered by some a relief from strict counterpoint, and by others the path to musical ruin, the new "fashion" had its roots in ornamentation, tempo rubato, articulation of the theme, homophony, and condensed patterns of movements. The solo sonata, which in its central slow movement was the instrumental counterpart to the opera aria, gave the greatest impetus to the practice of instrumental embellishment. Since in writing a solo sonata the composer was relatively unconcerned with the discipline of strict counterpoint, rigid rules carried less weight with him than freely formulated ideas. He valued the latter for the simple reason that they sounded pleasant to him. He could concentrate upon furbishing the melody with dazzling runs, broken chords, and intricate figural work based on a harmonic rather than a contrapuntal conception. Melodic decoration was of such importance that it was even considered to have harmonic implications. Quantz demonstrated that the appoggiatura was not merely a melodic ornament, but also a factor in the harmony of a composition.

Appoggiaturas in playing are not only a means of ornamentation, but are also a necessary thing. Without them a melody often sounds very lean and simple. In order for a melody to appear *galant*, it must always have more consonances than dissonances. If many consonances appear in succession, and if after several quick notes a long consonance follows, the ear can easily become fatigued. The dissonances, therefore, must reawaken it from time to time. To this end the appoggiaturas can contribute much, because, if they stand before the third or sixth, counting from the fundamental tone, they become dissonances, namely fourths and sevenths. However, they receive their proper resolution through the following note.[44]

Whereas the French delighted in composed ornamentation, the Italians left the embellishments to the performer. French compositions exhibited a basic picture of the *style galant*. Every detail was there, every finely etched adornment. Although it was the duty of the performer to interpret individual signs of ornamentation correctly, to decide whether the trill ran for eight notes or sixteen, and whether the appoggiatura came on the beat or off, he was aided to the extent that the French clearly indicated the type of ornament desired and the place where they intended it to appear. In contrast, despite the fact that it was actually easier to play the written notes of an Italian work, it was harder to play an Italian composition in a finished manner, since a share of the burden of invention lay with the performer. When an instrumentalist, unacquainted with the style of embellishment, undertook the performance of a composition, the effect was apt to be seriously inconsistent with the composer's conception.

44 Quantz, *op. cit.*, chap. viii, par. 1.

Existing documents enable us to observe the differences between improvised embellishments of the baroque style and those of the *style galant*. More specifically, one may compare Corelli's method of performance with that of his pupil, Geminiani. The titles of Amsterdam publications of the first part of Corelli's Op. 5 include the words, "Embellishments are added to the Adagios of the first six sonatas of this work, composed by Mr. A. Corelli, as he plays them." Estienne Roger (*ca.* 1712), and then Pierre Mortier, published Corelli's decorations on a staff over the original part.[45] There was some question as to the authenticity of these ornaments. According to Hawkins, in order to satisfy the dubious, Roger, "in one of his printed catalogues, signified that the original copy of them, as also some letters of the author on the subject, were open to the inspection of the curious at his shop." [46] In London John Walsh and J. Hare must have agreed that the embellishments were genuine because their edition in 1711 also boasted "ye advantage of having ye Graces to all ye Adagios and other places where the author thought proper." [47]

Upon examination, it becomes apparent that Corelli, or the contemporary who added the embellishments, did not aim at glutting the music with frills. Not every note is decorated. Most elaborate is the subdivision of notes originally long in value, such as half or quarter notes, into shorter notes, distributed within the limits of the larger value according to the fancy of the performer. Corelli returned to the original line on the note following the basic half or quarter note. Apart from these scalewise diminutions, the ornamentation amounted to inserting a neighboring note, or a passing tone to fill in the leap of a third. Also, two eighth notes might be converted into a dotted eighth followed by a sixteenth.

It should be noted that, in accordance with the custom of the time, Corelli embellished only the slow movements of his *sonate da chiesa*. Since an allegro, because of its lively tempo, allowed little room for improvisation, Corelli and his contemporaries at the most decorated the repetition of a section already heard unadorned. But in an adagio, what was written down was intentionally a mannequin, the draping of which was a test of the artist's talent. Burney looked back on the early eighteenth-century adagio with the observation that "It was formerly more easy to compose than play an *adagio* which generally consisted of a few

[45] Cf. Andreas Moser, "Zur Frage der Ornamentik in ihrer Anwendung auf Corellis Op. 5," *Zeitschrift für Musikwissenschaft*, I (1919), 290.

[46] John Hawkins, *A General History of the Science and Practice of Music* (London, 1776), IV, 316.

[47] Edward Dannreuther, *Musical Ornamentation* (London, 1893–1895), p. 115.

notes that were left to the taste and abilities of the performer; but as the composer seldom found his ideas fulfilled by the player, *adagios* are now made more *chantant* and interesting in themselves, and the performer is less put to the torture for embellishments." [48] The fact that the publishers of the Corelli sonatas tried to recapture in sober print embellishments which were supposed to be extemporaneous showed that the performer desired guidance in this ephemeral art of improvisation.

Geminiani's embellishments of Corelli's Op. 5 sonatas are interesting by way of contrast, for they are in the *style galant*. The most glaring difference between the methods of ornamentation practiced by Geminiani and Corelli was in the extent of decoration. Whereas Corelli embellished only the adagio of the *sonata da chiesa,* Geminiani decorated all the movements in both the *sonata da chiesa* and the *sonata da camera*. A comparison of the ninth sonata as Corelli wrote it with the improvised versions of Corelli and Geminiani reveals that the latter, in addition to applying flourishes more copiously, did not follow the original line as closely as did Corelli.[49] Geminiani used such devices as displacing a note from its beat by inserting a chordal tone or an accented neighboring note, converting a run into a line with leaps, transposing the figuration into a higher and more brilliant register, and recasting a concentrated melodic line with harmonic implications into a display of double stopping. He altered the notes to a degree beyond embellishment; actually, he revised. In the fourth movement he remodeled the rhythm so completely by the injection of triplets that the gavotte nature of the movement is obscured.

Geminiani was well versed in the *style galant* both as a composer and performer. An interesting light on the importance attached to performance is shed by a commentary on how Geminiani's rendition of one of his own solos was received after he lost the agility to do the work justice as a virtuoso. In 1760, on the invitation of his pupil Matthew Dubourg, Geminiani went to Dublin for a concert which, though a financial success, was not very well received, according to a letter written the next day by Mrs. Delaney, formerly a friend of Handel.[50] In the performance of a *galant* work, because the solo instrument had autonomous rights, a fully qualified executant was essential. The *style galant* became inconsequential once a performer could no longer manage a flawless trill or an impeccable turn.

There are a variety of reports concerning the French reception of Ital-

[48] Burney, *op. cit.,* III, x.   [49] Hawkins, *op. cit.,* V, 393.
[50] W. H. Grattan Flood, "Geminiani in England and Ireland," *Sammelbände der Internationalen Musikgesellschaft,* XII (1910), 111.

ian improvised ornamentation. Burney relates how [in 1747] André-
Noel Pagin, who had studied with Tartini, "had the *honour* of being
hissed at the *Concert Spirituel* for daring to play in the Italian style,
and this was the reason of his quitting the profession." [51] The main basis
for complaint was that the added ornaments made all compositions sound
alike. Louis Bollioud de Mermet in his *Corruption of Taste in French
Music* (1746) lamented that a musician "so hampers and entangles the
subject of the piece with haphazard tones and superfluous ornaments,
that one can no longer recognize it. He plays ten sonatas in such a way
that one believes one hears the same sonata because these turns are under
his fingers and he places them everywhere in the same fashion." [52] Rousseau, on the contrary, approved of ornamenting popular melodies which
existed in the virtuoso repertoire solely for the purpose of display.[53]

Among the Germans, Franz Benda (1709–1786) and Telemann reflected the relationship between Geminiani's type of embellishment and
Corelli's. Whereas Telemann (like Corelli) had limited the decoration
to the slow movements, Benda (like Geminiani) usually embellished all
the movements of the sonata. Mersmann's examination of a volume containing the scores of thirty-three Benda violin sonatas with ornamented
versions of the violin parts discloses that the technique of embellishment
is the same in all the movements: the same figures and turns, the same
laws of resolution.[54] In his adagios, by diminishing a note or a group of
notes into a fast run without exact time-value for each note, Benda revealed a propensity toward rubato decoration corresponding to that
prevalent among the Italians. He achieved variety by avoiding the use
of one principle of ornamentation twice in succession. To alter a repetition he might change the direction of a run, substitute an arpeggio for a
scale, break through to new registers by exceeding the upper limit of the
original motive, vary the entrances of the theme, or raise a theme an
octave higher and underline it with double stops. In order to reserve the
climax for a later place in the composition, Benda might remove the
embellishments from the repetition, for example, by converting an
eighth note motion into quarter notes. Subsequently, when he height-
ened the diminution to sixteenth notes, the rhythmical intensity of the
original line was not only reached, but surpassed.

[51] Charles Burney, *The Present State of Music in France and Italy* (London, 1771),
p. 43.
[52] Lionel de la Laurencie, *L'École française de violon de Lully à Viotti* (Paris,
1922–1924), III, 198.
[53] Jean-Jacques Rousseau, *Dictionnaire de musique* (Paris, 1768), p. 531.
[54] Hans Mersmann, "Beiträge zur Aufführungspraxis der vorklassischen Kammermusik in Deutschland," *Archiv für Musikwissenschaft*, II (1920), 119.

In the *style galant,* ornamentation was supplemented by tempo rubato. When Tosi warned the Italian singer that the factor of keeping time should not be sacrificed to his "beloved passages and divisions," [55] he was advocating control, but not complete rigidity, in the matter of tempo. Further on in the same work he gave his approval of freedom with regard to tempo. "Whoever does not know how to steal the Time in Singing, knows not how to compose, nor to accompany himself, and is destitute of the best Taste and greatest Knowledge." [56] John Ernest Galliard (1687–1749), who translated Tosi's book into English (1742), brought it up to date for the *galant* world by means of a preface and footnotes.[57] Galliard, assuming the voice as "a Standard to be imitated by Instruments," [58] observed that the expression,

stealing the Time [tempo rubato] . . . regards particularly the Vocal, or the Performance on a single Instrument, in the *Pathetick* and *Tender;* when the Bass goes an exactly regular Pace, the other Part retards or anticipates in a singular Manner, for the Sake of Expression, but after That returns to its Exactness, to be guided by the Bass. Experience and Taste must teach it. A mechanical Method of going on with the Bass will easily distinguish the Merit of the other Manner.[59]

The ingenuity with which one was able to restore the normal tempo was crucial to a proper use of the tempo rubato.

Carl Philipp Emanuel Bach, who discussed tempo rubato first with reference to the clavier alone, applied the same criteria to a soloist with accompaniment, since the solo instrument was equivalent to the right hand of the clavier player. Furthermore, he observed that the introduction of tempo rubato was actually smoother when two instrumentalists were performing. When there was only one performer, the right hand had to contradict the tempo of the left; when there were two performers, the one playing the bass played in strict time while the other deviated.[60]

Although two performers may produce tempo rubato more easily than one, beyond two the difficulties of both tempo rubato and ornamentation obviously mount in direct proportion to the number of additional players. One soloist may give free rein to his fancy, when he knows that he has a reliable accompanist at the keyboard. When two, three, or four soloists are playing together, each cannot independently

[55] Pier. Francesco Tosi, *Observations on the Florid Song* (London, 1743), p. 99.
[56] *Ibid.,* p. 156.
[57] Galliard was born in Hanover where he was a pupil of A. Steffani.
[58] *Ibid.,* p. 159, note.   [59] *Ibid.,* p. 156, note.
[60] Carl Philipp Emanuel Bach, *Essay on the True Art of Playing Keyboard Instruments* [*Versuch über die wahre Art das Clavier zu spielen,* 1759 and 1762], trans. and ed. William J. Mitchell (New York, 1948), chap. iii, par. 28.

improvise his own adornments and take individual liberties with the tempo. Nevertheless, even though *style galant* composers preferred the solo sonata, they were not able to ignore the trio sonata completely. Where there were two treble melodic instruments, one refrained from embellishment unless the other had a chance to imitate it. When the melodic instruments were in thirds or sixths, they fared better without additional embellishments, for then the two main parts themselves were construed as being ornamental.[61] In the quartet there was still less freedom for introducing tempo rubato and arbitrary decorations than in the trio. Quantz noted that the trio "has the following advantage over the quartet: one can place in the trio more *galant* and agreeable thoughts, since there is one less concerted part." [62]

Aside from the increase in ornamentation and tempo rubato, the *style galant* differed from the baroque style in still another respect. A baroque melody was often constructed of winding motives and repeated notes, buried in the midst of passage work before and after it. Leclair's *da chiesa* trio sonatas, which are in this old tradition, featured themes without rests or repetitions, with syncopations, and with long series of notes of equal value. Sometimes the demarcation between the entrance of the theme in the second violin or cello and the preceding material was entirely neglected. Instead of holding these instruments in reserve for a clear statement of the theme, Leclair allotted countersubjects to them beforehand, thereby dulling the incisiveness of their thematic entries.[63] At times he was indefinite about the very formation of the theme. The second violin might enter with the theme minus its initial note; [64] or the first violin might begin with a passage only the first three notes of which were related to the theme as subsequently stated by the second violin and bass.[65]

In contrast to this amorphous type of thematic construction was the subjective theme which appeared with the *style galant*. Leclair himself was more enterprising and modern in his solo sonatas than in his trio sonatas. But the outstanding figure in the early *galant* transition from the baroque to the classical style was Giovanni Battista Pergolesi (1710–1736), whose interest was in the theme for its own sake and in the clarity and untrammeled elegance with which it could be set off. Pergolesi stressed, not the ingenious combinations to which the theme might lend

---

[61] Quantz, *op. cit.*, chap. xvi, par. 24.   [62] *Ibid.*, chap. xviii, par. 45.

[63] M. Leclair l'aîné, *Trio Sonata in B Flat Major* [Op. 4, No. 2, *ca.* 1730], ed. A. Moffat (London, 1934), second and fourth movements.

[64] *Ibid.*, fourth movement.

[65] M. Leclair l'aîné, *Trio Sonata in D Minor* [Op. 4, *ca.* 1730], ed. A. Moffat (London, 1934), second movement.

itself, but its emergence as a sharply defined unit. He was most anxious
for the listener to hear clearly the difference between theme and shape-
less background material. Pergolesi opened his Trio Sonata in G Major
with a pliable, well-delineated theme presented by the first violin: [66]

THEME FROM TRIO SONATA IN G MAJOR, BY PERGOLESI

The repetition of the first two-measure motive has an ending on the
dominant of G which could either remain in the key or modulate to
D major. Pergolesi utilizes the dual meaning of this cadence, in the
exposition by modulating to the secondary tonal area, and at the end
of the movement by repeating the secondary material in the original key
without further preparation. It proved a serviceable expedient which
Haydn later often utilized. Whereas in the above example a strategically
placed rest serves to articulate the theme, in his B♭ major trio sonata
(first movement) a well-placed partial repetition, involving a neat change
of pace from two sixteenths to a tied quarter, fulfills the same function: [67]

THEME FROM TRIO SONATA IN B♭ MAJOR, BY PERGOLESI

In spite of the advance in thematic delineation and formal design,
composers of the *style galant* wrote in a homophonic fashion which in
some respects echoed the old *da camera* style and the pseudo-fugal entry
of parts already prevalent in harpsichord music. In particular, the lazy
bass, which rarely had melodic movement, was reminiscent of the *da
camera* style. Schubart gave a remarkably perspicuous account of Pergolesi's music, stressing not only the unaffected bass but the general simplicity and economy:

All of his pieces which we possess are prized more highly than gold by all
friends of music. His setting is extremely plain: with two violins, a viola, and a
very simple bass he accomplishes much more than some of the most modern

[66] *Collegium musicum*, No. 29.   [67] *Ibid.*, No. 30.

composers with the tempestuous uproar of trumpets, drums, French horns, oboes, flutes, bassoons and all other wind instruments. Also his modulations, as well as his harmonic passages, are of the greatest simplicity, and for the expression of his thoughts he uses as few notes as possible.[68]

So far as the pseudo-polyphonic fugato was concerned, its place in the sonata was admissible on the same terms as the strict fugue. Both, according to Scheibe, were employed in the last movement, which was, "vigorous and fast, but generally more pleasant and flowing than the first fast or lively movement. Consequently it does not have so much fugal material, although both upper parts must contain a good and convincing melody throughout. But here also, some good masters make use of greater freedom, and even put a strict fugue at the end." [69]

For harpsichord music, Domenico Scarlatti demonstrated the feasibility of relating fugal entrances to homophony. This fusion became characteristic of chamber works in the *style galant*. A fugato, entailing free imitation and a bass which mostly accompanied, embodied a technique different from the voice leading of the old polyphonic fugue. For example in the last movement of Pergolesi's Trio Sonata in G Major, fugato: presto, the composer stimulated the listener by means of polyphonic thematic entrances which were relinquished after two or three measures, independent parts abandoned soon after their introduction. The three parts never are polyphonically independent of each other. When three parts are sounding at once there are only isolated measures where one part is not accompanying a second part homophonically, in thirds or sixths.

Both Hawkins [70] and Burney were dubious about whether the sonatas published under Pergolesi's name were written by him. One wonders how the sonatas under discussion could have been among those upon which Burney made the following judgment:

If the SONATAS ascribed to Pergolesi, for two violins and a base, are genuine, which is much to be doubted, it will not enhance their worth sufficiently to make them interesting to modern ears, accustomed to the bold and varied compositions of Boccherini, Haydn, Vanhal, &c. They are composed in a style that was worn out when Pergolesi began to write; at which time another was forming by Tartini, Veracini, and Martini of Milan, which has been since polished, refined, and enriched with new melodies, harmonies, modulation, and effects.

No fair and accurate judgment can be formed of the merit of a composer of past times, but by comparing his works with those of his predecessors and immediate competitors. The great progress that has been made in instrumental

---

[68] Schubart, *op. cit.*, p. 49.   [69] Scheibe, *op. cit.*, p. 678.
[70] Hawkins, *op. cit.*, V, 375. Also see C. L. Cudworth, "Notes on the Instrumental Works Attributed to Pergolesi," *M&L* XXX, p. 327.

Music, since the decease of Pergolesi, will not diminish his reputation, which was not built on productions of that kind, but on vocal compositions.[71]

Undoubtedly Pergolesi's reputation still rests on his vocal compositions. Yet, some of the very characteristics for which his vocal works are honored, their rhythmic tension and directness of melodic expression, were transferred by Pergolesi to his chamber music. Pergolesi's style must have had more bearing on that of Tartini, Veracini, and Sammartini than Burney admitted.

From the work of Francesco Maria Veracini (1690–1750) there was much to be gained in the way of freedom and individuality in tonality.[72] Tartini, zealous for musical guidance, was greatly impressed by Veracini when he heard the esteemed violin virtuoso in Venice (1714). Tartini was a prolific composer. According to J. A. Hiller, "The number of manuscript sonatas alone which are in the possession of music lovers mount up to more than two-hundred." [73] Besides the *Devil's Trill Sonata*, published posthumously, he wrote two books of sonatas, for a violin and bass, of which the first was published in Amsterdam in 1734 and the second in Rome in 1745. In Tartini's later sonatas, as contrasted with his earlier works, the motives were longer breathed and more varied, and the passage work was more organically integrated into the composition.

The stylistic advances of Veracini and Tartini were consolidated in the works of Giovanni Battista Sammartini (not to be confused with his brother, Giuseppe San Martini, the oboist).[74] Contemporaries in England and France ignored Giovanni, but lauded the music of Giuseppe. Early French editions, consequently, capitalized on Giuseppe's reputation by printing all the works of the Martini brothers under his name, and musicologists are still straightening out the confusion.[75]

The minuet was incorporated by Sammartini as the finale of a three-movement design which began with a fast movement, a plan typical of the trio sonata in the 1730s and 1740s. Although Giovanni Legrenzi had already used the minuet in Italian instrumental music, it was not until Sammartini that the minuet achieved a completely balanced construction. The word "balance" does not imply that the theme was constructed mechanically of two phrases each four measures long. Sammartini, like

[71] Burney, *A General History of Music,* IV, 557.
[72] Francesco Maria Veracini, *Sonate per violino,* in *Raccolta nazionale della musiche italiane,* ed. I. Pizzetti (Milan, 1919).
[73] Johann Adam Hiller, *Lebensbeschreibungen berühmter Musikgelehrten und Tonkünstler neuerer Zeit* (Leipzig, 1784), p. 276.   [74] See p. 69 f.
[75] G. de St. Foix, "Chronologie de l'oeuvre instrumentale de J. B. Sammartini," *Sammelbände der Internationalen Musikgesellschaft,* XV (1914), 310.

Pergolesi, knew the value of repeating a motive in order to give the line a clear enunciation. Witness the minuet of Sammartini's Sonata Op. 1, No. 3, from the 1730s.[76]

Sammartini also used an interesting two-movement plan: an initial movement, either fast or slow, followed by a minuet. When the original four-movement pattern had been sheared of the opening largo, there remained three movements, with thematic construction concentrated in the opening fast movement.[77] Now the opening allegro was discarded and the three-movement pattern reduced to two, of which the first was an andante, and the second a minuet. By writing two movements which were analogous in construction, Sammartini came as close to a one-movement pattern as he dared in a composition of supposedly larger dimensions.[78]

Sammartini helped to set the pace in style as well as pattern. He renounced counterpoint for the aria style with its repetitions and cadences; and like Pergolesi, he concentrated on the melody above, relying upon a lazy bass to effect the minimum of required cohesion. Only a more expressive and flowing melody, rising over the *galant* complication of short notes and ornaments, symmetrical formations, and melodic sequences, was now required to bring the classical style into view. In the *galant* music a sequence could be created with little inner drive from within the music itself. In decorating a line, a composer actuated by the *style galant* might impulsively expand it with momentary sequences, or create a sequence by using a standard figure on succeeding scale steps of the original line. As the classical style emerged, the overdressed *galant* music was disencumbered of excessive ornament. A clear, airy, simple line emerged. Sammartini passed on to the future, not the insignificance of *galant* filigree and polish, but the large sweep of Italian melody. He worked his way free from a motivically and rhythmically limited style, and emerged into the clarity, simplicity, and grace of the preclassic era.

[76] *Collegium musicum,* No. 28.   [77] See p. 105.
[78] Robert Sondheimer, "Giovanni Battista Sammartini," *Zeitschrift für Musikwissenschaft,* III (1920), 85–87.

V: SOLO INSTRUMENTATION

*D*URING the mid-eighteenth century the composer usually left to the performers the task of determining whether one player or several should be apportioned to each part other than the thorough bass. Fashion of composition, the fact that a work was either *da chiesa* or *da camera,* learned or *galant* in style, aided the performers in making a decision. Although, at the end of the seventeenth century, composers rarely commented on this matter, J. A. Schmierer did differentiate between orchestral and chamber setting in the preface to his *Zodiacus* (1698). The work, for an ensemble of four stringed instruments and harpsichord, consists of several eight-movement compositions, each introduced by an overture. Schmierer's directions covered the playing of the solo passages and the various way of reinforcing the *tutti:* typical instructions for concerto instrumentation. But, he added, should the lack of performers necessitate it, "the work could be set simply and, as it is called, be played *alla Camera.*" [1]

In general, however, performers relied on the fashion in which the composition was written for guidance. They could assume, for example, that in the *da chiesa* style the composer desired an imposing fullness of sound which was beside the point in the *da camera* style. Consequently, they performed the *sonata da chiesa* orchestrally and the *sonata da camera* with one player to a part. Mattheson in *Das beschützte Orchestre* (1717) included under the name *Symphonie* "all works written for a larger ensemble of instruments," namely, "concerti grossi, sinfonie *in specie,* overtures, strong sonatas and suites." [2] He qualified "sonata" by the word "strong" (*stark*) because there were two kinds of sonatas: those set for a reinforced ensemble and those intended for a group of soloists. The "strong sonata" was considered just as much an orchestral composition as the Venetian opera symphony in which there were no soloists. At the end of the century Sulzer contrasted the multiple instrumentation of the *sonata da chiesa* with the solo setting of the *sonata da camera.*

There are trios which are set in the learned and strict church style containing well-shaped fugues. They generally consist of two violin parts and a bass part,

[1] *Denkmäler deutscher Tonkunst,* X, 90.
[2] Johann Mattheson, *Das beschützte Orchestre* (Hamburg, 1717), p. 129.

and are even called church trios. These must be set with more than one instrument to a part: otherwise they have no power. The strict fugue which, on solemn occasions and in strongly set musical performances, moves all people by the sonority, solemnity and uniformity of its progression, has no appeal for the amateur of feeling in a chamber trio where each part is set only singly. It is only appealing to the connoisseur, for whom art in any form is welcome.[3]

Voluminous sound, however, was a typical baroque trait which, to some extent, also affected the *sonata da camera*. Even where the upper parts had solo instrumentation, thorough-bass practice insured the reinforcement of the bass part. Yet, in spite of this reinforcement a tendency was manifest toward solo performance in the bass register, although chamber style in the modern sense was not achieved until after the thorough bass had not only been opposed, but decisively rejected. The cello part was often divorced from the fundamental keyboard bass, a differentiation fostered by concerto grosso instrumentation, where the presence of a *concertino* encouraged a distinction in function among the instruments participating in the bass.

From the *da camera* style the *style galant* derived a penchant for solo instrumentation. In fact, solo playing was so closely associated with the *style galant* that the two terms were often used synonymously. When Quantz spoke of playing in a *galant* manner, he referred to the liberties with tempo and bowing characteristic of solo playing. He pitted the *style galant*, or solo style, against the ripieno style, thus:

Experience shows that those who are trained in good bands of musicians and have played for dancing many times, are better ripieno players than those who have played a single type of music in the *style galant* alone. In a like manner, for example, a fine stroke of the brush has a less desirable effect in a theatrical set—which one can see only by illumination and from a distance—than in a miniature. Thus the all too *galant* style and a long, drawn, or *spiccato* bow is not as good for accompanying in a large orchestra as in a solo or in a small chamber performance.[4]

Both as a composer and theoretician Quantz helped immensely toward clarifying chamber instrumentation. As chamber musician to Frederick the Great, he wrote both solo sonatas and solo concertos (*Kammerconcerte*) for the king to perform on the flute. Whereas the solo sonata, with soloist and thorough bass, was unequivocally in the chamber style of the period, whether or not the solo concerto was in chamber style rested on the nature of the accompaniment. In contrast to the concerto grosso which had several solo, or concerted, instruments, collectively

[3] Johann George Sulzer, *Allgemeine Theorie der schönen Künste* (Leipzig, 1792–1799), IV, 599.

[4] Johann Joachim Quantz, *Versuch einer Anweisung die Flöte traversiere zu spielen* (*1752*) (Leipzig, 1906), chap. xvii, sec. 1, par. 11.

called the *concertino,* the "chamber concerto" had only one solo instrument. While the *concertino* of the concerto grosso had to be balanced by the *tutti,* a robust accompanying orchestral body, the single concerted instrument of the chamber concerto could be accompanied either by a mass of instruments with more than one player to each part, or by a group of solo instruments. Quantz himself made the distinction clear:

> There are also two types of concerto with one concerted instrument, or so-called *chamber concerto.* Some demand a strong accompaniment, like the concerto grosso, but others a light accompaniment. If this is not observed, neither one will create the desired effect. From the first ritornelle one can see what kind of a concerto it is. That which is composed seriously, majestically, and more harmonically than melodically, and also is interspersed with many unisons, where the harmony does not change by eighths or quarters but half or whole measures, must have a strong accompaniment. But that which consists of an elusive, humorous, gay or cantabile melody, and has sudden changes of harmony, has a better effect with a small number of instruments in the accompaniment.[5]

This above quotation alone provides ample guide for determining which "chamber concertos" should be considered orchestral compositions in spite of their title, and which fall within the category of chamber music. Multiplying the instruments in the *tutti* helps to supply a suitable background for the more pompous solo. However, the real chamber concerto, in the narrower sense of the word "chamber," is a more delicate composition with fast changes, more adequately presented by a smaller group of performers to a more intimate gathering.

With regard to instrumentation, the solo sonata and the solo concerto differed in that the former had only a *continuo* accompaniment, while the latter had a composed accompaniment in addition to the *continuo.* There was also a divergence in style between the solo part of the solo sonata and the solo concerto. The concerto, replete with passage work and an accumulation of technical difficulties, was designed to give the virtuoso an opportunity for brilliant display, sometimes at the expense of expression. As instrumental virtuosity advanced during the eighteenth century, the concerto gained in importance. By the end of the century theorists like Koch were clamoring for the bygone days when the sonata was prized for its expressiveness:

> Since there is no doubt that the solo better suits the intention of art than the concerto, and since it is known well enough that the virtuosos who flourished in the middle of the past century . . . preferred, by far, to be heard in a solo rather than in a concerto, the strong attachment of our modern virtuosos for the concerto, and their aversion toward being heard in a solo, do not seem to

[5] *Ibid.,* chap. xviii, par. 32.

be a hearty compliment for the highly prized taste of the time. In short, the extraordinary preference for the concerto, and the complete neglect of the solo shows (at least with regard to the virtuosos) more the deterioration than the rise of fine taste.[6]

For those who could not recall the old days, Koch advised comparing the number of sonatas with the number of concertos written by C. P. E. Bach, Benda, [Gaetano] Pugnani (1731–1798), and [Jakob Friedrich] Kleinknecht (1722–1794).

In some cases the composer specified that the task of deciding whether a composition should be performed with a single player to a part or with many was at the discretion of the performers. Johann Stamitz's Op. 1, published in Paris under a ten-year General Privilege for instrumental music obtained in 1755, was entitled *Six Sonatas for Three Concerted Parts Which are Written for Performance Either by Three [Players] or with the Whole Orchestra*.[7] Stamitz probably intended here the practice associated in the first quarter of the eighteenth century with the French *Sonate en trio*, which could be performed either in chamber style with three or four players, or amplified into a small symphony. Both *Sonate en trio* and *Symphonie en trio* appeared side by side in the Op. 17 (n.d.) of Jean-Baptiste Quentin.[8] In the same vein, there is the London publication of twelve sonatas by Pergolesi for *Two Violins and a Bass or an Orchestra* mentioned by Johann Friedrich Reichardt.[9]

Advertisements and prefaces in France by the mid-eighteenth century at times specifically recommended solo instrumentation. Guillemain called for four instrumentalists in the preface to his *Six Sonates en quatuors ou conversations galantes et amusantes*, Op. 12 (1743), which he wrote for concerted flute and violin with the bass gamba and harpsichord mostly accompanying:

I thought that I could not dispense with warning the people who perform the quartets that, in order to render them in their true style, only one instrument, different from the rest, is necessary for each part, so that the clarity of which they are capable may be heard better. Do not rush the tempi too much, especially in the Allegros, and play the arias without slackening. Also take care not to strain, so that each instrument can be distinguished by the delicacy of its performance. If one wishes to use the harpsichord, one need accompany only on a small instrument, and play the chords in the Italian style.[10]

[6] Heinrich Christoph Koch, *Musikalisches Lexikon* (Frankfort on the Main, 1802), p. 1412.

[7] *Denkmäler der Tonkunst in Bayern*, III Jahrg. 1 Bd., p. xxxiv.

[8] Lionel de la Laurencie, *L'École française de violon de Lully à Viotti* (Paris, 1922–1924), I, 369. Quentin's first four works appeared between 1724 and 1729.

[9] Johann Friedrich Reichardt, *Briefe eines aufmerksamen Reisenden die Musik betreffend* (Frankfort and Leipzig, 1774), I, 138.   [10] La Laurencie, *op. cit.*, II, 27.

Indeed, the French had never been as interested in doubling the bass in the *continuo,* as had the Italians and Germans. The French provided ample precedent for Stamitz, who in turn influenced others to write works designated alternately for either chamber or orchestral performance. When Stamitz became known in Paris in 1751, François Gossec (1734–1829) was seventeen years old, a formative age in the career of a composer. Shortly thereafter Gossec entered the orchestra of Alexandre le Riche de la Pouplinière which Stamitz conducted from 1754–1755. The titles of Gossec's works showed the trend toward solo instrumentation. A clear example was his Op. 9, entitled *Six Trios for Two Violins, Bass and Horns ad libitum of Which the First Three Should Be Performed Only by Three People and the Three Others by Large Orchestra* (1766).[11] The chain kept on growing. In obvious imitation of Gossec, with whom he studied, Marie-Alexandre Guénin (b. 1744) entitled his Op. 1 (composed before 1769), *Six Trios of Which the First Three Should Be Performed by Three [Players] and the Others with the Whole Orchestra,* and dedicated them to Gossec.[12]

ELIMINATION OF THE THOROUGH BASS

In the discussion of solo instrumentation, emphasis has been placed thus far on parts other than the bass. So far as the lowest part was concerned, where the designation "bass" appeared, the performer could imply the use of a cello or a harpsichord, or both unless the number of performers was limited. Until the thorough bass fell into disfavor, it was impossible to stipulate for chamber performance only one instrument to a part in all registers, including the bass. As the common denominator for all styles in the first half of the eighteenth century, the *basso continuo,* with its doubling and improvisation of inner parts, hindered the formation of a crystallized chamber style. But it was in the music of the chamber that composers pioneered in dispensing with the *continuo,* and their efforts were abetted by the type of clavier style fostered by the *style galant.*

One phase of the disappearance of the thorough bass is accounted for in the transference of *continuo* material to an obbligato clavier part. It is possible to observe the actual process of converting a trio sonata with *continuo* into a "solo sonata" with obbligato clavier by comparing Johann Sebastian Bach's Trio Sonata for Two Flutes and Figured Bass in G Major,[13] with the transcription thereof which he made for obbligato

11 Georges Cucuel, *Etudes sur un orchestre au XVIIIme siècle* (Paris, 1913), p. 42; *Collegium musicum,* No. 47.

12 La Laurencie, *op. cit.,* II, 398.

13 *Johann Sebastian Bach's Werke* (Leipzig, 1851–1926), IX, 260.

clavier and viola da gamba.[14] In the transcription the part which was originally allotted to the second flute is transposed down an octave for the viola da gamba, the first flute part is transferred to the right hand of the clavier, while the bass remains in the left hand. In the process of transference and transposition the upper lines remain intact. Long notes sustained by the flute for three and four measures appear in the right hand of the clavier part without alteration. Perhaps the clavier player, who was not as yet entirely relieved of his improvisational duties, was expected to break up these extended values. But, on the whole, the inconsistencies were minor. There was little need for Bach to make elaborate changes in the solo sonata for, although the bass figures were omitted, he realized them fully in the parts themselves. Only in the bass lines did he feel compelled to modify and reshape. In the third movement, instead of the drum bass of the trio version, the revision has broken octaves in the left hand. Further on, in place of an alternation of quarter note and rest, the left hand has broken intervals in eighth notes.

Bach's procedures showed foresight into future methods of achieving fullness in a three-part composition without the use of the thorough bass and its attendant practices. The *continuo* type of accompaniment tended to disappear as composers, who had formerly relied upon it in the trio sonata to supplement or complete the chordal harmony, now began to write out the harmony explicitly, to the fullness desired, in sonatas with obbligato clavier. The process, as we shall see, was not completed at one stroke. Thorough-bass extemporization did not abruptly disappear in the sonata with obbligato clavier, but there was less and less for the keyboard player to realize at sight. In the near future, unequivocal specification of the chordal blocks and the equally unequivocal rejection of subsidiary extemporization were to render the thorough bass superfluous.

The relationship between the trio sonata and the solo sonata with obbligato clavier was, as one can gather from the Bach example just mentioned, quite important in this development, and the practice of converting (as J. S. Bach had done) the one into the other was furthered by men like Johann Gottlieb Graun and Franz Benda.[15] A particularly fine example of the interplay between the two, as well as of flexibility of instrumentation, was provided by a work which C. P. E. Bach composed in three alternate versions: as a *Trio a due violini e basso,* as a *Trio a flauto traverso, violino e basso,* and as a *Sonata a cembalo obligato e*

14 *Ibid.,* p. 175.
15 Hans Mersmann, *Die Kammermusik* (Leipzig, 1933), I, 162.

flauto (1754).[16] The word "trio" was also carried over to the solo sonata, for with the obbligato clavier providing two parts and the solo melodic instrument the third, three real parts (or a "trio") were present. Thus, in the catalogue of the musical bequest of C. P. E. Bach, all six of J. S. Bach's sonatas for clavier and violin were listed as "trios," and the first is specifically designated *Trio in B Minor for Obbligato Clavier and One Violin.*[17]

Continuo figuration, however, was not completely suppressed even in the presence of an obbligato clavier. J. S. Bach, Richter, and Schobert continued, upon occasion, to supply the obbligato clavier with a set of numerals. The word *accompagnando* was also used in certain passages (e.g., J. S. Bach's fifth violin sonata) to indicate that improvised additions were still required.[18] However, the figured passages appear when the solo melodic instrument has the theme and the right-hand part for the clavier is left empty. It is obvious that the harpsichordist was expected to complete the missing right-hand part in *continuo* style. In those passages where both hands are occupied with obbligato parts, it is difficult to determine how far the two parts were supplemented and who did the completion; although two possibilities for supplying the extemporaneous padding suggest themselves. Either a keyboard instrument in addition to the one designated as obbligato was used for accompanying, or obbligato parts and improvised accompaniment were played on one harpsichord.

Both these methods were probably used, depending on the composition and the virtuosity of the clavier player. An amateur might find it difficult merely to play the notes placed before him; but a skilled professional, no doubt, could manage not only the written part, but the addition of chord tones to complete the harmony. A copy of Bach's six sonatas for clavier and violin, calling for two keyboard instruments, was made by his pupil Kirnberger, who designated them "trios" with a *fundamento.*[19] The two upper parts, *violino* and *cembalo,* were in treble clef, while the *fundamento* was in bass clef. As with Telemann, the number of obbligato parts, not the number of instruments, determined the title of the composition.[20] Additional evidence of the use of two

---

[16] Alfred Wotquenne, *Catalogue thématique des oeuvres de Charles Philippe Emmanuel Bach* (Leipzig, 1905), Nos. 157, 152 and 85.

[17] *Philipp Emanuel Bachs musikalischer Nachlass,* ed. Heinrich Miesner, in *Bach-Jahrbuch,* XXXVI (1939), 87. The customary order of the six sonatas for clavier and violin by J. S. Bach appears here: B minor, A major, E major, C minor, F minor, G major.   [18] *Johann Sebastian Bach's Werke,* IX, 136.

[19] Hans Joachim Moser, "J. S. Bachs sechs Sonaten für Cembalo und Violine," *Zeitschrift für Musik,* CV (1938), 1221.   [20] See p. 79.

keyboard instruments is found in compositions for melodic instrument, obbligato harpsichord, and thorough bass. In Telemann's *Triosonate für Blockflöte, konzertierendes Cembalo und Generalbass (ca.* 1721) the thorough-bass part, except for the additional figures, coincides with the left hand of the concerted harpsichord. The *continuo* keyboardist supplies simple chords to round out the whole.

There were other compositions with obbligato keyboard which, in some movements, had chordal accompaniments written out completely, and in others had independent melodic lines that would be blurred by too much padding. For the homophonic movements no further accompaniment usually was necessary, and for the polyphonic movements the single harpsichord can provide the extemporaneous notes required. That the skilled harpsichordist was thought capable of improvising the few notes to be added to the obbligato parts was shown by the solo sonatas of Handel for melodic instrument and figured bass.[21] The violin was often given a whizzing theme, subsequently transferred to the keyboard; and the harpsichordist was expected to manage this theme without interrupting his interpretation of the figures. Much was demanded of harpsichord players in the eighteenth century.

As the harpsichord, formerly merely an accompanying instrument in chamber music, began to participate in melodic presentation and development, the melodic instrument, in its turn, was forced to take its share of the accompaniment. The obvious starting point for an examination of this phenomenon is J. S. Bach.

Bach's six sonatas for violin and obbligato clavier (*ca.* 1720) showed two styles of composition, the learned and the free. The learned treatment derived from the trio sonata with three active parts. Where fugal entrances occur, the theme, accompanied by a harmonic bass in the left hand, is first stated either by the right hand of the clavier and then by the violin, or vice versa. That these sonatas are rooted in thorough-bass technique is shown, in the first place, by the fact that the bass is never the first to introduce the theme. The bass, although performed here on one instrument, retained from the trio sonata the double function of playing both the theme and harmonic basis. In the latter connection, the keyboard player still was expected to fill in when required. When the right hand states the theme first, accompanied by the bass, the composite sound is usually fuller than when the violin and bass enter first. The right hand and bass, being in the same medium, blend more easily.

When no obbligato part was prescribed for the right hand, aside from the demand for padding, there must have been an inward compulsion

[21] *Georg Friedrich Händel's Werke* (Leipzig, 1859–1894), Vol. XXVII.

for the keyboard player to use his right hand to accompany. A melodic instrument at rest was not pressed into service as a supplementary instrument; while, on the contrary, a keyboard instrument was given no rest because it still retained its status as an accompanist. Since the clavier could adequately handle both theme and bass, composers proceeded to remove all need for the *continuo* by filling in the remaining bare spots with obbligato notes. In the fourth movement of the second sonata for obbligato clavier and viola da gamba, Bach by-passed the intermediate steps leading to a keyboard ensemble style. He eradicated all signs of two rigid parts by introducing in its place an arpeggiated interplay between the two hands.[22]

Within the free style of writing two main subdivisions, deduced on the basis of solo and accompaniment, were evident. In the first type, one instrument might dominate throughout the movement while the other accompanied. When the clavier was self-contained, the violin accompanied by introducing double or triple stops, reinforcing the clavier part in thirds or sixths, or by pursuing other techniques devoid of thematic import. Bach carried the independence of the clavier to an extreme when, in the third movement of the sixth violin sonata, he omitted the violin entirely. Conversely, the violin might have the solo while the clavier provided a chordal accompaniment. Or else, each instrument might fulfill the double function of soloist and accompanist within the same movement. In the third movement of the third violin sonata, the violin is the first to present the theme supported by a composed *continuo* type of chordal accompaniment in the clavier. Roles are then exchanged, the theme, in the relative major, moving to the right hand of the clavier part, while the violin, in a version reduced to double stops, presents what had just been the right-hand chordal accompaniment of the clavier. Except for the transposition, the left hand is identical in both cases.

Solo and accompaniment composition was too varied for a single center of influence to account for all types. Where the violin solo was accompanied by the clavier, the treatment of the solo instrument was drawn from the solo sonata and the solo concerto; where the clavier solo was accompanied by the violin, procedures were derived from the growing literature for clavier alone, as well as from the development of the harpsichord as a solo instrument in the concerto.

We may conclude, then, that an obbligato accompaniment was an outgrowth of the improvised thorough bass both in polyphonic movements, and in those homophonic movements where the melodic instru-

[22] *Johann Sebastian Bach's Werke,* IX, 201.

ment has the solo. The many treatises on the art of playing accompaniments show how ornaments, imitations of the melody, and fantasy arpeggios were worked into a figured bass accompaniment. The difference between an improvised and a composed accompaniment lay primarily in the execution. When the accompanying keyboard instrument also had a solo part in the right hand, the former, extemporaneous style of accompaniment had to be altered. Improvising and playing an obbligato clavier part simultaneously, or using two claviers, both cumbersome expedients, were necessarily superseded in time. The groundwork was laid for writing out a clavier part explicitly and without hindrance, so that its performance would agree with the composer's intention.

If this aim could be achieved in chamber music with a clavier, then an obbligato ensemble using a combination of instruments without a clavier was not far off. At a period when interest in the trio sonata was waning, it is significant that both Geminiani and Leclair took solo sonatas which they had written in former years and rewrote them as trios. To insert an extra part was, in effect, to acknowledge the diminishing importance of the thorough bass. Leclair, in 1753, reworked as *Sonates en trio*, Op. 13, several earlier solo sonatas which seemed "most suitable for this genre and whose effect would be most agreeable." [23] With the addition of a second violin, he revitalized the compositions, adding imitative entrances and melodic phrases, and replacing, with distinct parts, chords which had been indefinitely marked "arpeggio." This revision is historically important, not because it prolonged the life of the trio sonata, but because it indicated a turn toward composing the middle parts.

For compositions greatly dependent on the *basso continuo*, the practice itself furnished the elements for reintroducing the independent parts. Theorists explained how keyboard improvisation could be devised to make the sound fuller, as if a recognizable inner part were indicated by the figures. Quantz mentioned a specific technique for making a solo sound like a trio:

When the bass in slow pieces has to repeat several notes on the same tone, which are figured $\begin{smallmatrix} 5 & 6 & 7 & 6 & 5 \\ 3 & 4 & 5 & 4 & 3 \end{smallmatrix}$ and the like, where the main part usually realizes the upper figures in its melody: then it sounds very well if the accompanist plays the upper figure lower [reverses the intervals], and thus converts the thirds which both parts make with each other into sixths. This will not only sound more harmonious, but will give the piece more the air of a trio than a solo.[24]

23 M. Leclair l'aîné, *Ouverture et sonates en trio*, Op. 13 (Paris, *ca.* 1753).
24 Quantz, *op. cit.*, chap. xvii, sec. vi, par. 22.

Although the growing practice of writing out the middle parts is noticeable in combinations of instruments without an obbligato clavier, the disappearance of the *continuo* is even more obvious in compositions with a prescribed clavier part. An obbligato melody in the right hand of the harpsichord rendered one of the two upper melodic instruments of the trio sonata superfluous. Nevertheless, the instrument in excess was not immediately eliminated. There were transitional compositions for melodic instruments and obbligato clavier in which the lines of one or more of the melodic instruments were identical with corresponding lines in the harpsichord part.[25] Similarly, the custom of using a melodic instrument in the bass, self-evident in *continuo* practice, persisted to some extent when the clavier part was obbligato. J. S. Bach, in the title of a partly autograph manuscript of the above-mentioned six sonatas for clavier and violin, admitted the possibility of including a string bass: *Six Sonatas for Concerted Harpsichord and Solo Violin with an Optional Accompanying Bass Viola da Gamba* (1730).[26] The retention of a string bass for reinforcing the lowest line in the obbligato clavier part was likewise specified in clavier trios for harpsichord, violin (or flute), and bass by the Mannheimers, Franz Xaver Richter (1709–1789), Giuseppe Toeschi (1724–1788), Anton Filtz (1730–1760), and Ernst Eichner (1740–1777).[27] Richter's *Sonata da camera a cembalo obligato, flauto traverso o violino concertato e violoncello* in A major, is a transitional piece in that the cello, with few exceptions, is identical with the bass of the clavier part.[28] In the title the terms *concertato* and *obligato* both appear, the former referring to the violin and the latter to the harpsichord. The two instruments actively engage in the presentation of themes and important motives; yet they differ in style as well as in detail of performance. Although, in general, the harpsichord part has two concerted lines, Richter occasionally writes out the realization of a hypothetical *basso continuo* for the clavier in block chords, exactly as it would have been if figured and improvised. Chords which would have been extemporaneous formerly are obbligato here, in a sense that is far from *concertante*. Furthermore, as J. S. Bach does in some of his sonatas, Richter sometimes handles the harpsichord in thorough-bass fashion by using numerals when the violin has thematic material.

The disappearance of the thorough bass was affected, not only by the transference of *continuo* material to an obbligato clavier part, but also

---

[25] Hans Mersmann, "Beiträge zur Aufführungspraxis der vorklassischen Kammermusik in Deutschland," *Archiv für Musikwissenschaft*, II (1920), 102.
[26] *Bach's Werke*, IX, xvi.   [27] *Denkmäler der Tonkunst in Bayern*, Vol. XVI.
[28] *Collegium musicum*, No. 18.

by solo keyboard composition, a field in which the *continuo* had no place. In the early eighteenth century the association between solo keyboard style and chamber style was founded fundamentally upon the deficiency of clavier instruments with regard to tone production. Its inability to sustain tone gave the harpsichord a crisp and exact character. The composer, seeking a singing style of melody, resorted either to the embellishments of the *style galant,* or doubled the harpsichord part with one or more melodic instruments. Stringed instruments combined with the harpsichord reinforced the tone and highlighted the essential lines. In consequence, the harpsichord's development as a solo instrument also affected its relations with the strings in chamber music. As the style of the great keyboard masters of the late seventeenth century found its way into classical chamber music, the pendulum swung toward the harpsichord as the concerted instrument, and the violin was the accompanist, ad libitum.

In Germany the starting point for chamber music with obbligato keyboard was the ensemble; in France the focal point was the keyboard itself. The titles of some French harpsichord compositions in the beginning of the eighteenth century indicated that stringed instruments were optional. The *Six Suites de clavessin divisées en ouvertures, allemandes, courantes, sarabandes, gavottes, menuets, rondeaux & gigues composées & mises en concert part Monsieur Dieupart pour un violon ou flûte avec une basse de viole ou un archilut* is a full-bodied work, many movements of which are written essentially in two parts with supplementary parts intermittently appearing and disappearing.[29] In view of its listing in Estienne Roger's catalogue of 1702, the opus was probably published between 1700 and 1702. The editor sold either the complete work or only the harpsichord "score," since the melodic instruments were optional. J. S. Bach knew this music, for a manuscript in Bach's handwriting contains two suites by Dieupart.[30] In a similar vein were the *Pièces de clavecin qui peuvent se jouer sur le viollon* by Elisabeth Claude Jacquet de la Guerre (1707). If a violinist were available, the harpsichordist could consign the upper part to him and realize the figured bass with two hands.[31]

In both instances the situation was in exact reverse of that noted in connection with the trio sonata. Instead of the harpsichord playing parts written for stringed instruments, melodic instruments were allowed to

29 Charles Dieupart, *Six Suites pour clavecin,* ed. Paul Brunold (Paris, 1934).
30 Edward Dannreuther, *Musical Ornamentation* (London, 1893–1895), I, 137.
31 Marc Pincherle, *J. C. de Mondonville, Pièces de clavecin en sonates* (Paris, 1935), Introduction, p. 17.

take parts originally conceived for the harpsichord. The following quotation, taken from a contemporary description of a violin accompanying a harpsichord, which appeared in the *Mercure de France* (1729), is revealing: "Mademoiselle Couperin, daughter of Monsieur Couperin, organist to the king, had the honor of playing several harpsichord pieces before the queen several times this month. . . . She was accompanied only by Monsieur Besson, ordinary of the chamber music of the king, who has made a special study of playing this sort of piece perfectly, softening his violin extremely." [32] Corrette corroborated this type of playing in the preface to his *Sonates pour le clavecin avec accompagnement de violon* (1741), where he warns, "The violin must play in a subdued fashion." [33]

When the violin was given material which did not merely double the harpsichord line, even these accompaniments were, as Raguenet noted in 1702, "for the most part no more than single strokes of the bow, heard at intervals, with no connected and continuous melody, serving only to have certain chords heard from time to time." [34]

This state of affairs continued for many years until, at long last, in 1734 Jean-Joseph de Mondonville essayed a more substantial violin part in his *Pièces de clavecin en sonates avec accompagnement d'un violon*. It was obviously his intention here to place harpsichord and violin on an equal footing. In this particular respect, Mondonville was not a man of his time, but rather one who looked ahead to the instrumental balance of the latter part of the eighteenth century. Even in a fugal movement he strove for greater fullness of tone by introducing broken octaves and intervals, not only in subsidiary figurations, but in the theme itself.[35] In all the sonatas the harpsichord technique is advanced. There are octave doublings in the left hand and crossing of the hands.

Although Mondonville ostensibly avoids use of the *continuo* in these sonatas, he nonetheless introduced figures into the aria of the fifth sonata. In this aria, he allotted the melody to the violin and an accompanying motive to the right hand of the harpsichord. Content merely with indicating the motive, he wrote *"sempre,"* followed on the lower staff by intervals for the left hand, and on the upper staff by figures from which the motive is to be realized in the right hand. Wherever the accompaniment varied from the given motive, it was written out.[36]

---

[32] *Ibid.,* p. 22.   [33] *Loc. cit.*

[34] François Raguenet, *Parallèle du Italiens et des François en ce qui regarde la musique et les opéra* (Paris, 1702), p. 54 f.

[35] Second movement of the first sonata.

[36] J. C. de Mondonville, *Six Sonates or Lessons for the Harpsichord Which May Be Accompanied with a Violin or German Flute* (London, *ca.* 1750). The small notes in the quotation are Pincherle's realization of the figures.

EXCERPT FROM ARIA OF SONATA V, BY MONDONVILLE

This is a crossbreed between the thorough bass and obbligato accompaniment, since two notes are given in the left hand instead of just the bass. Nevertheless, Mondonville was so explicit in his directions that it would be difficult for the harpsichordist to misinterpret his intentions. In the first movement of the fourth sonata he wrote out block chords in *basso continuo* style to accompany scalewise passages in the violin.[37] But the notes were written out, and it was an outgrowth of the *continuo* style that survived here, rather than the *continuo* itself.

Mondonville's second movements are always arias. In some the melody is in the right hand of the clavier, and in others in the solo violin part. He could not indicate more clearly that he regarded the two instruments as equals.

Succeeding composers who wrote pieces with obbligato harpsichord parts lacked Mondonville's grasp of equality of instrumentation. Instead, they resumed the direction of Dieupart and La Guerre, and a

37 For Richter's use of this technique see p. 130.

series of pieces for solo harpsichord with string parts ad libitum appeared. Dieupart and La Guerre, however, did not compose separate
parts for the strings, but merely advised doubling the harpsichord parts,
whereas the composers of the newer works provided ad libitum string
parts which, although optional, nevertheless had a certain measure of
independence from the harpsichord. In these compositions, a correct
and complete performance demanded the presence of the stringed instruments. The situation was analogous to the performance of sonorous
thorough-bass compositions without the accompanying harpsichord; in
spite of the depth of sound within the texture of the composition, such a
performance sounded empty to many ears.

Rameau's advice to performers given in his *Pièces de clavecin en concerts, avec un violon ou une flûte, et une viole ou un deuxième violon*
(1741)—harpsichord pieces with added string parts—is interesting from
the standpoint of solo and accompaniment.

Advice to the performers:
   I have written some small concerted compositions for harpsichord, a violin
or flute, and a gamba or a second violin. Four parts usually prevail. I thought
they should be published in score, because not only must the three instruments
blend well together, and the performers understand each other's role, but,
above all, the violin and gamba, while yielding to the harpsichord, must distinguish that which is only accompaniment from that which is part of the subject,
by softening still more in the first case. All the long notes should be played
softly rather than forcibly, the short notes extremely sweetly, and those which
follow each other without interruption should be mellow.
   These pieces performed on the harpsichord alone leave nothing to be desired; one does not even suspect then that they admit any other treatment.[38]

In France, partiality for the clavier affected even violinists. Gabriel
Guillemain, in connection with his *Pièces de clavecin en sonates avec
accompagnement de violon* (Op. 13, 1745), wrote,

When I composed these sonatas, my first idea was to assign them to the harpsichord alone without any accompaniment, since I had observed that the violin
is somewhat too overbearing, a quality which prevents perception of the real
subject. But in order to conform to the present taste, I felt compelled to add
that part, which must be performed quite softly in order that the harpsichord
alone may be heard without difficulty. One may, if one wishes, perform these
sonatas with or without accompaniment. They will lose none of their melody
since it is complete in the harpsichord part. This will be more convenient for
people who do not always have a violin at their disposal when they want to
play some of these pieces.[39]

[38] Jean-Philippe Rameau, *Œuvres complètes* (Paris) Vol. XX.
[39] Pincherle, *op. cit.*, p. 23 f.

The epitome of the sonata for keyboard instrument and violin ad libitum was reached by Johann Schobert (1720–1767), whose Op. 1, 2, 3, and 10 are entitled *Sonatas for the Harpsichord Which May Be Played with the Accompaniment of the Violin*.[40] The phrase *qui peuvent se jouer avec l'accompagnement du violon* was transformed to *avec accompagnement du violon ad libitum* in Op. 5, 6, 7, 9, and 14. The accompanying stringed instrument is missing only in Op. 8 and in some works published after Schobert's death. Riemann, quoting Méreaux's version of the violin part as a "third hand ad libitum" an octave higher, felt that Méreaux and Pauer went too far in publishing Schobert's sonatas as mere clavier works, since the violin did have some share in the ensemble.[41]

The most obvious element in Schobert's keyboard writing was its virtuosity. Italian contemporaries, such as Giuseppe Antonio Paganelli (b. 1700), Pietro Domenico Paradisi (1710–1792), Baldassare Galuppi (1703–1785), Alberti, and Giovanni Battista Pescetti (1704–1766), as well as the Viennese, represented by Wagenseil, have often been mentioned as influencing Schobert in this respect. Schobert covered the keyboard with motives well suited to it, filled out the space between high and low notes with arpeggios, and made frequent use of both keyboard tremolo and Alberti bass. He placed the violin in unison with any part including the momentary bass, and in octaves, thirds, or sixths above or below the melody. For the violin he simplified motives to accompany the more elaborate versions allotted to the clavier, and he used the instrument to reinforce the strong beats with chord tones. The clavier dominated. Passages where Schobert bows to the *continuo* by writing a figured bass instead of working out the clavier part are infrequent.[42]

The connection between works with *continuo*, those with obbligato clavier, and those without clavier either written or improvised, was made clear in the compositions of Leopold Mozart. He was one of the few composers between 1740 and 1760 who kept a strict account of which compositions were to be played with *continuo* and which without.[43] The line of change may be followed easily. In 1740 L. Mozart wrote trio sonatas for two violins and thorough bass, *Sonate sei per chiesa e da camera a tre: due violini e basso. E basso* alone is a noncommittal designation, but the layout of the works, as well as the combination of instruments, bespeaks the old trio sonata tradition. The next

---

[40] *Denkmäler deutscher Tonkunst*, XXXIX, viii.   [41] *Ibid.*, p. ix.
[42] *Ibid.*, p. 57. B♭ Major Trio, Op. 16[1], first movement, after the double bar.
[43] *Denkmäler der Tonkunst in Bayern*, IX[2].

stage for L. Mozart was that of the clavier trio or *divertimento* for ob-bligato harpsichord, violin, and cello, *Trio: cembalo principalo, violino unisono ò violone cello (ca.* 1750). In these compositions the violin part corresponds to the right hand of the clavier while the cello is similar to the left hand. The more faithful adherence of the cello to the left hand, in contrast to a somewhat more venturesome relationship between the violin and right hand, is an indication that a break with the *continuo* was not an easy matter. However, after thus exploring the possibility of writing out the clavier part in an ensemble, L. Mozart confirmed the fact that music could be conceived with or without thorough bass. In 1755 he wrote two types of symphony: *Sinfonia di camera,* for solo setting, with figures which demanded *continuo* accompaniment, and symphonies for orchestral setting, not requiring a *continuo.* Finally, in the *Divertimenti à due violini e violoncello* of 1760, L. Mozart achieved a trio without *continuo.* The phrase *e violoncello* in the title indicated the use of cello without clavier doubling.[44] Although Mozart's divertimentos of 1760 are the height of his artistic achievement, the totality of his production deserves the historian's attention; for, presented in chronological order, his work represents a methodical account of the stages through which the thorough bass disappeared.

Sandberger, interestingly enough, traced the entire process of the disappearance of the *continuo* through the evidence offered by the titles themselves. The phrase *con violoncello e basso continuo* signified that the *continuo* was essential; *col basso continuo ossia violoncello* meant that the *continuo* was optional, and *e violoncello* implied that the clavier was omitted.[45] The cello could either accompany, assume equal rank with the clavier, or displace the clavier. In general, the three stages may be assigned to three decades. Through the 1750s the *continuo* was an essential fixture, by the 1760s it was often ad libitum, and in the 1770s it was to a considerable extent already displaced by the cello. Nat-urally, unless this scheme of dates is regarded as elastic, freaks will ap-pear "out of place." For instance, an early tendency to suppress the *continuo* is evident in the *XII Sonate a due violini, e violoncello, e cem-balo, se piace, opera terza,* by Giuseppe San Martini (London, *ca.* 1745), where the option of *continuo* or cello was offered the performer fifteen years before 1760. On the other hand, works with figured bass continued to appear after 1770. As a matter of course, until 1780 many London and Amsterdam publications of chamber music provided figures regard-

---

[44] Adolph Sandberger, "Zur Geschichte des Haydnschen Streichquartett," in *Ausgewählte Aufsätze zur Musikgeschichte* (Munich, 1921), I, 240.
[45] *Ibid.,* p. 244 f.

less of whether or not the composer had included them. The publishers, then as now, apparently felt that the old-fashioned market in music was the safest, or else they operated on the principle that compositions without figures were not necessarily those least in need of them.

Solos and Duets.—Mendelssohn in 1847 and Schumann in 1854 felt compelled to add piano accompaniments to some of Bach's unaccompanied violin sonatas. Yet, in an age when accompaniments were the accepted fashion, Bach, along with Johann Georg Pisendel (1687–1755), Nicola Matteis, Junior (d. 1737), Angelo Ragazzi (1680–1750), and Francesco Geminiani, chose to let the violin manage a sonata quite alone.[46] Bach directed his attention toward creating music which he considered to be full bodied in itself, and, it would seem, he accepted the limitations imposed by the performing instrument quite consciously as a challenge. The unaccompanied violin solos contained movements which also appeared in Bach's clavier and organ compositions. Although Bach achieved more sonority in the keyboard version by amplifying the chords in the lower regions, and by projecting subsidiary parts which were but barely hinted at by the violin, the fact remains that he conceived the solo violin version as an entity and deliberately ignored the *continuo* accompaniment.

In general, however, the unaccompanied solo for a melodic instrument, because it imitated the role of the keyboard solo on a type of instrument much less suitable for performing music in several parts, could have had only slight bearing, if any, on the disappearance of the thorough bass. More important in this respect was a species allied to the unaccompanied solo—the unaccompanied duet, either for two similar or two different melodic instruments. The unaccompanied solo and duet were types of chamber composition with one instrument to a part, to the exclusion of the thorough bass. Both were artistic mediums, although both also served to some extent as vehicles for amateur or pedagogical purposes. In contrast to polyphonic violin solos demanding the utmost skill in performance were the unaccompanied solo compositions written for instruments like the flute or oboe, which individually had no polyphonic capabilities. But among the duets for two melodic instruments without bass there was a contrapuntal duet in which the two parts were equivalent throughout, as well as a homophonic duet in which the parts clung to progressions of parallel thirds and sixths. In the contrapuntal duet, the lower part was to be considered, not as a

[46] Andreas Moser, *Geschichte des Violinspiels* (Berlin, 1923), p. 137 ff.

modified bass, but as a matched contestant with the upper part. Since each part had a well-constructed line, their combination was so rich harmonically that there was no need for a bass part to give the music support and direction. Double counterpoint was essential to this type of polyphonic construction, and crossing of parts was one of its common characteristics.[47]

The polyphonic duet eventually was neglected in favor of the homophonic duet. Koch, who upheld the latter, suggested that each type should have its own name in order for one to know which kind of duet to expect from the title.[48] In practice, however, the two types of duet were not so distinguishable as theorists would like to imagine. Often sonatas written for two equivalent violins had to be modified to the point where one instrument dominated and the other largely accompanied. Because of the absence of the *continuo,* the composer at times felt constrained to descend to the lower limits on one of the violins, or to include many double stops. On the other hand, the homophonic duet would indeed have been boring without a measure of independence in the lower part. A favorite procedure was to contrast homophonic slow movements with polyphonic fast movements in the same composition.

The French fostered the duet with similar instruments. While the violin gave impetus to the unaccompanied solo, the flute inspired composers toward the unaccompanied duet. Between the years 1709 and 1728, Hotteterre le Romain, Michel de la Barre (1675–1743), Pierre Philidor (1681–1731), Jean-Jacques Naudot (composed 1726–1740), and Michel Blavet (1700–1768), all flute players, composed for two flutes without bass.[49] From the titles of their works, it was sometimes evident that two violins could be substituted for the flutes. Hotteterre sanctioned interchangeable instrumentation in his *Suite de pièces,* "for two trebles without *basso continuo,* for transverse flutes, recorders, viols, etc.," Op. 4 (1712). Joseph-Bodin de Boismortier (1691–1765) specifically demanded flutes for his duets, Op. 1 and 2 (1724), and violins for his Op. 10 (1725), whereas Louis Gabriel Guillemain reverted to a choice of instruments. The *Mercure de France* in 1739 explained that since Guillemain's Op. 4 was written "precisely for two violins, involv-

[47] M. de Bethizy, *Exposition de la théorie et de la pratique de la musique* (Paris, 1754), p. 249.

[48] Heinrich Christoph Koch, *Musikalisches Lexikon* (Frankfort on the Main, 1802), p. 502.

[49] L. Fleury, "Music for Two Flutes without Bass," *Music and Letters,* VI (1925), 110–118.

ing double stops, the composer, recognizing this, has just published a fifth opus in the same genre, which differs from the other in that it may be performed by two transverse flutes as well as by two violins. He hopes that these sonatas will not have less success than the preceding, being in the reach of people more or less skillful." [50]

The accompanying role of the second instrument was emphasized when a duet was for two different instruments. Boismortier in his *Sonatas for a Transverse Flute and a Violin in Chords, without Bass,* Op. 51 (1734), had the violin accompany with incessant double and triple stops.[51] In the middle of the 1770s Haydn wrote string compositions for violin and viola which he originally entitled *Solo per il violino.* As the accompanist, the viola was so definitely subsidiary that Haydn omitted mention of it in the title. However, its presence could not be so completely ignored, and the title was altered to read *6 Violin Solo mit Begleitung einer Viola.*[52] Yet they were not really "duets," and he refrained from using that word in the heading.

A bona fide duet between two different instruments was described by Burney who, having received a letter of introduction from Felice Giardini (1716–1796), visited the Besozzi brothers, Alessandro and Antonio.[53]

The eldest plays the hautbois, and the youngest the bassoon, which instrument continues the scale of the hautbois, and is its true base. Their compositions generally consist of select and detached passages, yet so elaborately finished, that, like select thoughts or maxims in literature, each is not a fragment, but a whole: these pieces are in a peculiar manner adapted to display the powers of the performers; but it is difficult to describe their style of playing. Their compositions, when printed, give but an imperfect idea of it. So much expression! such delicacy! such a perfect acquiescence and agreement together, that many of the passages seem heartfelt sighs, breathed through the same reed. No brillancy of execution is aimed at, all are notes of meaning. The imitations are exact; the melody is pretty equally distributed between the two instruments; each *forte, piano, crescendo, diminuendo,* and *appogiatura,* is observed with a minute exactness, which could be attained only by such a long residence and study together. The eldest has lost his under front teeth, and complained of age; and it is natural to suppose that the performance of each has been better: however, to me, who heard them now for the first time, it was charming. If there is any defect in so exquisite a performance, it arises from the *equal perfection* of the *two parts;* which distracts the attention, and renders it impossible to listen to both, when both have dissimilar melodies equally pleasing.[54]

[50] La Laurencie, *op. cit.,* II, 5.   [51] *Ibid.,* III, 128.
[52] J. P. Larsen, *Die Haydn-Überlieferung* (Copenhagen, 1939), p. 226.
[53] See p. 70.
[54] Charles Burney, *The Present State of Music in France and Italy* (London, 1773), pp. 67–69.

Such understanding between performers and interchange of melody between the instruments made for perfection in the construction and presentation of a duet. In an effort to criticize something adversely, Burney could find fault only with the independence of the parts!

A more likely cause for complaint were the incessant successions of parallel thirds and sixths fashionable in duets toward the end of the eighteenth century. Conscious of the omission of the *continuo* bass, composers tried to compensate for its absence by using intervals and progressions which sounded full to the ear harmonically. The development of the unaccompanied duet, a reincarnation from pre-*continuo* days, constituted one of the factors in the neglect and ultimate disappearance of a well-established *continuo*.

Music Performed Out of Doors.—With respect to ensembles of more than two instruments, performance without thorough bass was sanctioned out of doors before it was accepted in the chamber. The obvious inconveniences in carrying a keyboard instrument about, largely accounted for its exclusion in open-air performance.

Outdoor music-making was associated most frequently with the type of composition called *divertimento,* cassation, and serenade.[55] These titles, however, were not completely dependent on the locale of performance, for a composition for obbligato clavier with accompanying strings, performed indoors, might also be called a *divertimento.* The function of music performed out of doors, like the function of music performed in the chamber, was to entertain. All the names above mentioned referred to popular compositions, written in many movements and assigned to several instruments. Cassation might be proffered by students to their *amours;* the serenade might honor an engaged couple or a person of distinction; the *divertimento* might serve to put a hunting party in the right spirit. The purpose of all three types could be summed up in the Italian word *divertimento* meaning amusement.

Outdoor compositions had long been associated with nocturnal musical activity. The serenata or serenade was orginally performed during the serene (Italian, *serena*) evening by a singer accompanied in simple fashion on the guitar or mandolin. In the mid-eighteenth century Rousseau, lamenting the custom of relegating the serenade to the lower classes, remarked, "The silence of the night, which banishes all confusion, makes the music preferable, and renders it more delicious." [56] The Austrian serenade was quite another matter: "They do not give the serenades here to send their sighs to the air, or to declare their love, for

---

[55] Other titles were: *Notturno, Scherzando, Parthie,* and *Concertante.*
[56] Jean-Jacques Rousseau, *Dictionnaire de musique* (Paris, 1768), p. 429.

which here there are a thousand more suitable opportunities, but these serenades consist of trios, quartets, mostly from operas, for several voices, for wind instruments, often for a whole orchestra, and they perform the greatest symphonies." [57] As early as 1684 it was reported that Vienna was overflowing with musicians and that "scarcely an evening goes by that we do not have a serenade [*Nachtmusik*] before our windows on the streets." [58] By the 1720s the serenade was well in vogue.

For elaborate occasions there were orchestral serenades, and for private performance there were those for a small number of single instruments. Just as indoor music, depending on the circumstances, consisted of orchestral works as well as of works for chamber performance, the outdoor serenade sometimes had single, sometimes multiple instrumentation. However, the popular purpose of the outdoor pieces accounted for their propensity toward single instrumentation. The serenade comprised a loose succession of movements, usually with a march at the beginning or end, and with one or more minuets in between. J. J. Fux wrote a sixteen-movement *Serenada* with three minuets in his *Concentus musico-instrumentalis* (1707).[59] As was so often the case in this type of composition, Fux scored the work for a mixture of strings and wood winds.

Many derivations have been suggested for the word "cassation," which, with its carefree, charming melodies represented the development of bourgeois interest in naïve folk music, and a reaction away from the earlier, more stereotyped handling of the dance in the suite. Various lexicographers have traced the term "cassation" to *gassatim gehen*, an expression which Praetorius used in his definition of serenata: [60] It is an evening song with interspersed *Ritornelli*, for three or more parts, performed while promenading on the street in the evening (*Gassaten gehen*). At the universities they use it to serenade young girls." [61] However, because of the introductory march in the cassation, Riemann believed the word to be related to *cassa*, Italian for a large drum. He thought this logical since a drum is usually used at the beginning and the end of a march.[62] Somewhat later, Wyzewa and St. Foix connected the term with the French *casser*, to break, on the grounds that a cassation was a small symphony having rests between the indi-

[57] Vienna Theater Almanac, 1794, in C. F. Pohl, *Joseph Haydn* (Berlin, 1875), I, 107.
[58] Ed. Browne, in Pohl, *op. cit.*, I, 106.
[59] *Denkmäler der Tonkunst in Österreich*, XXIII², 7.
[60] Otto Jahn, *W. A. Mozart* (Leipzig, 1889–1891), I, 847 f., note by Hermann Deiters, ed.
[61] Michael Praetorius, *Syntagma musicum* (*1619*) (Leipzig, 1916), p. 31.
[62] Hugo Riemann, *Musik Lexikon* (Berlin, 1929), I, 864.

vidual movements, which were not necessarily played in order.[63]

Possible derivations aside, it is important for our purpose to note that when the cassation and *divertimento* were performed indoors by a group of soloists, they fell within the category of chamber music. Yet, it is often difficult to decide whether an individual *divertimento* was written for solo performers or for orchestra, since in early classical times *divertimento*, symphony, and quartet were not clearly distinguished. In general, however, the title *divertimento* was reserved for compositions which were pert, carefree, and vaporous by nature. The movements were short, void of polyphonic intricacies, and contrived mainly to delight the ear rather than to create a profound impression on the listener.

[63] T. de Wyzewa and G. de Saint-Foix, *W. A. Mozart* (Paris, 1936), I, 201.

VI: CONSOLIDATION OF THE ELEMENTS
INTO THE CLASSICAL CHAMBER STYLE

*M*OVEMENTS strung together without inner connection, sweet mixtures of tones without penetration, and a flavor which had mostly local appeal were fair ingredients for casual music-making, but music, to be of a consistent character, required more logic and unity than was offered in the *divertimento*. To obviate any deficiency which might result from surrendering the thorough bass, composers, nearing the classical chamber style, consolidated the elements discussed above; they coördinated the developments which had been made concerning the relationship of styles, disposition of instruments, use of instruments for their individual characteristics, assignment of one instrument to a part, and the union of the homophonic and polyphonic idioms.

With regard to the relationship of styles, there was a certain amount of crossing over from one branch of musical composition to another. For example, Italian opera composers like Nicola Jommelli (1714–1774), Nicola Piccinni (1728–1800) and Johann Adolph Hasse (1699–1783), developed the thematic ideal which was taken over into instrumental music. Rests themselves were made to speak, and contrasts which formerly would have been considered as two separate moods were welded into a living, sensitive, impulsive theme. Schubart attributed to Jommelli "the more exact designation of musical color; and especially the universally effective crescendo and decrescendo." [1] Although Jommelli himself was not an important figure in the chamber style, the advances he made in opera were transferred to the chamber by other composers. Schubart admitted, "In the chamber style Jommelli worked much too carelessly for his composition in that species to merit much approbation." [2]

In Germany the sweep toward the classical theme was accelerated by the orchestral works of Johann Stamitz, Franz Beck, C. P. E. Bach, and Wagenseil. The heterogeneous elements within the theme constituted latent energy which, when set free, gave rise to a conflict to be carried out and then resolved. Not all the themes were based on contrasts. Yet even where there was consistency in motive, dynamics, articulation, and

[1] C. F. D. Schubart, *Ideen zu einer Ästhetik der Tonkunst* (Vienna, 1806), p. 47.
[2] *Ibid.,* p. 48.

accompanying parts, the nature of the theme tended strongly toward
the classical style. Whereas the old presto gigue could be slowed down
to an andante,[3] the tempo of a movement was now often inherent in
the theme itself. The effect of the prestissimo theme is analogous to that
of a painting viewed from a distance. When the observer approaches the
canvas too closely he sees what appears to be a mass of indeterminate
brush strokes. Likewise, the prestissimo theme disintegrates if played
at slow-motion tempo. Its profile is preserved only at a breakneck speed.

Allied to thematic delineation is the technique of dispersing the
theme through all the parts to such an extent that the successive efforts
of the whole ensemble of instruments are required for the presentation
of one musical line. This uniformity of texture originated in the solo
clavier style, whence it was transferred to chamber music. Bernardo Pas-
quini (1637–1710), successor of Frescobaldi, transported the free parts
of the toccata to the clavier sonata. This process was completed by Domenico Scarlatti before the heritage, with slight modification, passed to
chamber style. On the clavier a single scalewise or arpeggiated part was
divided between two hands which crossed frequently; in the string ensemble a single part was apportioned among three, four, or five melodic
instruments. By emancipating the bass in their trio sonatas from the
usual unbroken line of the *continuo* so that the cello could join in the
melodic interplay with the other instruments, Sammartini, Gluck,[4] and
Stamitz helped to remove the boundaries which encased each part as
a melodic entity. Thus they paved the way for the technique in which
one melody passed through all the parts like a filigree.

With regard to the disposition of instruments, except for the omission of the thorough bass, the chamber trio for two violins and cello was
essentially a continuation of the trio sonata. As late as 1777 Mozart's
trio, K.V. 266, for two violins and bass, still had the constant crossing
of the two violins and the accompanying bass characteristic of the old
Italian trio sonata.[5] In the species as a whole, any effort toward filling
the gap between the violins and bass was concentrated in the second
violin part, where repeated double stops, accentuating triple stops, and
chordal figuration were aimed at compensating for the missing *continuo*. The string trio with two violins persisted until the end of the
1760s when differentiation of the two violins led to the replacement of
the second violin by a viola. Luigi Boccherini's trios for two violins and
cello, Op. 2 (1760), were followed by trios for violin, viola, and cello,

---

[3] The loss of dance character through such tampering has already been indicated.
See p. 104.   [4] *Collegium musicum*, Nos. 32–37.
[5] W. A. Mozart, *Gesamtausgabe* (Leipzig, 1876–1905), Ser. 24, 23a.

Op. 9. Because of this change in instrumentation Choron and Fayolle maintained that, "Boccherini is the first who, towards 1768, gave the trio a permanent character. After him come (Fred) Fiorillo, Cramer, Giardini, Pugnani, finally Viotti." [6]

Many composers, including Boccherini, Dittersdorf, Gossec, Haydn, and Beethoven, utilized the string trio as a steppingstone to the quartet.[7] According to Carpani, while Haydn was in the service of Baron von Fürnberg, the latter, pleased with six Haydn trios performed at the castle, urged him to try his hand at the quartet.[8] The baron enjoyed chamber music and considered it an excellent way to entertain his guests. He provided for daily ensemble music, to be performed by the following instrumentalists: Haydn, then only slightly over twenty years of age; a cellist named Albrechtsberger, who may have been a relative of Johann Georg Albrechtsberger, and two other members of the estate who were not professional musicians, the cleric and the administrator.[9] Within a short space of time Haydn composed eighteen quartets for this group of players. Despite the fact that they were written for four players, they were called, not quartets, but cassations, *divertimenti*, and *notturni*, appropriate names in view of their gay, popular demeanor. Accordingly, in the first draft of the *Entwurf-Katalog* (a thematic catalogue of Haydn's compositions started in 1765 by Haydn and the copyist Joseph Elssler), his nineteen trios for two violins and bass had the separate heading *Trio*,[10] while the early quartets, individually labeled *Cassatio* or *Divertimento à quattro*, were listed along with the other *divertimenti* for varying numbers of instruments.[11] Two of the cassations, now quartets Op. 2, Nos. 3 and 5, originally called for horns besides.[12] Due to the overlapping in instrumentation, when the cassation and *divertimento* merged into the string quartet, it was most natural for the same patterns of movements to be familiar under all three names. The importance of the minuet in the *divertimento* was reflected in Haydn's first twelve quartets, each of which has two minuets distributed among a total of five movements.

[6] Al. Choron and F. Fayolle, *Dictionnaire historique des musiciens* (Paris, 1817), I, lxiij.

[7] Boccherini's first six quartets, engraved as Op. 1, were actually written after his trios published as Op. 2.

[8] Giuseppe Carpani, *Le Haydine ovvero lettere su la vita e le opere del celebre Maestro Giuseppe Haydn* (Milan, 1812), p. 85.

[9] Georg August Griesinger, *Biographische Notizen über Joseph Haydn* (Leipzig, 1810), p. 15; Ernst Ludwig Gerber, *Historisch-biographisches Lexicon der Tonkünstler* (Leipzig, 1790), II, 595.

[10] *Drei Haydn Kataloge in Faksimile*, ed. Jens Peter Larsen (Copenhagen, 1941), p. 15.   [11] *Ibid.*, p. 5.   [12] C. F. Pohl, *Joseph Haydn* (Berlin, 1875), I, 338 f.

Quartets of the preclassic era were a species dependent, not only on the *divertimento,* but also on the trio sonata, concerto, and symphony. The adherence of the quartet to the distribution of instruments in the trio sonata is evidenced in the concentration on treble and bass parts. Frequently the middle lines of the quartet either paralleled the activity of the outer parts in octaves, thirds, or sixths, or they simulated the type of padding previously allotted to a *continuo* keyboard instrument. Not until the smallest note values gained admittance to the middle parts, not until the viola was emancipated from the bass, not until every part was understood as a potential vehicle for the melodic motives, was the string quartet a reality.

Theoretically, with regard to instrumentation, the easiest way to convert a string trio into a string quartet was to insert a viola between the two violins and the bass. Such a mechanical conversion was occasionally attempted. In Buckingham Palace there is a manuscript of Handel's sonatas for two violins and bass, Op. 5 (1739) [13] which was copied in the latter half of the eighteenth century. The fourth sonata in this copy is of special interest because of the addition of a part for viola ad libitum. On the basis of Chrysander's observation that the viola part is in a different handwriting from the rest,[14] it appears that someone after 1750 desired to transform this trio sonata into a quartet. However, the arranger fell short of his aim, for the viola part lacks individuality, and merely serves to complete a four-part harmony.

Another source for the disposition of instruments in the quartet lay in the solo performance of concertos. Whereas the typical Italian concerto grosso, under the influence of Corelli, had a *concertino* for two violins and a cello, Geminiani added a viola, thus creating a quartet *concertino* with a middle part containing independent interest. In the first edition of Geminiani's Op. 3, published in London by J. Walsh under the title, *Concerti grossi con due violini viola e violoncello di concerti obligati e due altri violini e basso di concerto grosso* (1733), the four instruments of the *concertino* plus the three ripieno instruments constituted seven parts in all. In this version there was no viola prescribed for the *tutti.* However, twenty-two years later, when the concertos were printed in score, the quartet backbone of these concertos was emphasized by the addition of a viola di ripieno.

Since the soloists in some concerti grossi, besides playing their solo parts, also joined in the *tutti,* there was a body of concertos in which all the music could be played by the soloists alone. Charles Avison gave di-

---

[13] See p. 100 f.
[14] *Georg Friedrich Händel's Werke* (Leipzig, 1859–1894), XXVII, ii; music, p. 172.

rections to the soloists for differentiating the solo and *tutti* parts in the event that the ripieno performers were not present:

When Concertos are performed with three or four Instruments only, it may not be amiss to play the Solo Parts *Mezzo Piano;* and to know more accurately where to find them, the first and last Note of every Chorus should be distinguished thus (♩) and to prevent all Mistakes of pointing the *Forte* at a wrong Place, that also ought to have the same Mark: By this Means the Performer will be directed to give the *first* Note of every Chorus and Forte its proper Emphasis, and not suffer the *latter* to hang upon the Ear, which is extremely disagreeable.[15]

The concerto pared down to a string quartet retained the characteristics of a real concerto. Quantz outlined requisites applicable both to the concerto grosso and the chamber concerto. In each of its movements there should be "a stately ritornelle at the beginning which must be more harmonious than melodious, more serious than humorous, and mixed with unisons." [16] Transferred to the quartet, the unison of all the instruments was valuable in cases where the harmonic succession was well defined in the melodic line itself. Further on he urged, "The change of concerted instruments must be distributed so that one is not heard too much and the other too little," [17] advice which was likewise suitable for the quartet.

Dealing separately with the viola player, Quantz commented,

He must distinguish between arias, concertos, and other sorts of music which he has to accompany. In airs he does not have much to do, since he has to play mostly only a pure middle part, or with the bass in unison. But in concertos there is often more to do, because at times the viola, instead of the second violin, is given the imitation or a melody similar to the upper part. Likewise the viola also must at times play a singing ritornelle with the violins in unison, which in an adagio creates a specially good effect. If the violist, at such occasions, does not have a clear and agreeable delivery, the most beautiful composition can be spoiled by him, especially when in such a piece there is only one person playing each part.[18]

Echo effects copied from the concerto were self-explanatory when first transferred to chamber music. If a passage was repeated, the performers automatically played it loudly the first time and softly the next. According to Quantz, "On repetition or with similar thoughts consisting of half or whole measures, either on the same tones or in a transposition, the

15 Charles Avison, *An Essay on Musical Expression* (London, 1752), p. 126.
16 Johann Joachim Quantz, *Versuch einer Anweisung die Flöte traversiere zu spielen* (*1752*) (Leipzig, 1906), chap. xviii, par. 31.
17 *Loc. cit.* 18 *Ibid.*, chap. xvii, sec. iii, par. 4.

repetition may be played somewhat more softly than the first execution of it." [19] From this quotation one realizes that the old echo effect between phrases had gained a counterpart in contrast within a phrase, even within a short motive, on either strong or weak beats.[20] The individual components of a theme might be juxtaposed amid sudden changes of mood, or might be graded gradually, through a slow crescendo or decrescendo. The order of the day was neither strict fugal manipulation of a definite number of real voices, nor the transparent homophony of the *style galant* with lazy basses and syncopated middle parts. In the classical style preference was given to free imitation among a variable number of parts. A powerful unison phrase could be followed by a delicate phrase with some independence in the accompanying parts; an opening phrase with full harmony could be opposed by a soft, running melodic phrase with the harmony barely suggested. All the instruments together might play piano and a single instrument alone might play forte. Effects of loud and soft had been introduced into the concerto by pitting a larger body of sound against a smaller one. Now dynamic contrast could be achieved within a single body of sound, small or large.

The proximity between concerto grosso instrumentation and string quartet instrumentation, to the point of their overlapping, is shown in six concertos written by Alessandro Scarlatti between 1715 and 1725. Edward Dent observed that four of Scarlatti's *VI Concertos for Two Violins and Violoncello Obligato, with Two Violins More, a Tenor and Thoroughbass*, published by Dr. Benjamin Cooke (London, ca. 1740), were identical with a manuscript of four compositions copied by one of Scarlatti's regular copyists, entitled *Sonata à quattro; due violini violetta e violoncello; senza cembalo; del Sigr Cavalre Alesso Scarlatti.*[21] After putting the parts of the concerto version together, Dent saw that the seven parts could be condensed to four, since the soloists played throughout and the ripienists merely reinforced the sections where they joined in. Because of the preponderance of counterpoint in the compositions, the viola had much to do, and the harpsichord was omitted even at this early date.[22]

---

[19] *Ibid.*, chap. xvii, sec. vii, par. 26; cf. C. P. E. Bach, *Essay on the True Art of Playing Keyboard Instruments [Versuch über die wahre Art das Clavier zu spielen, 1759 1762]*, trans. and ed. William J. Mitchell (New York, 1948), chap. iii, par. 29.

[20] A. Heuss, "Die Dynamik der Mannheimer Schule," *Zeitschrift für Musikwissenschaft*, II (1919), 45.

[21] E. J. Dent, "The Earliest String Quartets," *Monthly Musical Record*, XXXIII (1903), 202–204.

[22] A. Scarlatti, *Sonata a Quattro in D Minor*, ed. H. David (New York, 1940).

The lack of distinction between concerto and string quartet prevailed until the middle of the eighteenth century. Tartini composed about 150 concertos, among which there are many *Sonate a quattro*.[23] It is interesting to observe that while Tartini was creating string quartets without *continuo,* he was still writing *Trio da camera* with *continuo.* Quartets, besides being related to the *divertimento* and concerto, were likewise considered a subdivision of the chamber symphony. For the *Sinfonia a quattro,* in vogue before 1750, it was the performers who determined whether the parts were to be played with single or multiple instrumentation. Tartini used both terms, *Sonata a quattro* and *Sinfonia a quattro,* to refer to three-movement compositions with a strong penchant for parallel thirds and sixths in the voice leading. Although he failed to designate the presence of the *continuo,* its function is recalled in the stiff bass part. On the other hand, the *Sinfonie a quattro* by Giovanni Battista Sammartini have more supple bass parts, with many rests. The "symphonies" which Sammartini wrote before the line between quartet and symphony had been clearly drawn, are as quartetlike as any other compositions of the preclassic era. The fact that Sammartini's basses had more vitality than was usually evident in the continuous sound of the customary thorough bass may have been one of the factors which induced Joseph Misliweczek (1737–1781) [24] to declare that Sammartini was Haydn's predecessor in the field of the quartet. Misliweczek's opinion, and more particularly Haydn's contradiction, has long since become legend. According to Griesinger,

the violinist Misliweczek, a Bohemian by birth, heard quartets performed during his stay in Milan, and when the already seventy-year-old Johann Baptista Sammartini was named as the composer of the same, he cried out completely astounded, "At last I know the predecessor of Haydn, and the model on which he was trained!" It seemed worthwhile to me to examine more closely the grounds for this declaration, since I had never heard doubt of Haydn's originality, especially in his quartets. I asked Haydn whether he had heard Sammartini's work in his youth, and what he thought of this composer. Haydn answered that he had previously heard Sammartini's music, but never prized it, for Sammartini is a dauber [*Schmierer*]. He laughed heartily, when I came forth with Misliweczek's pretentious discovery, and said that he recognized as his model only Emanuel Bach, and a subsequent completely accidental circumstance caused him to try his luck at the composition of quartets.[25]

Carpani told the tale as if he had himself been on the scene. With convincing assurance he declared, "I will never forget what occurred

---

[23] Adolph Sandberger, "Zur Geschichte des Haydnschen Streichquartett," in *Ausgewählte Aufsätze zur Musikgeschichte* (Munich, 1921), I, 245.

[24] A Bohemian composer who wrote string quartets.

[25] Griesinger, *op. cit.,* p. 14 f.

thirty years ago, with Misliweczek, in Milan, at a concert where they were playing some old symphonies by Sammartini . . ." [26] The rest of the story was essentially the same. It should be noted that Carpani referred to the Sammartini compositions as "symphonies," not "quartets." The idea that Haydn might have learned something about quartet composition from another master's orchestral works is perfectly plausible. Further on, Carpani gives exact information on how Haydn could have reached Sammartini's compositions.

Now it remains for me to explain to you how Haydn of Vienna could profit by numerous original compositions by Sammartini of Milan. It will not be difficult for me if you lend me your ear. Pallavicini had been preceded as governor of Austrian Lombardy by the Count of Harrach. He was the first to bring the music of Sammartini to Vienna. It was an immense success and a great vogue in that large capital, where music is regarded as the most agreeable pastime. Count Palfi, grand chancellor of Hungary, Count Schönborn and Count Mortzin were express rivals in procuring the newest compositions of Sammartini, which were heard in profusion in their concerts almost every day. Haydn, young and studious, could and did attend these concerts many times, but he heard the music of that composer still more often when he passed from the service of Count Mortzin to that of Prince Esterházy, . . . who, like Count Palfi, had attached to his service the distant pen of Sammartini. . . . The musical archives alone of the Palfi family contain more than a thousand pieces composed by that man.[27]

Since Sammartini's works were available to Haydn, it seems highly probable that he took advantage of the opportunity to peruse them. However, in view of the numerous types of composition which went into the making of the quartet, and in view of the many other composers whose works Haydn must have seen and heard, it seems unfair to attribute a preponderant influence to one source.

The title under which La Chevardière published Haydn's Op. 1, *Six Symphonies ou quatuors dialogués pour deux violons, alto et basse,* further indicated the relation of the orchestra to chamber music. As a substitute for the quartet in E♭, which had been listed in the *Entwurf Katalog* along with other compositions of the above opus, La Chevardière included a symphony in B♭. In pattern, the E♭ quartet, with five movements of which two are minuets, corresponds exactly to the other quartets composed at the time, whereas the B♭ composition, with a three-movement design derivative of the Italian symphony, is different from the remaining members of the opus. Perhaps the composition in E♭ was replaced because its movements are thin in substance as com-

[26] Carpani, *op. cit.,* p. 57.   [27] *Ibid.,* p. 61 f.

pared with the other compositions of Op. 1. Nonetheless, such conjectures do not obscure the fact that a symphony became a member of a group of compositions in chamber style. Through the discovery of authentic parts for two horns and two oboes, the orchestral nature of the composition in B♭ was established conclusively. Besides, an internal examination of the "quartet's" distribution of instruments reveals its orchestral character. As one criterion, the viola rarely moves beyond the chaperonage of the bass. Octaves between the viola and bass lingered longer as a standard procedure for the symphony than for the string quartet, after the two mediums eventually were severed. In the second movement of the work in B♭ the viola and bass are continually in octaves; in the other two movements there is only slight respite from reinforcement of the bass. The other quartets of Haydn's Op. 1 are hardly as persistent in the use of octaves, except in the minuets. The lean arpeggio formulas, the determined syncopations, and numerous scale passages of the three-movement composition also tend toward the orchestral.

Although wholesale octave doubling of the bass veered toward the orchestral style, in chamber style controlled doubling offered a desirable means for contrast, an effect which prompted Haydn to use the technique in upper parts as well as lower. In the *Vienna Diary* of 1766 the following evaluation of Haydn's cassations, quartets, and trios appeared: "The monotonous style of writing the parts in consonant octaves was originated by him. One cannot deny its agreeableness when it appears seldom and in Haydnlike garb." [28]

A reticent acceptance of octave doubling, tempered by the feeling that anything Haydn did was all right, was also displayed by Junker: "That he really introduced the octave progression—I am pleased to see; for it can often produce a great effect regardless of correctness or incorrectness; and, at least for the ear, has the exact ratio of an octave." [29]

Gerber's comments on octave doubling between the first and second violin indicate that Haydn derived this technique from the orchestra and transferred it to the quartet.

Already his first quartets, which became known about 1760, created a general sensation. People laughed and were pleased on the one side by the extraordinary simplicity and liveliness in them and on the other side they cried out against the degradation of music to comic trifling, and against unheard-of octaves.—For he was the one who first introduced into these, his quartets, the style of doubling the melody at the octave, or allowing the first and second violin to proceed in octaves, which had such a great effect in large orchestras at

28 Pohl, *op. cit.*, I, 373.
29 Carl Ludwig Junker, *Zwanzig Componisten* (Bern, 1776), p. 67.

expressive places. But people soon became accustomed to this style in spite of all the shouting. Yes, they finally imitated it themselves.[30]

Dies, however, denied Haydn's priority in the matter, although he granted the influence of Haydn's example. "Haydn was one of the first who made use of a melody doubled at the octave (de Lucca in [the periodical] *Das gelehrte Oesterreich* mistakenly called him the founder of the octave progression). Immediately it became a fashionable epidemic to reinforce the melody at the octave." [31]

Strengthening the melody in octaves was a technique which invited repeated comment. Concerning C. P. E. Bach's third sonatina, for concertato harpsichord and six obbligato instruments, J. A. Hiller wrote, "It consists of three movements, a largo, allegro and tempo di minuetto. A skillful strengthening of the melody by octaves in the clavier part is brought about in the opening largo, right in the beginning and towards the end. It has an incomparable effect." [32] Reinforcement of a flute by the clavier an octave below sometimes involved a slight adjustment in one of the parts to compensate for the nature of the instrument. In the first sonatina of C. P. E. Bach, for the same combination of instruments as the composition described by Hiller, the flute holds a note for over two measures while the clavier continues to restrike the note in an effort to shadow the flute an octave below.[33] In string writing, with the first violin echoed below by the second violin, no such alteration was necessary.

Still on the borderline of orchestral style was the *Quatuor concertant* of the Viennese composer Franz Asplmayr (*ca.* 1721–1786). In Op. 2, No. 2, for two violins, alto, and bass, Asplmayr presented the melody of the first movement in octaves between the two violins.[34] The fact that the viola and bass are harmonic, often in octaves, but not active melodically, indicates that the technique is still close to the orchestra, even though the title specifies a chamber setting. *Concertant,* in reference to the quartet, meant the use of one instrument to a part, rather than solo treatment in the sense of virtuosity. The quartet composer was soon to aim toward the cohesion of all instruments, allowing one instrument to surpass the rest in brilliant solo work only on intermittent occasions, and usually with a particular personage in mind. Tonal balance was the factor which

---

[30] Ernst Ludwig Gerber, *Historisch-biographisches Lexicon der Tonkünstler* (Leipzig, 1790), I, 611.

[31] Albert Christoph Dies, *Biographische Nachrichten von Joseph Haydn* (Vienna, 1810), p. 206.

[32] *Wöchentliche Nachrichten und Anmerkungen die Musik betreffend,* J. A. Hiller, ed. (Leipzig, 1766), p. 36.

[33] C. P. E. Bach. *Sonatine in C dur für Klavier, 2 Flöten, 2 Violinen, Viola und Violoncell,* ed. Hjalmar von Dameck (Berlin, 1922).

[34] *Collegium musicum,* No. 46.

was to segregate the classical string quartet from the symphony. Each of the instruments of the string quartet was to receive the treatment which its nature demanded, yet all were to blend together into a unified whole.

Because of the allotment of a single instrument to a part, there was a strong tendency toward experimenting with the individuality of the instrument. The personality of an instrument was often likened to the traits of a man. Bombet pictured the four instrumental conversationalists of an ensemble as four people, each with his own characteristics.

You know that quartetts are executed by four instruments, a first violin, a second violin, an alto, and a violoncello. An intelligent woman said, that when she heard a quartett of Haydn's she fancied herself present at the conversation of four agreeable persons. She thought that the first violin had the air of an eloquent man of genius, of middle age, who supported a conversation, the subject of which he had suggested. In the second violin, she recognized a friend of the first, who sought by all possible means to display him to advantage, seldom thought of himself, and kept up the conversation, rather by assenting to what was said by the others, than by advancing any ideas of his own. The alto, was a grave, learned, and sententious man. He supported the discourse of the first violin by laconic maxims, striking for their truth. The bass, was a worthy old lady, rather inclined to chatter, who said nothing of much consequence, and yet was always desiring to put in a word. But she gave an additional grace to the conversation, and while she was talking, the other interlocutors had time to breathe. It was, however, evident, that she had a secret inclination for the alto, which she preferred to the other instruments.[35]

Identification of the instruments of an ensemble as conversationalists was expressed in the word *dialogué*, which commonly appeared in chamber music titles. French publishers used the term profusely when printing works by composers of other nationalities, as well as of their own. The Mannheimer, Joseph Toeschi (1724–1788), wrote *Six quatuors dialogués* published in Paris by La Chevardière. Indeed, the "conversation" of Toeschi's Op. 1, No. 1, for flute, violin, viola, and cello was very thin in spots. In one passage for flute and cello alone, the instruments are over three octaves apart.[36] Except for the brief emancipation of the viola in order to effect a canonic entrance, the instrument merely accompanies, supplying chordal figures, sustaining given notes, going below the violin in thirds, or above the bass in octaves.

In an examination of preclassical quartets, not only their deficiencies, but also their merits must be taken into account. The basis for the classical quartet was there, awaiting development. Prudent contemporary commentators aided the course of chamber music by singling out the fine qualities of the music. Junker reported enthusiastically of Toeschi's

35 L. A. C. Bombet, *The Life of Haydn in a Series of Letters* (London, 1817), p. 63.
36 *Denkmäler der Tonkunst in Bayern*, XV, 79, meas. 17.

first flute quartet, that he "was astonished by the melodies, rushing one upon the other, by the fullness, by the harmonic connection; by the richness of each particular instrument,—by their interchange."[37] Further on he maintained, "In the history of music the flute quartets of Toeschi will always deserve an important place!—for they are epoch-making." [38] In fairness to Junker it must be noted that he did not sink all his faith in one man. He mentioned that for the taste of Joseph Alois Schmittbauer (1718–1809), Eichner, and Heinrich Joseph Riegel (1741–1799), "Toeschi was not stimulating enough. They composed the quartet in almost the same vein, but they avoided the uniformity, were more diverse, and imitated song more—were thus still more melodious." [39]

The conversation in the quartet spread to topics covering a wider and wider range. Its subject matter could be at times serious and contemplative, then frivolous and lively. All the conversationalists had to be ready to join in the discussion. Such a state of coöperation, however, was an ideal whose fulfillment was to take years of development. The greatest single factor in the development of instrumental conversation was the inclusion of counterpoint in an essentially homophonic style. Composers had long been concerned with combining polyphonic and homophonic styles. The intermixture of *da chiesa* and *da camera* styles in turn was superseded by the union of *galant* and learned styles. With regard to the external juxtaposition of styles a most common occurrence in a composition with several movements was the combination of an introductory homophonic movement and a closing fugal movement, such as the union of *galant* prelude and learned fugue. Paired movements appeared in the Viennese string quartets of Florian Leopold Gassmann (1729–1774). The first movement was slow, in the style of a prelude, followed by a second movement, in fugal style. The third movement, minuet, and the following finale were inconsequential in comparison with the preceding two movements.[40]

However, the blend of the strict and the free penetrated beyond the mere placement of the movements. The long-standing conflict between counterpoint and *continuo* practice was to be solved, not by alternating polyphonic and homophonic movements, but by developing a style which inwardly united the *galant* and learned. In the first half of the eighteenth century, although all theory was built on a chordal basis, from a melodic point of view counterpoint and thorough-bass practice were distinct. Counterpoint dealt with chords arising from the union of mel-

37 Junker, *op. cit.*, p. 96.   38 *Ibid.*, p. 97.   39 *Loc. cit.*
40 A. Einstein, "Mozart's Four String Trio Preludes to Fugues of Bach," *Musical Times*, LXXVII (1936), 211.

odies sounding at the same time, while thorough bass dealt with chords as they were used in accompaniment. Composers and theorists who achieved lasting fame were often well versed in both styles. Quantz, who studied counterpoint with Fux in Vienna (1717) and then with Francesco Gasparini in Rome (1724), wrote a mass consisting only of canons before he ventured into solo, duet, and trio composition. J. A. Hiller commented wisely on what counterpoint meant to Quantz: "After this instruction in eye-music, Quantz began to write for the ear, and composed solos, duets, trios and concertos. Even if he could not make use of all the stiff artistry of counterpoint in these musical compositions, yet through this schooling he had attained an advantage in composition which stood him in good stead in the completion of a trio or quartet." [41]

Fux furthered the cause of strict counterpoint, to a great extent, by training many composers personally and by reaching a host of others through his *Gradus ad Parnassum* (1725). Counterpoint even invaded the *divertimento*. That Antonio Caldara (1670–1736), who was assistant *Kapellmeister* to Fux, assimilated the latter's strong contrapuntal bent is evidenced in his six- and nine-part *Divertimenti musicali* (Vienna, 1729).[42]

Autobiographies and contemporary biographies of eighteenth-century composers often referred to the *Gradus ad Parnassum,* which was the standard work in the field of strict counterpoint. Ignaz Holzbauer (1711–1783), describing how he disobeyed his father's wishes by studying music, revealed,

I begged my sister until she finally gave me money to buy Fux's composition book. I understood Latin and so began to study it. The storage room was the place for it, since it could not be in my bedroom. I soon composed symphonies, concertos and all sorts of similar compositions, and these works of mine were always greeted with the greatest approbation from my masters. During a whole year I followed my instinct for music alone.[43]

Holzbauer, born in Vienna, eventually migrated to Mannheim. Other Viennese also took their point of departure from Fux. Dittersdorf, too, was referred to Fux's work at the very first composition lesson he took with Giuseppe Bonno (1710–1788).[44] Haydn, after having consulted

[41] J. A. Hiller, *Lebensbeschreibungen berühmter Musikgelehrten und Tonkünstler neuerer Zeit* (Leipzig, 1784), p. 223.

[42] Antonio Caldara, *Das Do-Re-Mi,* ed. Fritz Jöde (Wolfenbüttel, 1928). Contains twenty-eight three-part instrumental canons from Caldara's *Divertimenti musicali per campagna; canoni all' unisono a 3, 4, 5, 6 e à 9 voci; con altri d'altro genere à 2, 3, è 4.*

[43] F. Walter, *Geschichte des Theaters und der Musik am Kurpfälzischen Hofe* (Leipzig, 1898), p. 357.

[44] *The Autobiography of Karl von Dittersdorf,* trans. A. D. Coleridge (London, 1896), p. 76 f.

Carl Philipp Emanuel's *Versuch über die wahre Art, das Clavier zu spielen* and Mattheson's *Vollkommene Kapellmeister,* likewise turned to the *Gradus.* Griesinger described how Haydn was attracted to this "book which in old age he still praised as classical, and of which he had preserved a worn-out copy. With tireless energy Haydn sought to absorb Fux's theory. He went through his whole method in a practical manner. He worked out the lessons, set them aside for a few weeks, then surveyed them again, and polished them until he thought he had found the solution." [45]

Haydn's efforts to bring strict counterpoint in line with the taste of his time in one case involved a mere external juxtaposition of styles. He added preludes to fugues written by his predecessor at Esterháza, Gregor Joseph Werner (d. 1766). However, although Haydn was interested in strict counterpoint as a pedagogical discipline, in his own compositions his musicianship dictated liberties in the use of counterpoint. Dies quoted Haydn as saying,

I wrote what seemed good to me, and corrected it afterwards according to the rules of harmony. I never used other artifices. A few times I took the liberty of offending, not the ear, but the usual rules of the text-books, and at those places wrote the words: *con licenza.* They shouted, "A mistake!" and wanted to prove it by Fux. I asked my opponents whether they could prove by their musical ear that it was a mistake. They had to answer "No." [46]

Counterpoint was in the process of being reconciled with thorough-bass theory. Haydn took most of his "liberties" in the development section of the composition, while working out the materials of the theme. He had the art of development so well in hand that the theme itself was sometimes a secondary matter to him. The motives Haydn used in thematic construction while writing quartets in his youth do not vary essentially from the motives used in later years; the difference in his technique of development constitutes the difference in quartet construction.[47] By separation and dissection of motives, by contrapuntal imitation, by reintroducing parts from new angles, he could make much of an insignificant theme.

When his object was not to express any particular "affection," or to paint any particular images, all subjects were alike to him. "The whole art consists," said he, "in taking up a subject, and pursuing it." Often, when a friend entered, as he was about to commence a piece, he would say with a smile, "Give me a subject." Give a subject to Haydn! who would have the courage to do so?—

---

45 Griesinger, *op. cit.,* p. 10.   46 Dies, *op. cit.,* p. 59.
47 A. Hinderberger, *Die Motivik in Haydns Streichquartetten* (Turbenthal, 1935), p. 21.

"Come, never mind," he would say, "give me any thing you can think of;" and you were obliged to obey.

Many of his astonishing quartetts exhibit marks of this piece of dexterity. They commence with the most insignificant idea, but by degrees, this idea assumes a character; it strengthens, increases, extends itself, and the dwarf becomes a giant before our wondering eyes.[48]

Nevertheless, even in the development of motives, counterpoint did not obliterate the heritage left by the *continuo*. Counterpoint was used only for special effects, such as presenting the theme in the obbligato accompanying parts, or introducing appropriate motives to emphasize the subsidiary parts; at those times the accompanying parts were equivalent to the main melody-bearing part. Yet, for ordinary purposes the accompanying parts were coherent but subordinate participants whose services were required in one of the three flexible registers, upper, middle, or lower. Their duty in a homophonic or unison passage was merely to complement or reinforce; in a contrapuntal passage their rank was more prominent.

Haydn's early training, and his associations with church music and opera, provided the groundwork upon which he proceeded to chamber music. Prior to the composition of the Op. 1 quartets, he learned musical fundamentals in Vienna as a choir boy at St. Stephen's. After leaving the choir he met Nicolo Porpora, the famous Italian composer, who taught him composition and the Italian method of singing and accompaniment.[49] It was also through Porpora that he made contact with outstanding composers of the day. As clavier accompanist for Porpora, in 1753 Haydn went to Mannersdorf, a leading resort, where he met Gluck, Bonno, Dittersdorf, and Wagenseil. Through Wagenseil, Haydn became acquainted with the music of Mannheim; with Dittersdorf he established an intimate friendship conducive to the exchange of musical ideas.

Haydn's Op. 1 was flavored with all the elements which later were to be blended into the classical chamber style. It borrowed from the vocal medium traces of the chorale style [50] and a predominance of the first violin, sometimes in a flowing cantilena clearly vocal in nature,[51] at other times with a chromatic inflection reminiscent of opera.[52] Stylis-

---

48 Bombet, *op. cit.*, p. 111. Bombet plagiarized G. Carpani's *Le Haydine ovvero lettere su la vita e le opere del celebre Maestro Giuseppe Haydn* (Milan, 1812). This passage is a translation of Carpani, p. 40 f.

49 Dies, *op. cit.*, p. 35; Griesinger, *op. cit.*, p. 13.

50 No. 1, third movement. (For convenience, unless otherwise indicated, the numbering corresponds to the Eulenburg edition.)

51 The slow movement of No. 2 may be compared to an operatic arioso.

52 No. 2, second trio.

tically the most obvious influence was the Viennese *divertimento*.[53] However, the virtuosity of the solo violin concerto and the rapid touch of the keyboard style [54] also left their imprint.

Although the violin dominates in Op. 1, there are attempts at a more equitable allotment of responsibility and privilege among the instruments. As a relief from stodgy continuity in the bass, the cello is at times omitted.[55] Furthermore, the cello,[56] viola,[57] or second violin [58] are each entrusted with the melodic line on occasion. A genuine feeling for instrumental color is evident in a passage for muted first violin and pizzicato chordal accompaniment by the other three instruments.[59]

Strict canon,[60] as well as pseudo-canon with one part holding a tone while the other moves,[61] also appear in Op. 1. In the development sections there are already indications of the motivic workmanship in which Haydn was to excel. Dynamic shadings or sharp contrasts sometimes attend the dissection of the theme.

Contemporary publishers were too shortsighted to see that Haydn was already envisioning a new type of chamber music in his first three works. Everywhere but in Paris publishers persisted in adding a *continuo* to these compositions, although it was evident that Haydn's cello parts were developing a sense of the instrument's potential independence. In the first trio of Op. 2, No. 5, the cello is allotted a theme which is almost identical with that given to the first violin in the first trio of Op. 2, No. 2. Although the accompanying parts differ in the two trios, in both cases the melody is based on the same motive treated sequentially. The cello could command respect as well as the violin.

A device which offered the three upper instruments considerable opportunity for discourse was the theme and variations. Haydn introduced it twice in Op. 2, as the fourth movement of No. 3 and the first movement of No. 6. Haydn's variation technique in No. 6 is typical of what might be expected from him at this early period, in view of other such movements in his collected works. The framework for all the variations is the same: the bass of the theme is used as an ostinato in each variation, and the time signature, as well as the number of measures in each period, is constant. Haydn enhances this background with contrast-

---

[53] The third movement, presto, of No. 3, with the theme divided between the two violins, foretold the light dance character which was to feature in Op. 33.

[54] No. 3, last movement, climaxing at measure 20.

[55] Second trio of No. 6.   [56] Trios of both minuets of No. 3.

[57] First minuet of No. 2, measure 19.   [58] No. 3, first movement.

[59] No. 6, third movement.   [60] No. 4, second trio.

[61] No. 3, first movement, beginning with measure 15.

ing highlights in the three upper parts. In the variations, which are for the most part new counterpoints on a ground bass, he introduced melodies defined either by the contour of a phrase, or by the systematic exploitation of a motive. Only in the last variation of No. 6, consisting of alternations between a statement of half of the original theme and a diminution based thereon, does variation occur in the literal musical sense of the word. So far as the three upper instruments are concerned, when the first violin dominates in the second variation, the accompanying second violin and viola, not necessarily confined to the middle register, cross above the path of the first violin. In the following variation the contour of the line is divided between the second violin and the first. Whereas in Op. 2, No. 6, Haydn does not grant the viola any opportunity to distinguish itself, in the second minuet of Op. 2, No. 3, he contrives a series of variations in which the viola takes its turn as a well-defined individual. Pohl described the design of this movement as an *alternativo*.[62] The minuet and trio open the pattern; then a repetition of the minuet occurs after each of the three variations; a final repetition of the minuet closes the movement. Such a design more closely resembles a ritornelle than a theme and variations. With so many repetitions of the minuet Haydn must have realized that it would be tedious to confine the variations within the limits of an identical bass. Only in the second sections are the bass lines of the variations similar enough to be reduced to a fundamental scheme. Minus inorganic repetitions and insertions, the bass of the second sections may be generalized as follows:

BASS SCHEME FOR HAYDN'S QUARTET, OP. 2, NO. 3, 4TH MOVT.

The three alternating sections were variations based on the minuet, not the trio. Relationships may be read into this movement which are far more elaborate than those Haydn was apt to have conceived at the time. Actually, the harmony is based on fundamental formulas which occur in most works of this period, and the variations are in many respects episodes which bear resemblance to the minuet and to one another. From the point of view of instrumentation, No. 3 offers more diversity than the conventional theme and variation pattern of No. 6. In the first variation of No. 3 the viola has the dolce melody, and is accompanied by the other three parts. As if to compensate for this unusual

62 Pohl. *op. cit.*, I, 339.

procedure, Haydn omits the viola entirely in the second variation, and concentrates on the first violin. The third variation is a compromise, instrumentally speaking, with the viola and cello in thirds answered by the two violins in sixths or thirds.

Haydn likewise, with his inimitable sense of spontaneity, discovers and exploits opportunities for instrumental color and differentiation in several other movements of Op. 2, No. 3. In the third movement all four instruments are muted, and in the fifth movement the viola weaves itself boldly into the fabric of the conversation with figural work mounting to a high register. In the first movement, beginning at measure 58, the partial repetition of the main theme is disposed among the instruments differently from the statement in the exposition. A run played by the first violin in the theme is redistributed among second violin, viola, and cello in the recapitulation. Haydn definitely is seeking a less one-sided conversation. (See Excerpts on page 161.)

Op. 3 was an experimental work* in which Haydn abandoned the five-movement *divertimento* pattern of Op. 1 and 2. Although the majority of quartets in Op. 3 are based on the four-movement pattern: fast, slow, minuet and trio, fast, with the slow movement in a contrasting key, a three-movement pattern is utilized in No. 2 and a two-movement pattern in No. 4. The second quartet of this opus is the one which exhibits the greatest cohesion of diverse elements. A *Fantasia con variazioni*, based on a march theme, a favorite in the cassation, serves for the first movement. The cello, inexorably repeated in each variation, is the least flexible of the four instruments. In the first variation, the viola also has a line restated from the original section; only the two violins are set free, answering each other with triplet arpeggios. Variations two, three, and four are literally variations of the given theme in that the first violin parts are diminutions on the theme itself. The fourth variation is the most daring; yet the theme is clearly there, with the viola pursuing a relief motive based on extended leaps. Haydn customarily rounds out a theme and variation movement with a verbatim repetition of the theme in the final variation. But in this case, the redistribution of materials is carried to the point where the last is a true variation upon the theme rather than a repetition of it. The three lower parts carry the main burden, while the first violin, entering at the fourth measure, spins over them a delicate series of arabesques. In his early quartets, as in his maturest work, Haydn was constantly setting himself new problems and discovering new effects.

The second movement of Op. 3, No. 2 is a menuetto and trio, an apparently restricted pattern within which Haydn always seemed able to

*See "Preface," p. x.

discover new instrumental resources. In the first section of this minuet the two violins are in octaves, the cello mostly in thirds below, while the viola reiterates an eighth note drone.

The third and last movement of this quartet is characterized by Pohl as the lively finale of a comic opera.[63] Certainly the opera buffa devices

EXCERPTS FROM QUARTET, OP. 2, NO. 3, 1ST MOVT., BY HAYDN

63 *Ibid.*, I, 341.

are there: the unison arpeggios in eighth notes, the rising line of the two violins in thirds against an octave pedal point in the viola and cello, the increase of movement to repeated sixteenth notes, and the syncopation of the three upper instruments against the drum bass. As in opera buffa, this spirited instrumental introduction prepares for the cantabile line which begins in measure 39. However, although the techniques are borrowed from opera, the pattern into which Haydn weaves them belongs to instrumental music. The instrumental introduction corresponds to a tonic tonal area, while the cantabile theme starts the dominant tonal area. There is a development and a recapitulation. All the foregoing forms a large "A" section. A well-defined "B" section follows, based on a folklike tune, after which the "A" section is repeated. It is a sonata-rondo pattern.

The one other quartet in this opus with an unconventional number of movements, Op. 3, No. 4, is the only two-movement quartet Haydn composed, with the exception of the unfinished Op. 103. It is questionable whether the two movements of Op. 3, No. 4, one in B♭ major and the other in E♭ major, actually belong together. Yet, individually they are interesting. In the first movement, for example, the repetitious second theme is presented by the unusual combination of first violin and viola in octaves (measure 59); while in the second movement, a three-measure adagio in common time prefaces the presto exposition in $\frac{3}{4}$ time. The adagio is recalled later as a modulatory transition to the presto development and recapitulation. The result is a striking alternation of adagio, presto, adagio, presto.

The other four quartets of Op. 3 each have four movements of which the first and last are in fast tempo. Twice, in Nos. 5 and 6, the finales are labeled "scherzando." For his slow movements, Haydn offers a serenade in No. 5, and an arioso in No. 6, while his minuet-trio movements remain fertile soil for varied effects. The trio of No. 1 and the minuet of No. 6 contrast pizzicato and arco bowings. True to the literal sense of the word "trio," No. 5 uses only three instruments. A bagpipe is imitated in the minuet of No. 3, initially by the first violin playing both melody and inner drone with the cello supplying the bass, then in the recapitulation with the viola taking over the tricky double line. The minuet and trio movement was rapidly achieving that rich variety of detail and that comprehensive design which were to elevate it to a position of equality with the other movements of the quartet.

In his first eighteen string quartets, Haydn effected the same condensation of the five-movement *divertimento* which had taken place twenty years earlier in Vienna and Mannheim. Carlton Sprague Smith argued the possibility that Haydn's set of quartets for flute, violin, viola, and cello written in the middle of the 1750s, and known as Op. 5, originally may have been five-movement structures with two minuets, and that the omission of one of the minuets may have been effected later.[64] As in Op. 1 and 2, the quartets of Op. 5 were known by such various titles as *divertimentos, quatuors dialogués, quadri,* cassations, or symphonies.

Luigi Boccherini's six quartets, Op. 1 (1761), compared with Haydn's early quartets in cassation style, reveal Boccherini as one of the originators of the classical string quartet. Apart from the florid decorations derived from Sammartini, Boccherini's quartets display an independence of parts and an equilibrium of sonority far in advance of analogous productions of the time. Arguments about whether or not Boccherini preceded Haydn in the composition of quartets are futile. It has been contended on Boccherini's behalf that his Op. 1 was astonishing even in comparison with Haydn's Op. 9 (*ca.* 1769), which it antedated by about eight years. On occasion Boccherini united all four instruments by tossing an arpeggio from one to another.[65] He no longer required fugal technique in order to involve all his instruments on an equal basis, but he deployed them interchangeably in a single homophonic movement, even allotting the treble part to the cello and the bass to the second violin.[66] As befits a cellist of his caliber, he often lifted the cello part from obscurity; [67] but a comparable enthusiasm for the viola was rare.[68] This advanced instrumental conception, however, still alternated with passages in trio sonata style. Often his penchant for repeating part of a phrase and then discontinuing the repetition abruptly, resulted in rambling and loosely constructed themes. In accordance with Italian custom, the quartets were in three movements, some ending with a minuet-trio combination.

Boccherini was no more decisive about the designation of his first quartets than were the other quartet composers of his era. They were published in Paris by Venier in 1767 with the title *Six Symphonies or Quartets for Two Violins, Alto, and Obbligato Violoncello.*

The early works of both Haydn and Boccherini were on the threshold of the classical style. Since each of the two was influential in his own

---

[64] C. S. Smith, "Haydn's Chamber Music and the Flute," *Musical Quarterly,* XIX (1933), 439. Op. 5, No. 4, is reprinted in *Nagels Musik-Archiv,* No. 129, with four movements.

[65] Op. 1, No. 1, in C minor, first movement, measure 12. The six quartets of Boccherini's Op. 1 are contained in *Quartetti diversi, a due violini, viola e basso, di diversi compositori* (Rome, 1768), a manuscript in the Music Library at Columbia University.

[66] No. 2, in B♭ major, first movement.   [67] No. 1, second movement.

[68] No. 3, in D major, third movement.

right there is no need to negate the work of one in favor of the other. In later years, the mutual respect with which the two men regarded one another was documented in the correspondence files of Artaria, the publisher.[69]

Haydn made it clear to Domenico Artaria, who took over the business in 1802, that he preferred to recognize only the quartets after the first eighteen.[70] It was perhaps natural for the great composer to underrate his earlier and stylistically less mature productions. But it is fortunate that as maturer works were conceived the earlier compositions were not irrevocably destroyed. From the chamber enthusiast's point of view, these early quartets are still entertainment, as fresh and as engaging as ever; while to the historian they constitute an indispensable landmark in the early history of the classical chamber style.

[69] F. Artaria and H. Botstiber, *Joseph Haydn und das Verlagshaus Artaria* (Vienna, 1909), p. 23.   [70] *Ibid.*, p. 87.

CONCLUSION

CLASSICAL chamber style toward the end of the eighteenth century combined various attributes of church, theater, vocal, and orchestral music, fusing them into an intimate type of music requiring in performance only one player to each part. The resourceful composer was aware that instrumental chamber music was related to these various genres. He transferred vocal effects to his ensemble of instruments, not because he was ignorant of the aesthetic and practical differences between vocal and instrumental styles, but because he sought variety within the domain of chamber music. To create music suitable for chamber performance, the composer had to make his ideas conform to the choice of location. Although the foremost aim handed down from the transitory period was entertainment, his task was not an easy one, because there were no extramusical associations to divert the audience if the music in itself proved inadequate. Conversely, no nonmusical encumbrances encroached upon the freedom of his musical conceptions.

The trend of composition took many turns prior to the evolution of the classical notion that four-part harmony was most satisfactorily expressed by a chamber ensemble of four stringed instruments. Among the types of chamber music popular in the early eighteenth century, those founded upon the thorough bass were far in the lead—especially the trio sonata and the solo sonata. The concept of the thorough bass, obviating the need for explicitly written-out inner parts and providing for reinforcement of the bass line, was obviously contrary to the subsequent classical ideal of chamber music. Yet, when the emergence of chamber style is viewed in perspective, the era of thorough-bass practice falls naturally into place. Before the classical ideal of balance could be achieved—a balance seemingly homophonic perhaps, but in truth based upon a subtle fusion of the homophonic and polyphonic styles—it was essential that the dominance of a strictly polyphonic idiom be broken. Thorough bass stressed (perhaps to a certain degree, overstressed) by its strong doubling of the bass line, the harmonic foundation upon which a composition could securely rest, and through its system of figures made mandatory the erection of vertical columns of harmony to support the evolution of a freer melodic line. In this sense, although its specific practices ultimately outlived their usefulness, thorough bass helped pave the way for a more balanced style. Several well-established musical species—the vocal *canzonetta,* the instrumental *canzone* and *ricercare,* and the division on a ground—provided the basis for the disposition of parts in the trio sonata. The transformation from *canzone* to trio sonata was effected either by omission of parts (which, unless approximately replaced by the thorough bass, were sacrificed to the composite harmony) or by the absorption of parts, so that the trio sonata accounted for a total activity which heretofore had entailed a greater number of voices. The trio sonata itself was an important source from which the solo sonata derived its distribution of instruments. In this case, the process of transformation was effected by condensing the two upper lines into one, or by transferring the part for the second melodic instrument of the trio sonata to the right hand of the keyboard. In contrast to the trio and solo sonata, the unaccompanied solo and duo, without thorough bass, were relatively minor contenders for attention. The matter of writing for one, two, or even three melodic instruments without *continuo* posed the problem of accounting for the parts in a natural, unaffected manner. Substituting wind instruments for strings further increased the difficulty. And the inclusion of more than four instruments was hazardous for it tempted the composer beyond the confines of chamber music into orchestral territory. The relationship between species of composition still remained ambiguous, for the *divertimento* and the early quartet were in many respects identical.

With respect to the instruments of the quartet, the use of two violins was a well-established inheritance from the trio sonata. So far as their construction was concerned, stringed instruments in general developed to the point of classical perfection faster than either the clavier or the winds. Advance in violin technique set the pace for the other melodic instruments in the treble, bass, and middle registers. Even during the reign of the *continuo,* the middle register was never completely disregarded; and the viola, last of the standard stringed instruments to come into its own, eventually replaced the gamba in those four-part *quadri* which remained faithful to the polyphonic tradition. So far as clavier instruments were concerned, the harpsichord and clavichord drew the lion's share of both the *continuo* and the obbligato parts. When the piano was finally introduced to chamber music as a participant on equal footing with the violin family, its presence endangered the balance of the classical chamber style. The piano, with its capacity to play many parts at once, pitted itself as a separate entity against the entire group of melodic instruments. The conversation of four stringed instruments proved easier to manipulate than the combination of stringed instruments and piano. In the latter case, two opposing types of instrument had to be equated so that each could undertake either solo or accompaniment.

Yet, despite the difficulties inherent in blending certain instruments and distributing them within larger and smaller ensembles, composers of the classic era successfully wrote chamber music for a variety of combinations other than the string quartet. They were masters of musical design, of tasteful ornamentation, and of that judicious mixture of homophony and polyphony with which they could resolve many an awkward situation.

After the three active melodic parts in the first allegro of the *sonata da chiesa* had succumbed to dance influence, there was little left to distinguish the style from the *sonata da camera*. When *da chiesa* and *da camera* elements were unified in one work, the identification of each movement by its tempo designation, a usage fostered by the *da chiesa* style, took precedence over the inclusion of dance titles. Preference for character titles meant much in the formation of the classical chamber style, where extramusical associations were reduced to a minimum.

During the amalgamation of *da chiesa* and *da camera* styles, the number of movements in a given composition was sometimes considerably increased by appending to the three opening *da chiesa* movements a series of *da camera* dances; a procedure which, incidentally, tended to undermine the internal cohesion of the work. The *divertimento* suffered from a similar unwieldiness, until the fashion of composition turned toward a reduction in the number of movements and a tightening of the over-all design.

The *style galant* fared better with the solo sonata than with the trio sonata because of the former's greater adaptability to tempo rubato and decorative effect. Concomitant with the development of that sense of balance and economy of means characteristic of the classical chamber style was the transformation of the embellishments of the *style galant* from improvisation into a written line. Whereas the Italians continued to practice extempore decoration, the French incorporated their ornamentation into the written composition. The latter practice led to the classical precept that improvisation added to music already complete in itself was prone to result in the tasteless disfigurement of a composition, and, in any case, was an encroachment upon the prerogatives of the composer. In the classical era, such embellishments as he chose to utilize formed an integral part of the composer's conception.

A prerequisite for prescribed ornamentation throughout the parts was the complete absorption of the thorough bass by obbligato lines; embellishments could not be designated unless the part itself was written down. Suppression of the thorough bass was effected in connection with both trio sonata and solo keyboard composition. As the trio sonata with *continuo* developed into the solo sonata with obbligato clavier, the objective conditions emerged which enabled the composer to write down every note of the composition. Furthermore, it was discovered that *continuo* material could be transferred, not only to a chordal instrument, but to melodic instruments as well. On the other hand, when a composition for solo keyboard was reinforced with optional melodic instruments, a type of ensemble composition minus the *continuo* was anticipated.

The essential sense of balance, somewhat lacking at first, was achieved gradually. In the process, counterpoint, which had been obscured by the lazy basses and pseudo-polyphonic fugatos of the *style galant,* was discovered serviceable in the classical chamber style for both contrast and combination of parts. Counterpoint took its place along with homophonic techniques as a component of thematic development, or was slyly introduced into the accompanying parts as a device for projecting them into the conversation. While the first violin part was still the most prominent, the use of counterpoint prevented the other parts from being ignored. Imitation between the parts guarded, not only against the undue projection of any one member of the ensemble, but also against confusion arising from too many ideas going on at once. The theme, already conceived as a coördinated union of motives in the *style galant,* was now dissected and worked through the parts polyphonically, with the motives not juxtaposed but kneaded into the composition. Counterpoint alone, however, would have trimmed all the parts to the same dimension; homophony remained the basis of contrapuntal manipulation and the bulwark of the classical style in general.

Whether played by an ensemble of master musicians, or by a nobleman and those in his entourage, or by a group of amateurs from any rank in society, chamber music remained the aristocrat of the musical world. By definition, compositions belonging to the realm of chamber music were in a privileged class. The intimacy of instrumentation (one player to a part) made for exclusiveness, and the size of the audience, if any, was comparatively limited. Solo, duet, trio, quartet, quintet, sextet, or septet was called upon as the occasion demanded. Composers who wrote for these instrumental combinations drew freely from a wide variety of musical mediums, instrumental distributions, patterns, and fashions of composition. From this potpourri of elements—refined until the thorough bass was weeded out, until suitable musical designs were evolved, and until an appropriate fusion of homophony and polyphony was contrived—emerged the classical chamber style.

BIBLIOGRAPHY

Abbado, Michelangelo. "La 'scordatura' negli strumenti ad arco e Nicolò Paganini," *La rassegna musicale*, XIII (1940), 213–226.

Abert, Hermann. "Joseph Haydns Klavierwerke, Band I (Sonaten Nr. 1–22)," *Zeitschrift für Musikwissenschaft*, II (1920), 553–571.

—— *W. A. Mozart.* Leipzig, 1923.

Adler, Guido. *Handbuch der Musikgeschichte.* 2d ed. Berlin, 1930.

—— "Zu Biber's Violinsonaten," *Zeitschrift der Internationalen Musikgesellschaft*, IX (1907), 29–30.

Alembert, J. d'. *Élémens de musique théorique et pratique suivant les principes de M. Rameau.* Lyon, 1779.

Altmann, Wilhelm. *Handbuch für Streichquartettspieler.* Berlin, 1928.

—— *Kammermusik-Katalog.* Leipzig, 1931.

—— "Nachträge zu Hugo Riemanns Verzeichnis der Druckausgaben und thematischem Katalog der Mannheimer Kammermusik des XVIII Jahrhunderts," *Zeitschrift für Musikwissenschaft*, I (1919), 620–628.

Antoniotto, Giorgio. *L'arte armonica; or, A Treatise on the Composition of Musick;* written in Italian by Giorgio Antoniotto and translated into English. London, 1760.

Apel, Willi. *Harvard Dictionary of Music.* Cambridge, 1946.

Arnold, F. T. *The Art of Accompaniment from a Thorough-Bass.* London, 1931.

Artaria, F., and H. Botstiber. *Joseph Haydn und das Verlagshaus Artaria.* Vienna, 1909.

Avison, Charles. *An Essay on Musical Expression.* London, 1752.

Bach, Carl Philipp Emanuel. *Essay on the True Art of Playing Keyboard Instruments [Versuch über die wahre Art das Clavier zu spielen,* 1759 and 1762], trans. and ed. William J. Mitchell. New York, 1948.

—— *Sonatine in C dur,* ed. Hjalmar von Dameck. Berlin, 1922.

Bach, J. S. *Johann Sebastian Bach's Werke.* Leipzig, 1851–1926.

Baker's Biographical Dictionary of Musicians. 4th ed. New York, 1940.

Bartoli, Romeo, ed. *Composizioni vocali polifoniche a due, tre e quattro voci sole dei secoli XVI e XVII.* Milan, 1917.

Beckmann, Gustav. *Die Entwicklung des deutschen Violinspiels im 17. Jahrhundert.* Eisleben, 1916.

—— "Johann Pachelbel als Kammerkomponist," *Archiv für Musikwissenschaft*, I (1919), 267–274.

Bethizy, M. de. *Exposition de la théorie et de la pratique de la musique, suivant les nouvelles découvertes.* Paris, 1754.

Bitter, C. H. *Carl Philipp Emanuel und Wilhelm Friedemann Bach und deren Brüder.* Berlin, 1868.

Blainville, C. H. *L'Esprit de l'art musical.* Geneva, 1754.

Blom, Eric. "The Minuet-Trio," *Music and Letters*, XXII (1941), 162–180.

Bombet, L. A. C. *The Life of Haydn in a Series of Letters Written at Vienna,* trans. from the French. London, 1817.

Bonnet, Jacques. *Histoire de la musique, et de ses effets.* Amsterdam, 1725.

Brenet, Michel. *Les Concerts en France sous l'ancien régime.* Paris, 1900.

—— "La Librairie musicale en France de 1653 à 1790, d'après les registres de privilèges," *Sammelbände der Internationalen Musikgesellschaft,* VIII (1907), 401–466.

Brossard, Sébastien de. *Dictionnaire de musique.* Paris, 1705.

Brosses, Charles de. *Lettres familières écrites d'Italie en 1739 et 1740.* Paris, 1858.

Burney, Charles. *A General History of Music.* London, 1776–1789.

—— *The Present State of Music in France and Italy.* London, 1771.

—— *The Present State of Music in Germany, the Netherlands and United Provinces.* London, 1773.

Caldara, Antonio. *Das Do-Re-Mi,* ed. Fritz Jöde. Wolfenbüttel, 1928.

Cannon, Beekman C. *Johann Mattheson, Spectator in Music.* New Haven, 1947.

Carpani, Giuseppe. *Le Haydine ovvero lettere su la vita e le opere del celebre Maestro Giuseppe Haydn.* Milan, 1812.

Cartier, J. B. *L'Art du violon.* Paris, ca. 1803.

Cavalieri, Emilio de'. *La rappresentazione di anima, e di corpo (1600),* in *Prima fioriture del melodramma italiano.* Rome, 1912.

Cello-Bibliothek klassischer Sonaten. Mainz, 1930.

Choron, Al., and F. Fayolle. *Dictionnaire historique des musiciens.* Paris, 1817.

Cobbett, Walter Willson. *Cyclopedic Survey of Chamber Music.* London, 1929.

Corelli, Arcangelo. *Sonate a tre,* ed. Waldemar Woehl. Cassel, 1934–1939.

—— *Sonate a violino e violone o cimbalo . . . opera quinta . . . troisième edition ou l'on a joint les agréemens des adagio de cet ouvrage, composez par Mr A. Corelli comme il les joue,* Amsterdam, 1712.

Couperin, F. *Oeuvres complètes de François Couperin,* ed. Maurice Cauchie. Paris, 1933.

Cucuel, Georges. *Etudes sur un orchestre au XVIIIme siècle.* Paris, 1913.

—— *La Pouplinière et la musique de chambre au XVIIIᵉ siècle.* Paris, 1913.

Dannreuther, Edward. *Musical Ornamentation.* London, 1893–1895.

Daube, Johann Friedrich. *General-Bass in drey Accorden.* Leipzig, 1756.

David, F. *Die hohe Schule des Violinspiels.* Leipzig, ca. 1880.

David, Hans, and Arthur Mendel. *The Bach Reader.* New York, 1945.

Denkmäler der Tonkunst in Österreich. Vienna, 1894–1938.

Denkmäler deutscher Tonkunst. Leipzig, 1892–1931.

Denkmäler deutscher Tonkunst, zweite Folge: Denkmäler der Tonkunst in Bayern. Leipzig, 1900–1931.

Dent, Edward J. "The Earliest String Quartets," *Monthly Musical Record,* XXXIII (1903), 202–204.

—— "Italian Opera in the Eighteenth Century, and Its Influence on the Music of the Classical Period," *Sammelbände der Internationalen Musikgesellschaft,* XIV (1913), 500–509.

Dies, Albert Christoph. *Biographische Nachrichten von Joseph Haydn.* Vienna, 1810.

Dieupart, Charles. *Six Suites pour clavecin,* ed. Paul Brunold. Paris, 1934.

Dittersdorf, K. *The Autobiography of Karl von Dittersdorf*, trans. A. D. Coleridge. London, 1896.

Dommer, A. von. *Handbuch der Musikgeschichte*, ed. Arnold Schering. Leipzig, 1923.

Ecorcheville, Jules. *Vingt Suites d'orchestre du XVIIᵉ siècle français 1640–1670*. Paris, 1906.

Einstein, Alfred. "Mozart's Four String Trio Preludes to Fugues of Bach," *Musical Times*, LXXVII (1936), 209–216.

—— "Opus I," *Musical Quarterly*, XX (1934), 367–383.

—— "Vincenzo Galilei and the Instructive Duo," *Music and Letters*, XVIII (1937), 360–368.

—— "Zum 48. Bande der Händel-Ausgabe," *Sammelbände der Internationalen Musikgesellschaft*, IV (1902), 1,0–172.

—— "Zur deutschen Literatur für Viola da Gamba im 16. und 17. Jahrhundert," *Publikationen der Internationalen Musikgesellschaft, Beihefte, Zweite Folge*, I (1905), 1–120.

Eitner, Robert. *Biographisch-bibliographisches Quellen-Lexicon*. Leipzig, 1898.

Ferand, Ernst. *Die Improvisation in der Musik*. Czechoslovakia, 1938.

Fischer, Wilhelm. "Zur Entwicklungsgeschichte des Wiener klassischen Stils," *Studien zur Musikwissenschaft*, III (1915), 24–84.

Fleury, Louis. "The Flute and Flutists in the French Art of the Seventeenth and Eighteenth Centuries," *Musical Quarterly*, IX (1923), 515–537.

—— "Music for Two Flutes without Bass," *Music and Letters*, VI (1925), 110–118.

Flood, W. H. Grattan. "Geminiani in England and Ireland," *Sammelbände der Internationalen Musikgesellschaft*, XII (1910), 108–112.

Forkel, Johann Nikolaus. *Johann Sebastian Bach, His Life, Art, and Work* [*Über J. S. Bachs Leben, Kunst und Kunstwerke*, 1802], trans. Charles Sanford Terry. London, 1920.

Frescobaldi, G. *Collectio musices organicae*, ed. Fr. X. Haberl. Leipzig, 1889.

Fux, Johann Joseph. *Steps to Parnassus* [*Gradus ad Parnassum*, 1725], trans. and ed. Alfred Mann. New York, 1943.

Ganassi, Sylvestro. *Regola Rubertina* (*1542*), facsim. ed. Max Schneider. Leipzig, 1924.

Geiringer, Karl, ed. *Alte Meistersonaten für Geige und Klavier*. Vienna, *ca.* 1937.

—— *Haydn, a Creative Life in Music*. New York, 1946.

Geminiani, Francesco. *Twelve Sonatas for Violin and Piano*, ed. R. L. Finney. Northampton, *ca.* 1935.

Gerber, Ernst Ludwig. *Historisch-biographisches Lexicon der Tonkünstler*. Leipzig, 1790.

—— *Neues historisch-biographisches Lexikon der Tonkünstler*. Leipzig, 1812.

Gerhartz, Karl. "Die Violinschule in ihrer musikgeschichtlichen Entwicklung bis Leopold Mozart," *Zeitschrift für Musikwissenschaft*, VII (1925), 553–569.

Goldschmidt, Hugo. *Studien zur Geschichte der italienischen Oper im 17. Jahrhundert*. Leipzig, 1901.

Gradenwitz, Peter. "The Symphonies of Johann Stamitz," *Music Review*, I (1940), 354–363.

Griesinger, Georg August. *Biographische Notizen über Joseph Haydn*. Leipzig, 1810.

Haas, Robert. "Aufführungspraxis der Musik," in E. Bücken, *Handbuch der Musikwissenschaft*. Leipzig, 1928–1934. Vol. I.

—— *Die Estensischen Musikalien*. Regensburg, 1927.

Händel, G. F. *Georg Friedrich Händel's Werke*. Leipzig, 1859–1894.

Hausswald, Günter. *Johann David Heinichens Instrumentalwerke*. Wolfenbüttel and Berlin, 1937.

Hawkins, John. *A General History of the Science and Practice of Music*. London, 1776.

Haydn, F. J. *Joseph Haydns Werke*. Leipzig, 1907–1933.

—— *Sämtliche 83 Streichquartette*, ed. W. Altmann. Leipzig, *ca.* 1936.

—— *Haydn Quartet Opus 1, No. 1*, newly ed. after the original editions by Marion M. Scott. London, 1931.

Heinichen, Johann David. *Der General-Bass in der Composition*. Dresden, 1728.

Hellouin, Frédéric. *Feuillets d'histoire musicale française*. Paris, 1903.

Heuss, Alfred. "Die Dynamik der Mannheimer Schule," *Zeitschrift für Musikwissenschaft*, II (1919), 44–54.

Hiller, Johann Adam, *Anweisung zum Violinspielen*. Grätz, 1795.

—— *Lebensbeschreibungen berühmter Musikgelehrten und Tonkünstler neuerer Zeit*. Leipzig, 1784.

—— *Wöchentliche Nachrichten und Ammerkungen die Musik betreffend*. Leipzig, 1766–1768.

Hinderberger, Adolph. *Die Motivik in Haydns Streichquartetten*. Turbenthal, 1935.

Hull, Eaglefield A. "The Earliest Known String-Quartet," *Musical Quarterly*, XV (1929), 72–76.

Iselin, Dora J. *Biagio Marini, sein Leben und seine Instrumentalwerke*. Hildburghausen, 1930.

Jahn, Otto. *W. A. Mozart*, ed. Hermann Deiters. Leipzig, 1889.

Jalowetz, Heinrich. "Beethoven's Jugendwerke in ihren melodischen Beziehungen zu Mozart, Haydn und Ph. E. Bach," *Sammelbände der Internationalen Musikgesellschaft*, XII (1911), 417–474.

Junker, Carl Ludwig. *Zwanzig Componisten*. Bern, 1776.

Katz, Erich. *Die musikalischen Stilbegriffe des 17. Jahrhunderts*. Freiburg, 1926.

Kinkeldey, O. *Orgel und Klavier in der Musik des 16. Jahrhunderts*. Leipzig, 1910.

Kircher, Athanasius. *Musurgia universalis sive ars magna consoni et dissoni*. Rome, 1650.

Koch, Heinrich Christoph. *Musikalisches Lexikon*. Frankfort on the Main, 1802.

Kraus, Joseph Martin. *Wahrheiten die Musik betreffend*. Frankfort on the Main, 1779.

Kretzschmar, Hermann. "Einige Bemerkungen über den Vortrag alter Musik," *Jahrbuch der Musikbibliothek Peters*, VII (1900), 53–68.

Lachmann, Robert. "Die Haydn-Autographen der Staatsbibliothek zu Berlin," *Zeitschrift für Musikwissenschaft*, XIV (1932), 289–298.

La Laurencie, Lionel de. *L'École française de violon de Lully à Viotti.* Paris, 1922–1924.

—— "Un Émule de Lully: Pierre Gautier de Marseille," *Sammelbände der Internationalen Musikgesellschaft,* XIII (1911), 54.

Láng, Paul Henry. *Music in Western Civilization.* New York, 1941.

Larsen, Jens Peter. *Die Haydn-Überlieferung.* Copenhagen, 1939.

—— *Drei Haydn Kataloge in Faksimile.* Copenhagen, 1941.

—— "Haydn und das 'Kleine Quartbuch,' "*Acta Musicologica,* VII (1935), 111–123.

Le Blanc, Hubert, "Défense de la basse de viole contre les entreprises du violon et les prétentions du violoncel," *La Revue musicale,* IX^1 (1927–1928), 43, 136, 247, IX^2 (1928), 21, 138, IX^3 (1928), 187.

Leclair l'aîné, Jean-Marie. *Second Livre de sonates pour le violon et pour la flûte traversière avec la basse continue,* Op. 2. Paris, ca. 1728.

—— *Trio Sonata in B Flat Major* [Op. 4, ca. 1730], ed. A. Moffat. London, 1934.

—— *Trio Sonata in D Minor* [Op. 4, ca. 1730], ed. A. Moffat. London, 1934.

—— *Quatrième Livre de sonates à violon seul avec la basse continue,* Op. 9. Paris, ca. 1738.

—— *Ouvertures et sonates en trio, pour deux violons avec la basse continue,* Op. 13. Paris, ca. 1753.

Leemans, Adrien. *Six Quatuor.* Paris, ca. 1770.

Lichtenthal, Pietro. *Dizionario e bibliografia della musica.* Milan, 1826.

Lindsay, J. Maurice and W. Leggat Smith. "Luigi Boccherini (1743–1805)," *Music and Letters,* XXIV (1943), 74–81.

Loisel, J. "Les Origines de la sonate classique," *Le Courrier musical,* X (1907), 517–524.

Mace, Thomas. *Musick's Monument.* London, 1676.

Marpurg, Friedrich Wilhelm. *Handbuch bey dem Generalbasse.* Berlin, 1762.

—— *Historisch-kritische Beyträge zur Aufnahme der Musik.* Berlin, 1754.

Mattheson, Johann. *Das beschützte Orchestre.* Hamburg, 1717.

—— *Das neu-eröffnete Orchestre.* Hamburg, 1713.

—— *Der vollkommene Kapellmeister.* Hamburg, 1739.

Mennicke, Carl. *Hasse und die Brüder Graun als Symphoniker.* Leipzig, 1906.

Mersmann, Hans. "Beiträge zur Aufführungspraxis der vorklassischen Kammermusik in Deutschland," *Archiv für Musikwissenschaft,* II (1920), 99–143.

—— "Die Kammermusik" in Kretzschmar, Hermann, *Führer durch den Konzertsaal.* Leipzig, 1933. Vol. III.

Meyer, E. H. "Has Handel Written Works for Two Flutes without a Bass?" *Music and Letters,* XVI (1935), 293–295.

Miesner, Heinrich, ed. "Philipp Emanuel Bachs musikalischer Nachlass," *Bach-Jahrbuch,* XXXVI (1939), 81–112.

Moffat, Alfred, ed. *Meisterschule der alten Zeit.* Berlin and Leipzig, ca. 1899.

Mondonville, Jean-Joseph Cassanea de. *Pièces de clavecin en sonates avec accompagnement de violon,* published with an introduction by Marc Pincherle. Paris, 1935.

Monteverdi, C. *Tutte le opere di Claudio Monteverdi.* Asolo, 1926–1942.

Morley, Thomas. *The First Booke of Consort Lessons.* London, 1611.

Moser, Andreas. *Geschichte des Violinspiels.* Berlin, 1923.

—— "Zur Frage der Ornamentik in ihrer Anwendung auf Corellis Op. 5," *Zeitschrift für Musikwissenschaft*, I (1919), 287–293.

Moser, Hans Joachim. "J. S. Bachs sechs Sonaten für Cembalo und Violine," *Zeitschrift für Musik*, CV (1938), 1220–1223.

—— *Musik Lexikon*. Berlin, 1935.

Mozart, Leopold. *Versuch einer gründlichen Violinschule (1756)*. Vienna, 1922.

Mozart, W. A. *Wolfgang Amadeus Mozart's Werke*. Leipzig, 1876–1905.

Nagels Musik-Archiv. Hannover, 1927–1940.

Nef, Karl. *Geschichte der Sinfonie und Suite*. Leipzig, 1921.

—— "Zur Geschichte der deutschen Instrumentalmusik in der zweiten Hälfte des 17. Jahrhunderts," *Publikationen der Internationalen Musikgesellschaft, Beihefte*, V (1902), 1–79.

Nohl, Ludwig. *Die geschichtliche Entwickelung der Kammermusik*. Brunswick, 1885.

North, Roger. *The Musicall Gramarian (1728)*. London, 1925.

Organum, dritte Reihe: Kammermusik. Leipzig, 1929–1930.

Picquot, L. *Boccherini*, ed. Georges de Saint-Foix. Paris, 1930.

Pincherle, Marc. "On the Origins of the String-Quartet," *Musical Quarterly*, XV (1929), 77–87.

Pohl, C. F. *Joseph Haydn*. Berlin, 1875.

Praetorius, M. *Gesamtausgabe der musikalischen Werke von Michael Praetorius*. Wolfenbüttel-Berlin, 1928–1930.

—— *Syntagma musicum, Band III (1619)*, reprint ed. Eduard Bernoulli. Leipzig, 1916.

Prelleur, Peter. *The Modern Musick-Master*. London, 1730.

Purcell, Henry. *Complete Works*. London, 1878–1928.

Quantz, Johann Joachim. *Versuch einer Anweisung die Flöte traversiere zu spielen (1752)*, reprint ed. Arnold Schering. Leipzig, 1906.

Quartetti diversi, a due violini, viola e basso, di diversi compositori, manuscript. Rome, 1768.

Raguenet, François. *Parallèle des Italiens et des François en ce qui regarde la musique et les opéra*. Paris, 1702.

Rameau, Jean-Philippe. *Œuvres complètes*, ed. C. Saint-Saëns. Paris, 1895–1913.

—— *Traité de l'harmonie*, Paris, 1722.

Reichardt, Johann Friedrich. *Briefe eines aufmerksamen Reisenden die Musik betreffend*. Frankfort and Leipzig, 1774.

Reissmann, August. *Joseph Haydn, sein Leben und seine Werke*. Berlin, 1879.

Riemann, Hugo. "Der 'Basso Ostinato' und die Anfänge der Kantate," *Sammelbände der Internationalen Musikgesellschaft*, XIII (1912), 531–543.

—— *Collegium musicum*. Leipzig, ca. 1934.

—— *Handbuch der Musikgeschichte*. Leipzig, 1920.

—— *Musikgeschichte in Beispielen*. Leipzig, 1912.

—— *Musik Lexikon*, ed. Alfred Einstein. Berlin, 1929.

—— *Old Chamber Music (Alte Kammermusik)*. London, 1898–1902.

Rigler, Gertrude. "Die Kammermusik Dittersdorfs," *Studien zur Musikwissenschaft*, XIV (1927), 179–212.

Rothweiler, Hugo. *Zur Entwicklung des Streichquartetts im Rahmen der Kammermusik des 18. Jahrhunderts.* Tübingen, 1934.

Rousseau, Jean. *Traité de la viole.* Paris, 1687.

Rousseau, Jean-Jacques. *Dictionnaire de musique.* Paris, 1768.

Sachs, Curt. *The History of Musical Instruments.* New York, 1940.

Saint-Foix, G. de. "Chronologie de l'oeuvre instrumentale de Jean Baptiste Sammartini," *Sammelbände der Internationalen Musikgesellschaft,* XV (1914), 308–324.

Saint-Lambert, Michel de. *Nouveau Traité de l'accompagnement du clavecin, de l'orgue, et des autres instruments.* Amsterdam, ca. 1710.

Sandberger, Adolf. "Zu Haydns Repertoir in Eisenstadt und Esterhaz," *Jahrbuch der Musikbibliothek Peters,* XL (1933), 35–37.

—— "Zur Geschichte des Haydnschen Streichquartett," in *Ausgewählte Aufsätze zur Musikgeschichte.* Munich, 1921. Vol. I.

Scarlatti, A. *Sonata a Quattro in D Minor,* ed. H. David. New York, 1940.

Scheibe, Johann Adolph, *Critischer Musikus.* Leipzig, 1745.

Scheidt, Samuel. *Samuel Scheidts Werke.* Hamburg, 1923–1937.

Schein, Johann Hermann. *Sämtliche Werke.* Leipzig, 1901–1923.

Schering, Arnold. *Aufführungspraxis alter Musik.* Leipzig, 1931.

—— *Geschichte des Instrumentalkonzerts.* 2d ed. Leipzig, 1927.

—— *Geschichte der Musik in Beispielen.* Leipzig, 1931.

—— "Zur Geschichte der Solosonate in der ersten Hälfte des 17. Jahrhunderts," in *Riemann Festschrift.* Leipzig, 1909.

Schmid, Ernst Fritz. *Carl Philipp Emanuel Bach und seine Kammermusik.* Cassel, 1931.

Schneider, Max. *Untersuchungen zur Entstehungsgeschichte des Basso continuo und seiner Bezifferung.* Leipzig, 1917.

—— "Zu Biber's Violinsonaten," *Zeitschrift der Internationalen Musikgesellschaft,* VIII (1907), 471–474.

Schubart, Christ. Fried. Dan. *Ideen zu einer Ästhetik der Tonkunst.* Vienna, 1806.

Schweitzer, Albert. *J. S. Bach,* trans. Ernest Newman. London, 1923.

Scott, Marion M. "Haydn's Opus Two and Opus Three," *Proceedings of the Musical Association,* LXI (1934), 1–19.

—— "Maddalena Lombardini, Madame Syrmen," *Music and Letters,* XIV (1933), 149–163.

Seiffert, Max. "G. Ph. Telemann's 'Musique de Table' als Quelle für Händel," *Bulletin de la Société Union Musicologique,* IV (1924), 1–28.

——, ed. *Organum, dritte Reihe: Kammermusik.* Leipzig, 1924–1934.

Simpson, Chr. *The Division-Violist; or, An Introduction to the Playing upon a Ground.* London, 1659.

Smith, Carlton Sprague. "Haydn's Chamber Music and the Flute," *Musical Quarterly,* XIX (1933), 341–350, 434–455.

Sondheimer, Robert. "Die formale Entwicklung der vorklassischen Sinfonie," *Archiv für Musikwissenschaft,* IV (1921), 85–99.

—— "Giovanni Battista Sammartini," *Zeitschrift für Musikwissenschaft,* III (1920), 83–110.

—— "Die Sinfonien Franz Becks," *Zeitschrift für Musikwissenschaft,* IV (1922), 323–350, 449–484.

Spiess, R. P. Meinrado. *Tractatus musicus compositorio-practicus.* Augsburg, 1745.

Spitta, Philipp. *Johann Sebastian Bach,* trans. Clara Bell and J. A. Fuller Maitland. London, 1899.

Sulzer, Johann George. *Allgemeine Theorie der schönen Künste,* 2d ed. Leipzig, 1792–1799.

Tartini, G. *A Letter from the Late Signor Tartini to Signora Maddalena Lombardini (Now Signora Sirmen),* trans. C. Burney. London, 1779.

Terry, Charles Sanford. *John Christian Bach.* London, 1929.

Thoinan, Ernest. *Les Hotteterre et les Chédeville.* Paris, 1894.

Torchi, Luigi. *L'arte musicale in Italia.* Milan, 1897–1900.

—— "La musica istrumentale in Italia nei secole XVI, XVII e XVIII," *Rivista musicale italiana,* IV (1897), 581–630.

Torrefranca, Fausto. "Le origini della sinfonia," *Rivista musicale italiana,* XX (1913), 291–346.

Tosi, Pier. Francesco. *Observations on the Florid Song,* trans. J. E. Galliard. London, 1742.

Tovey, Donald Francis. *Essays in Musical Analysis, Chamber Music,* ed. Hubert J. Foss. London, 1944.

Triest . . . "Bemerkungen über die Ausbildung der Tonkunst in Deutschland im 18ten Jahrhunderte," *Allgemeine musikalische Zeitung,* III (1801), 297–308.

Tutenberg, Fritz. "Die Durchführungsfrage in der vorneuklassischen Sinfonie," *Zeitschrift für Musikwissenschaft,* IX (1926), 90–94.

Veracini, Francesco Maria: *Sonate per violino,* in *Raccolta nazionale della musiche italiane,* ed. I. Pizzetti. Milan, 1919.

Walter, Friedrich. *Geschichte des Theaters und der Musik am Kurpfälzischen Hofe.* Leipzig, 1898.

Walther, Johann Gottfried. *Musicalisches Lexicon.* Leipzig, 1732.

Wasielewski, J. W. v. *Geschichte der Instrumentalmusik im XVI. Jahrhundert.* Berlin, 1878.

—— *Instrumentalsätze vom Ende des XVI. bis Ende des XVII. Jahrhunderts (als Musikbeilage zu "Die Violine im XVII. Jahrhundert").* Berlin, ca. 1874.

—— *Die Violine im XVII. Jahrhundert und die Anfänge der Instrumentalkomposition.* Bonn, 1874.

—— *Die Violine und ihre Meister.* Leipzig, 1927.

—— *Das Violoncell und seine Geschichte,* 3d ed. Leipzig, 1925.

Willaert, Adrian. *Ricercari a 3 voci,* ed. Hermann Zenck. Mainz and Leipzig, ca. 1933.

Wotquenne, Alfred. *Catalogue thématique des oeuvres de Charles Philippe Emmanuel Bach.* Leipzig, 1905.

Wyzewa, T. de, and G. St. Foix, "Un Maître inconnu de Mozart," *Zeitschrift der Internationalen Musikgesellschaft,* X (1908), 35–41.

—— *W. A. Mozart.* Paris, 1936.

Zarlino, Gioseffo. *Le istitutioni harmoniche.* Venice, 1558.

SUPPLEMENTARY BIBLIOGRAPHY

LITERATURE ON EARLY CHAMBER MUSIC

Abraham, Gerald. *Beethoven's Second-Period Quartets.* London: Oxford University Press, 1942; 2nd ed. 1943; 3rd ed. 1944.

Adler, Guido. "Haydn und die Wiener Klassik," *Österreichische Musikzeitschrift* XIV/5–6 (May–June 1959), 185–7.

———. "Schubert and the Viennese Classic School," *The Musical Quarterly* XIV/4 (October 1928), 473–85 (trans. by Theodore Baker).

Alain, Olivier. *La Musique de Chambre.* Paris: Société française de diffusion musicale et artistique, 1955.

Alker, Hugo. *Die Blockflöte: Instrumentenkunde, Geschichte, Musizierpraxis.* Vienna: H. Geyer, 1962.

———. *Blockflöten-Bibliographie.* Wilhelmshaven: Heinrichshofen, 1966.

Altmann, Wilhelm. *Handbuch für Klavierquartettspieler; Wegweiser durch die Klavierquartette.* Wolfenbüttel: Verlag für musikalische Kultur und Wissenschaft, 1937.

———. *Handbuch für Klavierquintettspieler; Wegweiser durch die Klavierquintette.* Wolfenbüttel: Verlag für musikalische Kultur und Wissenschaft, 1936.

———. *Handbuch für Klaviertriospieler; Wegweiser durch die Trios für Klavier, Violine, und Violoncell,* 4 vols. Wolfenbüttel: Verlag für musikalische Kultur und Wissenschaft, 1934.

———. *Kleiner Führer durch die Streichquartette für Haus und Schule.* Berlin-Halensee: Deutscher Musikliteratur-Verlag, 1950.

Anderson, Loren H. "Telemann's Music for Recorder," *American Recorder* VIII/1 (Winter 1967), 3–6.

Anglés, Higinio, and José Subirá. *Catálogo Musical de la Biblioteca Nacional de Madrid.* (Barcelona: Instituto Español de Musicología, 1949), III: *Impresos: Música Práctica.*

Apel, Willi, *Geschichte der Orgel- und Klaviermusik bis 1700.* Kassel: Bärenreiter, 1967.

———. "Solo Instrumental Music," in: *The New Oxford History of Music,* Gerald Abraham, ed. IV: *The Age of Humanism 1540-1630.* (London: Oxford University Press, 1968), 602–708.

Arnold, Cecily. "Early Seventeenth-Century Keyboard Parts," *Music and Letters* XXXIII/2 (April 1952), 151–3.

———, and Marshall Johnson. "The English Fantasy Suite," *Proceedings of the Royal Musical Association* LXXXII (1955–56), 1–14.

Arriaga, Emiliano de. *El Cuarteto, Su Origen, Desarrollo y Encantos.* Bilbao: Garmendia y Viciola, 1916.

Aschmann, Rudolf. *Das Deutsche Polyphone Violinspiel im 17. Jahrhundert.* Ph.D. diss.: Zurich, 1962.

Atabug, Alejandra Cumagun. *The Instrumental Music of Juan Crisostomo de Arriaga.* M.M. thesis: University of Illinois, 1963.

Aulich, Bruno, and Ernst Heimeran. *The Well-Tempered String Quartet; A Book of Counsel and Entertainment for all Lovers of Music in the Home,* trans. D. Millar Craig, revised ed. London: Novello, 1949.

Babitz, Sol. "Differences between 18th Century and Modern Violin Bowing," *The Score and I.M.A. Magazine* No. 19 (March 1957), 34–55.

————. "A Problem of Rhythm in Baroque Music," *The Musical Quarterly* XXXVIII/4 (October 1952), 533-65.

————, trans. See: Tartini,Giuseppe.

Bach, Carl Philipp Emanuel. *Autobiography,* facsimile of the original edition of 1773, with introduction by William S. Newman. Hilversum: Frits Knuf, 1967 *(Facsimiles of Early Biographies,* 4).

Bachmann, Werner. *Die Anfänge des Streichinstrumentenspiels,* 2nd ed. Leipzig: Breitkopf & Härtel, 1964.

Bader, Marga E. *Studien zu den Streichquartetten Op. 1–33 von Joseph Haydn.* Ph.D. diss.: Göttingen, 1945.

Baines, Anthony. *Woodwind Instruments and their History.* London: Faber & Faber; New York: W.W. Norton, 1957.

Barblan, Guglielmo. *Un Musicista Trentino, Francesco A. Bonporti (1672–1749); La Vita e le Opere.* Florence: Felice Le Monnier, 1940.

————. "Sui Rapporti Italo-Tedeschi nella Musica Strumentale del Settecento," *Analecta Musicologica* IV (1967), 1–12.

Barford, Philip. *The Keyboard Music of C.P.E. Bach Considered in Relation to his Musical Aesthetics and the Rise of the Sonata Principle.* London: Barrie & Rockliff, 1965.

Barnes, Marysue. *The Trio Sonatas of Antonio Caldara.* Ph.D. diss.: Florida State University, School of Music, 1960. (UM: 60–1403).

Baron, Ernst Gottlieb. *Untersuchung des Instruments der Lauten.* Nürnberg: J.F. Rüdiger, 1727; reprint, Amsterdam: Antiqua, 1965.

Bartha, Dénes, ed. *Joseph Haydn: Gesammelte Briefe und Aufzeichnungen,* Unter Benützung der Quellensammlung von H.C. Robbins Landon. Kassel: Bärenreiter, 1965.

Bartholomew, Leland Earl. *Alessandro Rauerij's Collection of Canzoni per Sonare (Venice, 1608).* Hays, Kansas: Fort Hays Kansas State College, 1965. *(Fort Hays Music Series, 1).*

Bartlett, Loren Wayne. *A Survey and Checklist of Representative Eighteenth-Century Concertos and Sonatas for Bassoon.* Ph.D. diss.: State University of Iowa, 1961.

Bate, Philip. *The Oboe: An Outline of its History, Development and Construction.* London: Ernest Benn, 1956.

Baudoiun-Bugnet, M. "La Musique de Chambre," in: *Encyclopédie de la Musique et Dictionnaire du Conservatoire,* Albert Lavignac and Lionel de la Laurencie, eds. (Paris: Librairie Delagrave, 1930), Deuxième Partie, V, 3144–78.

Bauer, Wilhelm A., and Otto Erich Deutsch, eds. *Mozart, Briefe und Aufzeichnungen, Gesamtausgabe,* 2 vols. Kassel: Bärenreiter, 1962.

Becker, Carl Ferdinand. *Die Hausmusik in Deutschland in dem 16., 17. und 18. Jahrhunderte.* Leipzig: Fest'sche Verlagsbuchhandlung, 1840.

————. *Systematisch-chronologische Darstellung der musikalischen Literatur von der frühesten bis auf die neueste Zeit.* Leipzig: R. Friese, 1836–39, reprint, Amsterdam: Frits Knuf, 1964.

Bell, A. Craig. "An Introduction to Haydn's Piano Trios," *Music Review* XVI/3 (August 1955), 191–7.

Bengtsson, Ingmar. *J.H. Roman och hans Instrumentalmusik: käll-och stilkritiska studier.* Uppsala: Almqvist & Wiksells, 1955. [With an English summary, p. 423].

Benton, Rita. "A la recherche of Pleyel perdu, or Perils, Problems, and Procedures of Pleyel Research," *Fontes Artis Musicae* XVII/1–2 (1970), 9–15.

————. *Form in the Sonatas of Domenico Scarlatti.* M.A. thesis: The State University of Iowa, 1951. (University of Rochester Microcard Publications in Music).

————. "Jean-Frédéric Edelmann, A Musical Victim of the French Revolution," *The Musical Quarterly* L/2 (April 1964) 165–87.

————. *Nicolas Joseph Hüllmandel and French Instrumental Music in the Second Half of the Eighteenth Century.* Ph.D. diss.: The State University of Iowa, 1961. (UM: 61–4019).

————. "Nicolas-Joseph Hüllmandel (1756–1823): Quelques Aspects de sa Vie et de son Oeuvre," *Revue de Musicologie* XLVII (December 1961), 177–94.

Berger, Jean. "Notes on Some 17th-Century Compositions for Trumpets and Strings in Bologna," *The Musical Quarterly* XXXVII/3 (July 1951), 354–67.

Bergmann, Walter. "Some Old and New Problems of Playing the Basso Continuo," *Proceedings of the Royal Musical Association* LXXXVII (1960–61), 31–43.

Bertini, Argia. *Roma: Biblioteca Corsiniana e dell' Accademia Nazionale dei Lincei; catalogo dei fondi musicali Chiti e Corsiniano.* Milan: Istituto Editoriale Italiano, 1964.

Besseler, Heinrich, "Mozart und die Deutsche Klassik," in: Erich Schenk, ed., *Bericht über den Internationalen Musikwissenschaftlichen Kongress Wien, Mozartjahr 1956.* (Graz–Köln: Hermann Böhlaus, 1958), 47–54.

Biales, Albert, *Sonatas and Canzonas for Larger Ensembles in Seventeenth-Century Austria,* 2 vols. Ph.D. diss.: The University of California at Los Angeles, 1962.

Biamonti, Giovanni. *I Quartetti di Beethoven.* Rome: Glingler, 1948.

Blume, Friedrich. *Der junge Bach.* Wolfenbüttel, Zürich: Möseler, 1967.

————. *Renaissance and Baroque Music; a comprehensive Survey,* trans. M.D. Herter Norton, New York: W. W. Norton, 1967.

————. *Syntagma Musicologicum; Gesammelte Reden und Schriften,* Martin Ruhnke, ed. Kassel: Bärenreiter, 1963.

————. "Eine unbekannte Violinsonate von J.S. Bach," *Bach-Jahrbuch* XXV (1928), 96–118.

Bock, Emil William. *The String Fantasies of John Hingeston (c.1616–1683),* 2 vols. Ph.D. diss.: State University of Iowa, 1956. (UM: 16–106).

Boewe, John Frederick. *The String Quintets of Johann Friedrich Peter.* M.M. thesis: University of Illinois, 1957.

Bol, Hans. "De triosonate op. 2 van Jean-Joseph Cassanéa de Mondonville," *Mens en Melodie* XXIII/12 (December 1968), 371-4.

Bonaccorsi, Alfredo. "Di alcuni 'Quintetti' di G.G. Cambini," *La Rassegna Musicale* XX/1 (January 1950) 32-6.

Bonta, Stephen. *The Church Sonatas of Giovanni Legrenzi,* 2 vols. Ph.D. diss.: Harvard University, 1964.

————. "The Uses of the *Sonata da Chiesa,*" *Journal of the American Musicological Society* XXII/1 (Spring 1969), 54–84.

Borrel, Eugène. *La Sonate.* Paris: Librairie Larousse, 1951.

Borroff, Edith. "The Instrumental Style of Jean-Joseph Cassanéa de Mondonville," *Recherches sur la Musique français classique* VII (1967), 165–203.

————. *The Instrumental Works of Jean-Joseph Cassanéa de Mondonville,* 2 vols. Ph.D. diss.: University of Michigan, 1959. (UM: 59–2099).

————. *An Introduction to Elisabeth-Claude Jacquet de La Guerre.* Brooklyn: Institute of Mediaeval Music, 1966. (Musicological Studies, 12).

Bottrigari, Hercole. *Hercole Bottrigari: Il Desiderio, or, Concerning the Playing Together of Various Musical Instruments,* Carol MacClintock trans. and ed. [Dallas] : American Institute of Musicology, 1962. (*Musicological Studies and Documents,* 9).

Boyden, David D. *The History of Violin Playing from its Origins to 1761 and its Relationship to the Violin and Violin Music.* London and New York: Oxford University Press, 1965.

————"The Missing Italian Manuscript of Tartini's *Traité des Agréments,*" *The Musical Quarterly* XLVI/3 (July 1960), 315–28.

Brainard, Paul. "Tartini and the Sonata for Unaccompanied Violin," *Journal of the American Musicological Society* XIV/3 (Fall 1961), 383–93.

————. *Die Violinsonaten Giuseppe Tartinis.* Ph.D. diss: Göttingen, 1960.

British Broadcasting Corporation. Central Music Library. *Chamber Music Catalogue,* (London: J. Smethurst & Co., 1965), I.

Brockmeier, Helen Frances. *The Theater Music of Henry Purcell: A Study of Songs and Instrumental Pieces for English Plays from 1680 to 1695.* M.A. thesis: University of Southern California, 1948.

Brofsky, Howard. *The Instrumental Music of Padre Martini.* Ph.D. diss: New York University, 1963. (UM: 64–6452)

————. "Padre Martini's Sonata for Four Trumpets and Strings," *Brass Quarterly* V (1961–62), 58–61.

Brook, Barry S. "The *Symphonie concertante:* an Interim Report," *The Musical Quarterly* XLVII/4 (October 1961), 493–516.

————. *La Symphonie Française dans la seconde Moitié du XVIIIe Siècle,* 3 vols. Paris: Publications de l'Institut de Musicologie de l'Université de Paris, 1962. [available through H. Baron, London].

————. ed. *The Breitkopf Thematic Catalogue: 1762–1787.* New York: Dover, 1966.

Brossard, Sébastien de. *Dictionnaire de Musique, contenant une explication des termes grecs, latins, italiens et françois les plus usitez dans la Musique . . . Et un Catalogue de plus de 900 auteurs qui ont écrit sur la Musique.* Paris: Christophe Ballard, 1703, reprint, Amsterdam: Antiqua, 1964.

Brown, Howard Mayer. *Instrumental Music Printed before 1600: A Bibliography.* Cambridge: Harvard University Press, 1965.

Brown, Maurice J.E. "Recent Schubert Discoveries," *Music and Letters* XXXII/4 (October 1951), 349–61.

Broyles, Michael E. "Beethoven's Sonata Op. 14, No. 1—Originally for Strings?" *Journal of the American Musicological Society* XXIII/3 (Fall 1970), 405–19.

Bruning, Patricia Jane. *A Study and Edition of the Six Trio Sonatas of Gaetano Franceschini (fl. ca. 1770–1800),* M.A. thesis: University of Iowa, 1960.

Brunold, Paul. *François Couperin,* trans. J.B. Hanson. Monaco: Lyrebird Press, 1949.

Bruun, Kai Aage. *Kammermusik fra Haydn til den unge Beethoven.* Copenhagen: Thaning & Appel, 1960.

———. *Kammermusik far Beethoven til Schubert.* Copenhagen: Thaning & Appel, 1962.

Buelow, George J. *Thorough-bass Accompaniment according to Johann David Heinichen.* Berkeley and Los Angeles: University of California Press, 1966.

———, and Robert Donington. "Figured Bass as Improvisation," *Acta Musicologica* XL/2–3 (1968), 178–9.

Bukofzer, Manfred F. "A Checklist of Instrumental Ensemble Music Before Haydn," *Music Teachers National Association Proceedings* Series 40 (1946), 470–9.

———"A Polyphonic Basse Dance of the Renaissance," in his *Studies in Medieval and Renaissance Music* (New York: W.W. Norton, 1950), 190–216.

———. *Music in the Baroque Era, from Monteverdi to Bach.* New York: W.W. Norton, 1947.

———. *Music of the Classic Period, 1750–1827,* revised ed. Berkeley: University of California, 1955. [Mimeographed syllabus.].

Carrell, Norman. *Bach the Borrower.* London: George Allen & Unwin, 1967.

Carse, Adam. *Eighteenth Century Symphonies: a Short History of the Symphony in the 18th Century with Special Reference to the Works in the two Series: "Early Classical Symphonies" and "18th Century Overtures".* London: Augener, 1951.

———. *The Orchestra in the XVIIIth Century.* Cambridge: W. Heffer, 1940.

Chailley, Jacques. "Sur la signification du quatuor de Mozart K.465, dit 'les dissonances', et du 7ème quatuor de Beethoven," in: Bjørn Hjelmborg & Søren Sørensen, eds. *Natalicia musicologica Knud Jeppesen septuagenario collegis oblata* (Hafniae: Wilhelm Hansen, 1962), 283–92.

Cherbuliez, A.E. "Bemerkungen zu den 'Haydn'-Streichquartetten Mozarts und Haydns 'Russischen' Streichquartetten," *Mozart-Jahrbuch* (1959), 28–45.

Cherry, Norman. "A Corelli Sonata for Trumpet, Violins, and Basso Continuo," *Brass Quarterly* IV/3 (Spring 1961), 103–13; IV/4 (Summer 1961), 156–8.

Chodkowski, Andrzej. "Z zagadnień formy sonatowej w twórczości kameralnej Beethovena," *Muzyka* XIII/4 (1968), 49–55.

Churgin, Bathia. "Francesco Galeazzi's Description (1796) of Sonata Form," *Journal of the American Musicological Society* XXI/2 (Summer 1968), 181–99.

———"New Facts in Sammartini Biography: The Authentic Print of the String Trios, op. 7," *Journal of the American Musicological Society* XX/1 (Spring 1967), 107–12.

————. *The Symphonies of G.B. Sammartini,* 2 vols. Ph.D. diss.: Harvard University, 1963.

Chusid, Martin. *The Chamber Music of Franz Schubert.* Ph.D. diss.: University of California at Berkeley, 1961.

————. "Schubert's Overture for String Quintet and Cherubini's Overture to *Faniska,*" *Journal of the American Musicological Society* XV/1 (Spring 1962), 78–84.

Clarke, Mary Gray. *The Violin Sonatas of F.M. Veracini: Some Aspects of Italian Late Baroque Instrumental Style Exemplified.* Ph.D. diss.: University of North Carolina, 1967. (UM: 68–6728).

Clercx, Suzanne. *Le Baroque et la Musique, Essai d'Esthétique Musicale.* Brussels: Édition de la Librairie Encyclopédique, 1948.

————. *Pierre van Maldere, Virtuose et Maître des Concerts de Charles de Lorraine 1729–1768.* Bruxelles: Palais des Académies, 1948.

Coates, William. "English Two-Part Viol Music, 1590–1640," *Music and Letters* XXXIII/2 (April 1952), 141–50.

Cobbett, Walter Willson, ed. *Cyclopedic Survey of Chamber Music,* with supplementary material edited by Colin Mason, 2nd edition, 3 vols. London and New York: Oxford University Press, 1963.

Cóeuroy, André, and Claude Rostand. *Les Chefs-d'oeuvre de la Musique de Chambre.* Paris: Librairie Plon, 1952.

Cohen, Albert. *The Evolution of the Fantasia and Works in Related Styles in the Seventeenth-Century Instrumental Ensemble Music of France and the Low Countries.* Ph.D. diss.: New York University, 1959. (UM: 59–2440).

————. "The *Fantaisie* for Instrumental Ensemble in 17th-Century France — Its Origin and Significance," *The Musical Quarterly* XLVIII/2 (April 1962), 234–43.

————, trans. and ed. See: Loulié, Etienne.

Cole, Malcolm S. "The Vogue of the Instrumental Rondo in the Late Eighteenth Century," *Journal of the American Musicological Society* XXII/3 (Fall 1969), 425–55.

Cooke, Deryck. "The Unity of Beethoven's Late Quartets," *The Music Review* XXIV/1 (February 1963), 30–49.

Cooper, Kenneth, and Julius Zsako, trans. "Georg Muffat's Observations on the Lully Style of Performance," *The Musical Quarterly* LIII/2 (April 1967), 220–45.

Coperario, Giovanni. *Rules How to Compose,* facsimile edition with introduction by Manfred Bukofzer. Los Angeles: Ernest E. Gottlieb, 1952.

Cosme, Luiz. *Música de Câmara.* Rio de Janeiro: Ministério da Educaçao e cultura, 1961.

Cowling, Elizabeth. *The Italian Sonata Literature for the Violoncello in the Baroque Era.* Ph.D. diss.: Northwestern University, 1967. (UM: 67–15,211).

Crane, Frederick. "The Derivation of Some Fifteenth-Century Basse-Danse Tunes," *Acta Musicologica* XXXVII (1965), 179–88.

————. *Materials for the Study of the Fifteenth Century Basse Danse.* Brooklyn, New York: The Institute of Mediaeval Music, 1968. (*Musicological Studies,* 16).

Crocker, Eunice Chandler. *An Introductory Study of the Italian Canzona for Instrumental Ensembles and Its Influence upon the Baroque Sonata,* 2 vols. Ph.D. diss.: Radcliffe College, 1943.

Croll, Gerhard. "Eine neuentdeckte Bach-Fuge für Streichquartett von Mozart," *Österreichische Musikzeitschrift* XXI/10 (Sondernummer 1966), 12–18.

Cudworth, Charles L. "Notes on the Instrumental Works Attributed to Pergolesi," *Music and Letters* XXX/4 (October 1949), 321–8.

Dadelsen, Georg von. *Beiträge zur Chronologie der Werke Johann Sebastian Bachs.* Trossingen: Hohner, 1958. *(Tübinger Bach-Studien, 4/5).*

———. *Bemerkungen zur Handschrift Johann Sebastian Bachs, seiner Familie und seines Kreises.* Trossingen: Hohner, 1957. *(Tübinger Bach-Studien, 1).*

Dahlhaus, Carl, ed. *Johann Theile: Musikalisches Kunstbuch.* Kassel: Bärenreiter, 1965.

Dann, Elias. *Heinrich Biber and the Seventeenth-Century Violin.* Ph.D. diss.: Columbia University, 1968.

Dart, Thurston. "The Earliest Collections of Clarinet Music," *The Galpin Society Journal* IV (June 1951), 39–41.

———. "A Hand-List of English Instrumental Music Printed Before 1681," *The Galpin Society Journal* VIII (March 1955), 13–26.

———. *The Interpretation of Music,* 2nd ed. New York: Harper & Row, 1963.

———. "Music and Musical Instruments in Cotgrave's *Dictionare* (1611)," *The Galpin Society Journal* XXI (March 1968), 70–80.

———. "The Printed Fantasies of Orlando Gibbons," *Music and Letters* XXXVII/4 (October 1956), 342–9.

———. "Purcell's Chamber Music," *Proceedings of the Royal Musical Association* LXXXV (1958–59), 81–93.

———. "Six Problems in Instrumental Music" [Performance Practice in the 17th and 18th Centuries], in: Jan La Rue, ed., *International Musicological Society, Report of the Eighth Congress, New York: 1961,* (Kassel: Bärenreiter, 1961), I, 231–5.

———. See: Morley, Thomas.

Davidsson, Åke. *Catalogue Critique et Descriptif des Imprimés de Musique des XVIe et XVIIe Siècles Conservés à la Bibliothèque de l'Université Royale d'Upsala* (Uppsala: Almqvist & Wiksells, 1951), "Musique Instrumentale," II, 131–56.

———. *Catalogue Critique et Descriptif des Ouvrages Théoriques sur la Musique, Imprimés au XVIe et au XVIIe Siècles, et Conservés dans les Bibliothèques Suédoises.* Uppsala: Almqvist & Wiksells, 1953.

Degrada, Francesco. "Il Clavicembalo nella Musica Strumentale de Camera nei Secoli XVII e XVIII," *Dal clavicembalo al pianoforte* I (1968), 29–33.

Dent, Edward J. *Alessandro Scarlatti: His Life and Works.* London: 1905, new impression with preface and additional notes by Frank Walker, London: Edward Arnold, 1960.

Deutsch, Otto Erich. "The Chronology of Schubert's String Quartets," *Music and Letters* XXIV/1 (January 1943), 25–30.

———. *Handel: A Documentary Biography.* London: A & C Black; New York: W.W. Norton, 1955.

———. *Mozart: Die Dokumente seines Lebens.* Kassel: Bärenreiter, 1961.

———. *Schubert: Thematic Catalogue of all his Works in Chronological Order.* New York: W.W. Norton, 1950; London: Dent, 1951; reprint, New York: Kalmus, 1970.

Dolmetsch, Arnold. *The Interpretation of the Music of the XVIIth and XVIIIth Centuries revealed by Contemporary Evidence.* London: Novello, 1915, 1946; New York: H.W. Gray, 1923; New York: Washington Square Paperbacks, 1969.

Dolmetsch, Carl. "A Practical Approach to Bach's Violin Sonatas," *The Consort* No. 12 (July 1955), 15–17.

Donington, Robert. "The English Contribution to the Growth of Chamber Music," *Music Survey* IV/1 (October 1951), 334–43.

————. *The Interpretation of Early Music*, 2nd ed. London: Faber & Faber; New York: St. Martin's Press, 1963.

————, and Thurston Dart, "The Origin of the In Nomine," *Music and Letters* XXX/2 (April 1949), 101–6.

Dorian, Frederick. *The History of Music in Performance: The Art of Musical Interpretation from the Renaissance to our Day.* New York: W.W. Norton, 1942.

Doring, Ernest N., ed. "Dubourg's 'The Violin'," *Violins and Violinists* XI/3 (March–April 1950), 111–114; XI/4 (May–June 1950), 169–72.

Duckles, Vincent, and Minnie Elmer, with the assistance of Pierluigi Petrobelli. *Thematic Catalog of a Manuscript Collection of Eighteenth-Century Italian Instrumental Music in the University of California, Berkeley, Music Library.* Berkeley and Los Angeles: University of California Press, 1963.

Dufourcq, Norbert, ed. "Aspects Inédits de l'Art Instrumental en France," *La Revue Musicale* No. 226 (1955), 5–6.

Dunning, Albert, and Arend Koole. "Pietro Antonio Locatelli: Nieuwe Bijdragen tot de Kennis van zijn Leven en Werken," *Tijdschrift van de Vereniging voor Nederlandse Muziekgeschiedenis* XX (1967), 52–96.

Dürr, Alfred. "Johann Gottlieb Goldberg und die Triosonate BWV 1037," *Bach-Jahrbuch* XL (1953), 51–80.

Dürrenmatt, Hans-Rudolf. *Die Durchführung bei Johann Stamitz (1717-1757). Beiträge zum Problem der Durchführung und analytische Untersuchung von ersten Sinfoniesätzen.* Bern and Stuttgart: Paul Haupt, 1969. *(Publikationen der Schweizerischen Musikforschenden Gesellschaft*, Ser. II, Vol. 19).

Eggebrecht, Hans Heinrich. "Arten des Generalbasses im frühen und mittleren 17. Jahrhundert," *Archiv für Musikwissenschaft* XIV/1 (1957), 61–82.

————. "Terminus 'Ricercar'," *Archiv für Musikwissenschaft* IX/2 (1952), 137–47.

Einstein, Alfred. *Mozart, His Character, His Work*, trans. Arthur Mendel and Nathan Broder. London and New York: Oxford University Press, 1945.

————. *Schubert; A Musical Portrait.* London and New York: Oxford University Press, 1951.

Elmer, Minnie Agnes. *Tartini's Improvised Ornamentation, as Illustrated by MSS from the Berkeley Collection of Instrumental Music.* M.A. thesis: University of California at Berkeley, 1962.

Elsen, Josephine Caryce. *The Instrumental Works of Peter Ritter (1763–1846).* Ph.D. diss: Northwestern University, 1967. (UM: 67–15, 226).

Engel, Hans, "Die Quellen des klassischen Stiles," in: Jan La Rue, ed., *International Musicological Society, Report of the Eighth Congress, New York: 1961* (Kassel: Bärenreiter, 1961), I, 285–304.

Engelbrecht, E. "The Origins of the String Quartet," *Royal College of Music Magazine* LXIII/2 (1967), 44–6.

Engländer, Richard. *Die Dresdner Instrumentalmusik in der Zeit der Wiener Klassik.* Uppsala: Almqvist & Wiksells, 1956.

———. "Die Echtheitsfrage in Mozarts Violinsonaten KV 55–60," *Die Musikforschung* VIII/3 (1955), 292–8.

Eppstein, Hans "J.S. Bachs Triosonate G-dur (BWV 1039) und ihre Beziehungen zur Sonate für Gambe und Cembalo G-dur (BWV 1027)," *Die Musikforschung* XVIII/2 (April–June 1965), 126–37.

———. "Mozarts 'Fantasie' KV 396," *Die Musikforschung* XXI/2 (April–June 1968), 205–11.

———. *Studien über J.S. Bach's Sonaten für ein Melodieinstrument und obligates Cembalo.* Uppsala: Almqvist & Wiksells, 1966.

———. "Zur Problematik von J.S. Bachs Sonate für Violine und Cembalo G-dur (BWV 1019)," *Archiv für Musikwissenschaft* XXI/3 (September 1964), 217–39.

Evans, Peter. Seventeenth-Century Chamber Music Manuscripts at Durham," *Music and Letters* XXXVI/3 (July 1955), 205–23.

Farish, Margaret K. *String Music in Print.* New York: R.R. Bowker, 1965. Supplement, including composer index, New York: R.R. Bowker, 1968.

Feder, Georg. "Bemerkungen über die Ausbildung der Klassischen Tonsprache in der Instrumentalmusik Haydns," in: Jan La Rue, ed., *International Musicological Society, Report of the Eighth Congress, New York: 1961* (Kassel: Bärenreiter, 1961), 305–13.

———. "Lo Stato Attuale degli Studi su Haydn," *Nuova Rivista Musicale Italiana* II/4 (July–August 1968), 625–54.

———. "Die Uberlieferung und Verbreitung der handschriftlichen Quellen zu Haydns Werken (Erste Folge)," *Haydn-Studien* I/1 (June 1965), 3–42.

Federhofer, Hellmut. "Eine Angelica-und Gitarrentabulatur aus der zweiten Halfte des 17. Jahrhunderts," in: Ludwig Finscher, Christoph-Hellmut Mahling, eds., *Festschrift für Walter Wiora zum 30. Dezember 1966* (Kassel: Bärenreiter, 1967), 313–16.

———. *Musikpflege und Musiker am Grazer Habsburgerhof der Erherzöge Karl und Ferdinand von Innerösterreich (1564–1619).* Mainz: B. Schott, 1967.

———, and Friedrich Wilhelm Riedel. "Quellenkundliche Beiträge zur Johann Joseph Fux-Forschung," *Archiv für Musikwissenschaft* XXI/2 (August 1964), 111–40.

Feinland, Alexander. *The Combination of Violin and Violoncello without Accompaniment.* Panama, R. of P.: 1947.

Fellowes, Edmund H. *William Byrd*, 2nd ed. London: Oxford University Press, 1948.

Ferguson, Donald. *Image and Structure in Chamber Music.* Minneapolis: University of Minnesota Press, 1964.

Finscher, Ludwig. "Joseph Haydn und das italienische Streichquartett," *Analecta Musicologica* IV (1967), 13–37.

———. "Popularität und Volkstümlichkeit in der Kammermusik der Wiener Klassik," in: *Volks- und Hochkunst in Dichtung und Musik-Tagungsbericht eines Colloquiums 19.-22. 10 1966 Saarbrücken* (Saarbrücken: Mw. Inst. der U. des Saarlands, [1968]), 28–38.

———. "Zur Sozialgeschichte des Klassischen Streichquartetts," in: Georg Reichert and Martin Just, eds., *Bericht über den internationalen Musikwis-*

senschaftlichen Kongress Kassel 1962 (Kassel: Bärenreiter, 1963), 37–9.

Fischer, Hans. *Die Sonate.* Berlin: Chr. Friedrich Vieweg, 1936.

———. *Von Bicinium zum Liedduett.* Wolfenbüttel : Möseler, 1963.

Fischer, Kurt von. *Die Beziehungen von Form und Motiv in Beethovens Instrumentalwerken.* Strasbourg and Zurich: Editions Heitz, 1948.

Fischer, Wilhelm. "Mozarts Weg von der begleiteten Klaviersonate zur Kammermusik mit Klavier," *Mozart-Jahrbuch* (1956), 16–34.

Floros, Constantin. *Carlo Antonio Campioni als Instrumentalkomponist.* Ph.D. diss.: University of Vienna, 1955.

Flotzinger, Rudolf. "Die Gagliarda Italjana; zur Frage der barocken Thementypologie," *Acta Musicologica* XXXIX/1–2 (January–June 1967), 92–100.

———. *Die Lautentabulaturen des Stiftes Kremsmünster; Thematischer Katalog.* Vienna: Hermann Bohlaus, 1965. *(Tabulae Musicae Austriacae,* 2).

Fogaccia, Piero. *Giovanni Legrenzi.* Bergamo: Edizioni Orobiche, 1954.

Forsberg, Carl Earl. *The Clavier-Violin Sonatas of W.A. Mozart.* Ph.D. diss.: Indiana University, 1964. (UM: 65–3477).

Fortune, Nigel. "Continuo Instruments in Italian Monodies," *The Galpin Society Journal* VI (July 1953) 10–13.

———. "Giustiniani on Instruments," *The Galpin Society Journal* V (March 1952), 48–54.

Fred, Herbert W. *The Instrumental Music of Johann Christoph Pepusch.* Ph.D. diss.: University of North Carolina, 1961. (UM: 62–3121).

Frotscher, Gotthold. *Aufführungspraxis alter Musik.* Locarno: Heinrichschofen's Verlag, 1963.

Fruchtman, Caroline S. *Checklist of Vocal Chamber Works by Benedetto Marcello.* Detroit: Information Coordinators, 1967. *(Detroit Studies in Music Bibliography,* 10).

Fruchtman, Efrim. "The Baryton: Its History and Its Music Re-examined," *Acta Musicologica* XXXIV/1–2 (January–June 1962), 2–17.

———. *The Baryton Trios of Tomasini, Burgksteiner, and Neumann.* Ph.D. diss.: University of North Carolina, 1960. (UM: 60–6986).

Fuhrmann, Roderich. "Die Klavier-Kammermusik Peter Ritters," in: Horst Heussner, ed., *Festschrift Hans Engel* (Kassel: Bärenreiter, 1964), 111–16.

———. *Mannheimer Klavier-Kammermusik.* Ph.D. diss., University of Marburg: Fotodruck von Erich Mauersberger, 1963.

Funk, Floyd Donald. *The Trio Sonatas of Georg Philipp Telemann (1681–1767).* Ph.D. diss.: George Peabody College for Teachers, Nashville, 1954.

Gallico, Claudio. "Emblemi musicali negle 'Scherzi' di Monteverdi," *Rivista Italiana di Musicologia* II/1 (1967), 54–72.

Gallo, F. Alberto. "Il 'Saggio per ben sonare il flautotraverso' di Antonio Lorenzoni nella cultura musicale italiana del Settecento," *La Rassegna Musicale* XXXI/2 (April 1961), 103–11.

Ganassi, Sylvestro. *Opera Intitulata Fontegara (Venice: 1535),* Hildemarie Peter, ed., Berlin–Lichterfelde: Robert Lienau, 1959.

Garrido, Pablo. "Introduccion a la Escritura Violinistica de Juan Sebastian Bach," *Revista Musical Chilena* X/49 (April 1955), 23–41.

Gärtner, Gustav. "Stilkritische Argumente für die Echtheit der 'Romantischen Violinsonaten' W.A.Mozart's," *Mozart-Jahrbuch* [IX] (1958), 30–43.

Garnsey, Sylvia. "The Use of Hand-Plucked Instruments in the Continuo Body: Nicola Matteis," *Music and Letters* XLVII/2 (April 1966), 135–40.

Gaspari, Gaetano. *Catalogo della Biblioteca del Liceo musicale di Bologna, Conservatorio di Musica "G.B. Martini,"* 5 vols. (Bologna: Libreria Romagnoli dall' Aqua, 1890–1943, reprint, Bologna: Arnold Forni, 1961), IV, *Musica Strumentale.*

Gasparini, Francesco. *The Practical Harmonist at the Harpsichord,* trans. Frank S. Stillings; David L. Burrows, ed. New Haven: Yale University Press, 1968. (*Music Theory Translation Series*, 1).

Gates, Willis C. *The Literature for Unaccompanied Solo Violin.* Ph.D. diss.: University of North Carolina, 1950.

Geiringer, Karl, in collaboration with Irene Geiringer. *The Bach Family; Seven Generations of Creative Genius.* London and New York: Oxford University Press, 1954.

———, in collaboration with Irene Geiringer. *Johann Sebastian Bach: The Culmination of an Era.* London and New York: Oxford University Press, 1966.

———, in collaboration with Irene Geiringer. *Haydn, A Creative Life in Music.* New York: W.W. Norton, 1946; 2nd ed. Garden City, New York: Doubleday, 1963; 3rd ed. Berkeley and Los Angeles: University of California Press, 1968.

Geminiani, Francesco. *The Art of Playing on the Violin (1751),* facsimile ed., with an introduction by David D. Boyden. London and New York: Oxford University Press, 1952.

———. *A Treatise of Good Taste in the Art of Musick: Dedicated to His Royal Highness, Frederick, Prince of Wales.* London: 1749; reprint, with an introduction by Robert Donington, New York: Da Capo Press, 1969.

Gerber, Rudolf. "Harmonische Probleme in Mozarts Streichquartetten," *Mozart-Jahrbuch.* II (1924), 55–77.

———. "Unbekannte Instrumentalwerke von Christoph Willibald Gluck," *Die Musikforschung* IV/4 (1951), 305–18.

Gerson-Kiwi, Edith. See: Kiwi, Edith.

Giazotto, Remo. *Tomaso Albinoni. "Musico di Violino dilettante Veneto" (1671–1750).* Milan: Fratelli Bocca, 1945.

———. *Giovan Battista Viotti.* Milan: Curci, 1956.

———. *Antonio Vivaldi.* Milan: Nuova Accademia Editrice, 1965.

Gibson, Oscar Lee. *The Serenades and Divertimenti of Mozart.* Ph.D. diss.: North Texas State University, 1960. (UM: 60–2791).

Giegling, Franz. "Geminiani's Harpsichord Transcriptions," *Music and Letters* XL/4 (October 1959), 350–2.

Girard, Adrien. *Histoire et Richesses de la Flûte.* Paris: Librairie Gründ, 1953.

Girdlestone, Cuthbert. *Jean-Philippe Rameau, his Life and Work,* London: Cassell; New York: Dover, 1957.

———, trans. See: Tartini, Giuseppe.

Gleason, Harold. *Chamber Music from Haydn to Ravel,* 2nd ed. Rochester, N.Y.: Levis Music Stores, 1952. (*Music Literature Outlines*, Ser. IV).

Gołos, Jerzy. "Utwory Instrumentalne Zespołowe z Rękopesu BJ 123/56" [Pieces for Instrumental Ensemble in the Jagiellonian Library Ms 127/56], *Muzyka* XII/2 (April 1967), 24–31.

Gombosi, Otto. *Der Lautenist Valentin Bakfark, Leben und Werke.* Budapest: Magyar Nemzeti Museum, 1935; Zoltán Falvy, ed. Budapest: Akadémiai Kiadó, 1967. (*Musicologia Hungarica,* Neue Folge, 1).

Gore, Richard Taylor. *The Instrumental Works of Georg Muffat.* Ph.D. diss.: The University of Rochester, Eastman School of Music, 1955.

Gotwals, Vernon. *Joseph Haydn: Eighteenth-Century Gentleman and Genius.* A translation with introduction and notes of G.A. Griesinger: *Biographische Notizen über Joseph Haydn* and A.C. Dies: *Biographische Nachrichten von Joseph Haydn.* Madison: University of Wisconsin Press, 1963.

Gräser, Hans. *Georg Philipp Telemanns Instrumentalkammermusik.* Ph.D. diss.: Munich, 1925.

Grassineau, James. *A Musical Dictionary (1740).* Reprint, New York: Broude Brothers, 1968.

Gray Robert, and Mary Rasmussen. "A Bibliography of Chamber Music Including Parts for More Than One Different Brass Instrument," *Brass Quarterly* III/4 (Summer 1960), 141–54.

———. "A Bibliography of Chamber Music Including Parts for the Trombone," *Brass Quarterly* III/3 (Spring 1960), 93–102.

Green, Douglass Marshall. *The Instrumental Ensemble Music of Leonardo Leo against the Background of Contemporary Neapolitan Music.* Ph.D. diss.: Boston University, 1958. (UM: 58–3099).

Greer, David. "The Part-Songs of the English Lutenists," *Proceedings of the Royal Musical Association* XCIV (1967–68), 97–110.

Gregory, Julia. See: Library of Congress.

Haas, Ingrid. *Ferdinando Bertoni: Leben und Instrumentalwerke.* Ph.D. diss.: University of Vienna, 1958.

Halfpenny, Eric. "A Seventeenth-Century Oboe Consort," *The Galpin Society Journal* X (May 1957), 60–2.

Hamilton, Mary Neal. *Music in Eighteenth Century Spain.* Urbana: University of Illinois, 1937; reprint, New York: Da Capo Press, 1971. (See: Chapter V, "Chamber Music," 163–75.)

Hanley, Edwin H. *Alessandro Scarlatti's "cantate da camera": A Bibliographical Study.* Ph.D. diss.: Yale University, 1963.

Hansell, Kathleen Kuzmick. *The Origins of the Italian Trio Sonata.* M.M. thesis: University of Illinois, 1969.

Hansell, Sven Hostrup. *Works for Solo Voice of Johann Adolph Hasse (1699–1783).* Detroit: Information Coordinators, 1968. (*Detroit Studies in Music Bibliography,* 12).

Haselbach, Richard. *Giovanni Battista Bassani.* Kassel: Bärenreiter, 1955.

Hausswald, Günter. "Barocke Kammermusik ohne Generalbass," *Hausmusik* XXI/3 (May–June 1957), 74–9.

———. "Der Divertimento-Begriff bei Georg Christoph Wagenseil," *Archiv für Musikwissenschaft* IX/1 (1952), 45–50.

———. *Mozarts Serenaden: Ein Beitrag zur Stilkritik des 18. Jahrhunderts.* Leipzig: Breitkopf & Härtel, 1951.

———. "Zur Stilistik von Johann Sebastian Bachs Sonaten und Partiten für Violine allein," *Archiv für Musikwissenschaft* XIV/4 (1957), 304–23.

———. "Johann Dismas Zelenka als Instrumentalkomponist," *Archiv für Musikwissenschaft* XIII/3–4 (1956), 243 –62.

Haydn, Joseph. *The Collected Correspondence and London Notebooks of Joseph Haydn*, trans. & ed. by H.C. Robbins Landon. London: Barrie and Rockliff, 1959.

————. *Gesammelte Briefe und Aufzeichnungen*, H.C. Robbins Landon, collator, Dénes Bartha, ed. Kassel: Bärenreiter, 1965.

Hayes, Gerald. "Instruments and Instrumental Notation," in: *The New Oxford History of Music*, Gerald Abraham, ed., IV, *The Age of Humanism 1540–1630* (London: Oxford University Press, 1968), 709–83.

Heartz, Daniel. "The Basse Dance. Its Evolution circa 1450–1550," *Annales musicologiques* VI (1958–63), 287–340.

————. "Hoftanz and Basse Dance," *Journal of the American Musicological Society* XIX/1 (Spring 1966), 13–36.

————, reporter. "Lute Music, in: Jan La Rue, ed. *International Musicological Society, Report of the Eighth Congress, New York: 1961* (Kassel: Bärenreiter, 1961), II, 72–6.

————. *Sources and Forms of the French Instrumental Dance in the Fifteenth Century.* Ph.D. diss.: Harvard University, 1957.

Hedlund, H. Jean. "Ensemble Music for Small Bassoons," *The Galpin Society Journal* XI (May 1958), 78–84.

Heinlein, Federico. "Mozart y su musica de camera," *Revista Musical Chilena* [Special Issue] (1957), 109–38.

Helm, Ernest Eugene. *Music at the Court of Frederick the Great.* Norman: University of Oklahoma Press, 1960.

Helm, Sanford Marion. *Catalog of Chamber Music for Wind Instruments.* Ann Arbor, Michigan: Braun-Brumfield, 1952. *(National Association of College Wind and Percussion Instrument Instructors,* Publication No.1). Reprint with corrections, New York: Da Capo Press, 1969.

Helm, Theodor. *Beethoven's Streichquartette. Versuch einer technischen Analyse dieser Werke im Zusammenhange mit ihrem geistigen Gehalt,* 3rd ed. Leipzig: C.F.W. Siegel, 1921.

Hemel, Viktor van. *De Kamermuziek: Geschiedenis, Komponisten, Befaamde Ensembles, Kamermuziekcompozities e.a.* Antwerp: Cupido-Uitgaven, 194–.

Henrotte, Gayle Allen. *The Ensemble Divertimento in Pre-Classic Vienna.* Ph.D. diss.: University of North Carolina, 1967.

Herbert, Ilse. "Tipuri de sonata de camera din secolul al XVIII lea privite din punctui de vedere al ansamblului executant" [Chamber sonata types of the 18th century seen from the point of view of the performing ensemble], *Lucrari de muzicologie* II (1966), 63–8. [Rumanian, with summaries in French, German, Russian].

Hermann-Bengen, Irmgard. *Tempobezeichnungen: Ursprung, Wandel im 17. und 18. Jahrhundert.* Tutzing: Hans Schneider, 1959.

Hertzmann, Erich. "Mozart's Creative Process," *The Musical Quarterly* XLIII/2 (April 1957), 187–200.

————. "Studien zur Basse Danse im 15. Jahrhundert, mit besonderer Berücksichtigung des brüsseler Manuskripts," *Zeitschrift für Musikwissenschaft* XI/7 (1928–29), 401–13.

Hess, Albert G. "The Transition from Harpsichord to Piano," *The Galpin Society Journal* VI (July 1953), 75–94.

Hess, Ernst. "Die 'Varianten' im Finale des Streichquintettes KV 593," *Mozart-Jahrbuch* (1960/61), 68–77.

Hess, Willy. "Der Erstdruck von Beethovens Flötensonate," *Neues Beethoven-Jahrbuch* VI (1935), 141–58.

———. "Die Teilwiederholung in der Klassischen Sinfonie und Kammermusik," *Die Musikforschung* XVI/3 (July-September 1963), 238–52.

Heyer, Anna Harriet. *Historical Sets, Collected Editions, and Monuments of Music: A Guide to Their Contents,* 2nd ed. Chicago; American Library Association, 1969.

Hitchcock, H. Wiley. "The Instrumental Music of Marc-Antoine Charpentier," *The Musical Quarterly* XLVII/1 (January 1961), 58–72.

Hoboken, Anthony van. *Joseph Haydn Thematisch-bibliographisches Werkverzeichnis* (Mainz: B. Schott's Söhne, 1957), I, *Instrumental Works.*

Höffer v. Winterfeld, Linde, and Harald Kunz. *Handbuch der Blockflöten-Literatur.* Berlin: Bote & Bock, 1959.

Hoffmann-Erbrecht, Lothar. "Der Nürnberger Musikverleger Johann Ulrich Haffner," *Acta Musicologica* XXVI/3–4 (August-December 1954), 114–26, "Nachträge," XXVII/3–4 (August–December 1955), 141–2.

Holtzapple, Jay Charles. *English Theorists, Tonality and the String Fancy, ca. 1590–1680.* M.M. thesis: University of Illinois, 1966.

Horsley, Imogene. *Fugue: History and Practice.* New York: The Free Press, 1966.

———. "Improvised Embellishment in the Performance of Renaissance Polyphonic Music," *Journal of the American Musicological Society* IV/1 (Spring 1951), 3–19.

———. "The Solo Ricercar in Diminution Manuals: New Light on Early Wind and String Techniques," *Acta Musicologica* XXXIII/1 (January–March 1961), 29–40.

Horstman, Jean. *The Instrumental Music of Johann Ludwig Krebs.* Ph.D. diss: Boston University, 1959. (UM: 59–3465).

Horton, John. "The Chamber Music," in: Gerald Abraham, ed. *Handel: A Symposium* (London: Oxford University Press, 1954), 248–61.

Hughes, David G., ed. *Instrumental Music: A Conference at Isham Memorial Library, May 4, 1957.* Cambridge: Harvard University Press, 1959; reprint, New York: Da Capo Press, 1971.

Hughes, Rosemary. *Haydn String Quartets.* London: British Broadcasting Corporation, 1966.

Hughes-Hughes, Augustus. *Catalogue of Manuscript Music in the British Museum.* London: Published by the order of the Trustees of the British Museum, 1909; reissue, 1965. III, *Instrumental Music, Treatises, etc.*

Hunt, Edgar. *The Recorder and its Music.* New York: W.W. Norton, 1963.

———. "The Recorder and its Music," *The Proceedings of the Royal Musical Association* LXXV (1948–49).

Husain, Imdad. "The Unaccompanied Violin Sonata," *The Strad* LX, No. 710 (June 1949), 52–4.

Hutchings, Arthur J.B. *The Baroque Concerto.* New York: W.W. Norton; London: Faber and Faber, 1961.

Jacobi, Erwin R. "G.F. Nicolai's Manuscript of Tartini's *Regole per ben suonar il Violino,*" *The Musical Quarterly* XLVII/2 (April 1961), 207–23.

Jacobs, Richard Morris. *The Chamber Ensembles of C.P.E. Bach Using Two or More Wind Instruments*. Ph.D. diss.: University of Iowa, 1963. (UM: 64–7926).

Jacquot, Jean, ed. *La Musique Instrumentale de la Renaissance*. Paris: Editions du Centre National de la Recherche Scientifique, 1955.

Jeffery, Brian. "Instrumentation in the Music of Antony Holborne," *The Galpin Society Journal* XIX (April 1966), 20–6.

Johansson, Cari. *French Music Publishers' Catalogues of the Second Half of the 18th Century*, 2 vols. Stockholm: Almqvist & Wiksells, 1955. (*Publications, Library of the Royal Swedish Academy of Music, 2*). Reprint, New York: Da Capo Press, 1971.

Johnson, Douglas. "Beethoven's Sketches for the Scherzo of the Quartet Op. 18, No. 6," *Journal of the American Musicological Society* XXIII/3 (Fall 1970), 385–404.

Johnson, Jane Troy. "How to 'Humour' John Jenkins' Three-Part Dances: Performance Directions in a Newberry Library MS," *Journal of the American Musicological Society* XX/2 (Summer 1967), 197–208.

Jordan, Henry Bryce. *The Music of Pelham Humfrey*. Ph.D. diss.: University of North Carolina, 1956.

Jung, Hans Rudolf. "Die Dresdener Vivaldi-Manuskripte," *Archiv für Musikwissenschaft* XII/4 (1955), 314–8.

———. *Johann Georg Pisendel (1687–1755): Leben und Werk. Ein Beitrag zur Geschichte der Violinmusik der Bach-Zeit*. Ph.D. diss.: Jena, 1956.

Kämper, Dietrich. "Das Lehr- und Instrumentalduo um 1500 in Italien," *Die Musikforschung* XVIII/3 (July–September 1965), 242–53.

Kahl, Willi. *Selbstbiographien deutscher Musiker des XVIII. Jahrhunderts; mit Einleitungen und Anmerkungen*. Cologne: Staufen-Verlag, 1948; reprint, Amsterdam: Frits Knuf, 1971.

Kast, Paul. *Die Bach-Handschriften der Berliner Staatsbibliothek*. Trossingen: Hohner, 1958. (*Tübinger Bach-Studien, 2/3*).

Keller, Hans. "The Chamber Music," in: H.C. Robbins Landon & Donald Mitchell, eds., *The Mozart Companion* (London and New York: Oxford University Press, 1956), 90–137.

———. "The Interpretation of Haydn String Quartets," *The Score* No. 24 (November 1958), 14–35.

Keller, Hermann. *Phrasing and Articulation; A Contribution to a Rhetoric of Music, with 152 Musical Examples*, trans. by Leigh Gerdine. New York: W.W. Norton, 1965.

Kelly, David Terrence. *The Instrumental Ensemble Fantasias of Adriano Banchieri*. Ph.D. diss.: Florida State University, School of Music, 1962. (UM: 62–4615).

Kelton, Raymond Harrison. *The Instrumental Music of Ascanio Mayone*. Ph.D. diss.: North Texas State University, 1961. (UM: 61–1297).

Kenton, Egon. *Life and Works of Giovanni Gabrieli*. [Dallas]: American Institute of Musicology, 1967. (*Musicological Studies and Documents, 16*).

Kerman, Joseph. *The Beethoven Quartets*. New York: A.A. Knopf, 1967.

Key, Donald Rochester. *Two Manuscripts of Instrumental Ensemble Music from the Elizabethan Period (British Museum Add. MS 31390 and Bodleian Library MSS D.212–216)*. Ph.D. diss.: Boston University, 1960. (UM: 60–3463).

King, Alexander Hyatt. *Chamber Music*. New York: Chanticleer Press, 1948.

————. *Mozart Chamber Music*. London: B.B.C. Publications, 1968. *(B.B.C. Music Guides)*.

————. *Mozart in Retrospect; Studies in Criticism and Bibliography*. London and New York: Oxford University Press, 1955; reissue, 1970.

————. "Mozart's 'Prussian' Quartets in Relation to His Late Style," *Music and Letters* XXI/4 (October 1940), 328–46.

Kinkeldey, Otto. *A Jewish Dancing Master of the Renaissance: Guglielmo Ebreo*. New York: The Alexander Kohut Memorial Foundation, 1929; reprint, Brooklyn: Dance Horizons, 1966.

Kinsky, Georg, and Hans Halm. *Das Werk Beethovens: thematisch-bibliographisches Verzeichnis seiner sämtlichen vollendeten Kompositionen*. Munich: G. Henle, 1955.

Kirby, Frank E. *A Short History of Keyboard Music*. New York: Free Press, 1966.

Kirkendale, Warren. *Fuge und Fugato in der Kammermusik des Rokoko und der Klassik*. Tutzing; Hans Schneider, 1966.

————. "The 'Great Fugue' Op. 133: Beethoven's 'Art of Fugue'," *Acta Musicologica* XXXV/1 (January–March 1963), 14–24.

————. "More Slow Introductions by Mozart to Fugues of J.S. Bach?" *Journal of the American Musicological Society* XVII/1 (Spring 1964), 43–65.

————. " 'Segreto Comunicato da Paganini'," *Journal of the American Musicological Society* XVIII/3 (Fall 1965), 394–407.

Kirkpatrick, Ralph. *Domenico Scarlatti*. Princeton; Princeton University Press, 1953.

Kish, Anne L. *Jean Baptiste Senallié: His Life, His Time and His Music*. Ph.D. diss.: Bryn Mawr College, 1964.

Kiwi, Edith. "Die Triosonate von ihren Anfängen bis zu Haydn und Mozart," *Die Zeitschrift für Hausmusik* III (1934), 37–63.

Klein, Deanne Arkus. *The Piano Trios of Joseph Haydn and their Significance in the Development of the Piano Trio Genre*. M.A. thesis: Queens College of CUNY, 1964.

Klenz, William. *Giovanni Maria Bononcini of Modena, a Chapter in Baroque Instrumental Music*. Durham, N.C.: Duke University Press, 1962.

Klingenbeck, Josef. "*Ignaz Pleyel, Sein Streichquartett im Rahmen der Wiener Klassik*," *Studien zur Musikwissenschaft*. Beihefte der Denkmäler der Tonkunst in Österreich XXVI (1962), 276–97.

Klitz, Brian Kent. *Solo Sonatas, Trio Sonatas, and Duos for Bassoon Before 1750*. Ph.D. diss.: University of North Carolina, 1961. (UM: 61–6125).

Köchel, Ludwig Ritter von. *Chronologisch-thematisches Verzeichnis sämtlicher Tonwerke Wolfgang Amadé Mozarts*, 6th ed., by Franz Giegling, Alexander Weinmann, Gerd Sievers. Wiesbaden: Breitkopf & Härtel, 1964.

Köhler, Karl-Heinz. *Die Triosonate bei den Dresdener Zeitgenossen Johann Sebastian Bachs*. Ph.D. diss.: Jena, 1956.

————. "Zur Problematik der Violinsonaten mit obligatem Cembalo," *Bach-Jahrbuch* XLV (1958), 114–22.

Kolneder, Walter. *Antonio Vivaldi (1678–1741); Leben und Werk*. Wiesbaden: Breitkopf & Härtel, 1965.

————. *Aufführungspraxis bei Vivaldi*. Leipzig; Breitkopf & Härtel, 1955.

————. "Die Musikalisch-Soziologischen Voraussetzungen der Violinentwicklung," in: Siegfried Kross and Hans Schmidt, eds. *Colloquium Amicorum*

Joseph Schmidt-Görg zum 70. Geburtstag (Bonn: Beethovenhaus, 1967), 179–96.

———. "Die Vivaldi Forschung; Geschichte, Probleme, Aufgaben," *Österreichische Musikzeitschrift* XX/6 (June 1967), 313–9.

———. "Zur Frage der Vivaldi-Kataloge," *Archiv für Musikwissenschaft* XI/4 (1954), 323–31.

Koole, Arend Johannes Christiaan. *Pietro Antonio Locatelli da Bergamo (1695–1764).* Amsterdam: Jasonpers Universiteitspers, 1949.

Kunze, Stefan. *Die Instrumentalmusik Giovanni Gabrielis,* 2 vols. Tutzing: Hans Schneider, 1963.

Laing, Millard Myron. *Anton Reicha's Quintets for Flute, Oboe, Clarinet, Horn, and Bassoon.* Ed. D. diss.: The State University of Iowa, 1952. (UM: 3697).

Lang, Paul Henry. "Bach: Six Trio Sonatas," *The Musical Quarterly* LIV/2 (April 1968), [Review of Records].

———. *George Frideric Handel.* New York: W.W. Norton, 1966.

Landon, Howard Chandler Robbins. "Doubtful and Spurious Quartets and Quintets attributed to Haydn," *The Music Review* XVIII/3 (August 1957) 213–21.

———. "Haydn and Authenticity: Some New Facts," *The Music Review* XVI/2 (May 1955), 138–40.

———. "On Haydn's Quartets of Opera 1 and 2: Notes and Comments on Sondheimer's *Historical and Psychological Study,*" *The Music Review* XIII/3 (August 1952), 181–6.

———. *The Symphonies of Joseph Haydn.* London: Universal, 1955.

———. *Supplement to the Symphonies of Joseph Haydn.* London: Barrie and Rockliff, 1961.

———. "The Symphonies of Joseph Haydn: Addenda and Corrigenda (I)," *The Music Review* XIX/4 (November 1958), 311–19.

———. "The Symphonies of Joseph Haydn: Addenda and Corrigenda (II)," *The Music Review* XX/1 (February 1959) 56–70.

———, trans. and ed. See: Haydn, Joseph.

Langwill, Lyndesay G. *The Bassoon and Contrabassoon.* London: Ernest Benn; New York: W.W. Norton, 1965.

Larsen, Jens Peter. "Some Observations on the Development and Characteristics of Vienna Classical Instrumental Music," *Studia Musicologica* IX/1–2 (1967), 115–39.

LaRue, Jan. "Bifocal Tonality: An Explanation for Ambiguous Baroque Cadences," in: *Essays on Music in Honor of Archibald Thompson Davison, by his Associates,* foreword by Randall Thompson. (Cambridge Department of Music, Harvard University, 1957), 173–84.

———. "Dittersdorf Negotiates a Price," in: Wilfried Brennecke and Hans Haase, eds., *Hans Albrecht in Memoriam* (Basel: Bärenreiter Kassel, 1962), 156–9.

———. "Handel's Clarinet," *The Music Review* XXI/3 (August 1960), 177–8.

———. "Union Thematic Catalogues for 18th Century Chamber Music and Concertos," *Fontes Artis Musicae* VII/2 (July–December 1960), 64–6.

Leavis, Ralph. "Mozart's Flute Quartet in C, K. App. 171," *Music and Letters* XLIII/1 (January 1962), 48–52.

Lee, Douglas Allen. *The Instrumental Works of Christoph Nichelmann*. Ph.D. diss.: University of Michigan, 1968.

Lefkowitz, Murray. *The English Fantasia for Viols*. M.M thesis: University of Southern California, 1951.

———. *William Lawes*. London: Routledge & Kegan Paul, 1960.

Lehmann, Ursula. *Deutsches und Italienisches Wesen in der Vorgeschichte des Klassischen Streichquartetts*. Würzburg–Aumühle: K. Triltsch, 1939.

le Fils, L'Abbé. *Principes du Violon, 1761* [Facsmile]. Introduction by Aristide Wirsta. Preface by Jacques Chailley. Avant propos, Eugène Borrel. Paris: L'Institut de Musicologie de l'Université, 1962.

Lesure, François. "Éstienne Roger et Pierre Mortier: Un épisode de la guerre des contrefaçons à Amsterdam," *Revue de Musicologie* XXXVIII/1 (July 1956), 35–48.

———. "Die 'Terpsichore' von Michael Praetorius und die französiche Instrumentalmusik unter Heinrich IV," *Die Musikforschung* V/1 (1952), 7–17.

———. *Recueils Imprimés XVIe–XVIIe Siècles*. Munich: Henle, 1960. *Répertoire International des Sources Musicales*.

———. *Recueils Imprimés XVIIIe Siècle*. Munich: Henle, 1964. *Répertoire International des Sources Musicales*.

———. *Pierre Trichet: Traité des Instruments de Musique (vers 1640)*. Neuilly-sur-Seine: Société de Musique d'Autrefois, 1957.

Letz, Hans, comp. *Music for the Violin and Viola*. New York: Rinehart, 1948.

Levy, Janet M. *The "Quatuor Concertant" in Paris in the Latter Half of the Eighteenth Century*. Ph.D. diss.: Stanford University, 1971.

Lewis, Edgar Jay, Jr. *The Use of Wind Instruments in Seventeenth-Century Instrumental Music*, 2 vols. Ph.D. diss.: University of Wisconsin, 1964. (UM: 64–3928).

Leyden, Rolf Van. "Die Violinsonate BWV 1024," *Bach-Jahrbuch* XLII (1955), 73–102.

Library of Congress: Catalogue of Early Books on Music (Before 1800). by Julia Gregory prepared under the direction of O.G. Sonneck. Washington: Government Printing Office, 1913; reprint, New York: Da Capo Press, 1969.

———. *Supplement*, by Hazel Bartlett. Washington: Government Printing Office, 1944; reprint, New York: Da Capo Press, 1969.

Liebner, Janos. "The Baryton," *The Consort* XXIII (1966), 109–28.

Liess, Andreas. *Die Trio-Sonaten von J.J. Fux*. Berlin: Junker & Dünnhaupt, 1940.

Lincoln, Stoddard M. *John Eccles: the Last of a Tradition*. Ph.D. diss.: Oxford University, 1963.

Lonchampt, J. *Les Quatuors à cordes de Beethoven*. Paris: Société française de Diffusion Musicale et Artistique, 1956. (*Journal Musical Français*, 15).

Loulié, Etienne. *Elements or Principles of Music*, Albert Cohen trans. and ed. Brooklyn: Institute of Mediaeval Music, [1965].

MacArdle, Donald W. "The Artaria Editions of Beethoven's C Major Quintet," *Journal of the American Musicological Society* XVI/2 (Summer 1963), 254–7.

———. "Beethoven, Artaria, and the C major Quintet," *The Musical Quarterly* XXXIV/4 (October 1948), 567–74.

————. "Beethoven's Quartet in B flat, Op. 130: An Analysis," *The Music Review* VIII/1 (February 1947), 11–24.

————. "A Check-List of Beethoven's Chamber Music," *Music and Letters* XXVII/1 (January 1946), 44–59; XXVII/2 (April 1946), 83–101; XXVII/3 (July 1946), 156–174; XXVII/4 (October 1946), 251–7.

MacClintock, Carol, trans. and ed. See: Bottrigari, Hercole.

Mace, Thomas. *Musick's Monument*. London: 1676; reprint, New York: Broude Brothers, 1966.

Mackerness, E.D. "Bach's F Major Violin Sonata," *The Music Review* XI/3 (August 1950), 175–9.

Mansfield, Orlando A. "Cherubini's String-Quartets," *The Musical Quarterly* XV/4 (October 1929), 590–605.

Marguerre, K. "Mozarts Klaviertrios," *Mozart-Jahrbuch* (1960/61), 182–94.

————. "Die Violinsonate KV. 547 und Ihre Bearbeitung für Klavier Allein," *Mozart-Jahrbuch* (1959), 228–33.

Marliave, Joseph de. *Beethoven's Quartets*, trans. by Hilda Andrews. London: Oxford, 1928; reprint, with introduction by Jean Escarra, New York: Dover, 1961.

Marx, Joseph. "The Baroque Era and Woodwinds," *Woodwind Magazine* (November 1948), 3 & 7.

Marx, Klaus. *Die Entwicklung des Violoncells und seiner Spieltechnik bis J.L. Duport (1520–1820)*. Regensburg; Gustav Bosse, 1963. *(Forschungsbeiträge zur Musikwissenschaft,* 13).

Mason, Daniel Gregory. *The Quartets of Beethoven*. New York and London: Oxford University Press, 1947.

McArtor, Marion E. *Francesco Geminiani, Composer and Theorist*. Ph.D. diss.: University of Michigan, 1951. (UM: 2363).

Meier, Adolf. *Konzertante Musik für Kontrabass in der wiener Klassik. Mit Beiträgen zur Geschichte des Kontrabassbaues in Oesterreich*. Worms: Bärenreiter Antiquariat, 1969.

Mellers, Wilfrid. *François Couperin and the French Classical Tradition*. London: Dennis Dobson, 1950. New York: Dover, 1951.

————. *The Sonata Principle (from c. 1750)*. London: Rockliff, 1957; Fair Lawn, N.J.: Essential Books, 1957.

Mendel, Hermann. *Musikalisches Conversations-Lexikon*, 11 vols. Leipzig: List & Francke, 1870–83.

Mersenne, Marin. *Harmonie Universelle, contenant la Théorie et la Pratique de la Musique*, 3 Vols., facsimile, introduction by François Lesure. Paris: Centre National de la Recherche Scientifique, 1963.

————. *Harmonie Universelle: The Book on Instruments*, trans. by Roger E. Chapman. The Hague: Martinus Nijhoff, 1957.

Mersmann, Hans. "Ein Programmtrio Karl Philipp Emanuel Bachs," *Bach-Jahrbuch* XIV (1917), 137–70.

Metcalfte, William C. "Dolce or Traverso? The Flauto Problem in Vivaldi's Instrumental Music," *The American Recorder* VI/3 (Summer 1965), 3–6.

Meyer, Ernst Hermann. "Die Bedeutung der Instrumentalmusik am Fürstbischöflichen Hofe zu Olomouc (Olmütz) in Kroměříž (Kremsier)," *Die Musikforschung* IX/4 (October–December 1956), 388–411.

————. "Concerted Instrumental Music," in: *The New Oxford History of Music,* Gerald Abraham, ed., IV, *The Age of Humanism 1540–1630* (London: Oxford University Press, 1968), 550–601.

————. "Deutsche Instrumentale Gruppenmusik gegen 1700," *Händel-Jahrbuch* X/XI (1964–65), 71–112.

————. *English Chamber Music: The History of a Great Art from the Middle Ages to Purcell.* London: Lawrence & Wishart, 1946; reissue, 1951; reprint, New York: Da Capo Press, 1971.

————. "Locke-Blow-Purcell- Drei Vorgänger Händels auf dem Gebiet des Instrumentalschaffen," *Händel-Jahrbuch* III (1957), 138–52.

Meyer, Eve Rose. *Florian Gassmann and the Viennese Divertimento.* Ph.D. diss.: University of Pennsylvania, 1963. (UM: 63–7068).

Meyer-Baer, Kathi. "Some Remarks on the Problems of the Basse-Dance," *Tijschrift voor Muziekwetenschap* XVII/4 (1955), 251–77.

Microcard Publications in Music: A Catalog of Early Music Books on Microcards. Rochester, New York: The University of Rochester Press, 1965.

Mies, Paul. "Ein Menuett von L. van Beethoven für Streichquartett," *Beethoven-Jahrbuch,* Zweite Reihe V (1961–64), 85–6 and facsimile.

————. "Quellenbewertung bei den Werken Ludwig van Beethovens: Allgemeine Bemerkungen und Beispiele aus den Klaviertrios op. 70," *Beethoven-Jahrbuch,* Zweite Reihe IV (1959–60), 72–84.

Misch, Ludwig. *Beethoven Studies,* trans. Geraldine de Courcy. Norman: University of Oklahoma Press, 1953.

Mishkin, Henry G. "Five Autograph String Quartets by Giovanni Battista Sammartini," *Journal of the American Musicological Society* VI/2 (Summer 1953), 136–47.

————. *The Function of the Episodic Sequence in Baroque Instrumental Music.* Ph.D. diss.: Havard University, 1938. [Summary in *Summaries of Theses,* Harvard University, 1940, 367–8].

————. "The Published Instrumental Works of Giovanni Battista Sammartini: A Bibliographical Reappraisal," *The Musical Quarterly* XLV/3 (July 1959), 361–74.

————. "The Solo Violin Sonata of the Bologna School," *The Musical Quarterly* XXIX/1 (January 1943), 92–112.

Mitchell, William J. "*The Beethoven Quartets* by Joseph Kerman," *The Musical Quarterly* LIII/3 (July 1967), 421–34. (Reviews of Books).

————. "Chord and Context in 18th-Century Theory," *Journal of the American Musicological Society* XVI/2 (Summer 1963), 221–39.

Monterosso, Raffaello. "Gasparo Visconti, Violinista Cremonese del Secolo XVIII," *Studien zur Musikwissenschaft: Beihefte der Denkmäler der Tonkunst in Österreich* XXV (1962), 378–88.

Mooser, Roy-Aloys. "Violonistes-Compositeurs Italiens en Russie au XVIIIe Siècle," *Rivista Musicale Italiana* XLII/3–4 (1938), 309–24; XLV/5–6 (1941), 264–80; XLVI/3 (1942), 273–93; XLVIII/2 (1946), 219–29; LII/1 (1950), 55–70.

Morley, Thomas. *A Plain and Easy Introduction to Practical Music,* R. Alec Harman, ed., with a foreword by Thurston Dart. London: Dent, 1952.

Moser, Hans Joachim. "Eine Pariser Quelle zur Wiener Triosonate des ausgehenden 17. Jahrhunderts: Der Codex Rost," in: Hans Zingerle, ed.

Festschrift Wilhelm Fischer (Innsbruck: Selbstverlag des Sprachwis-senschaftlichen Seminars der Universität Innsbruck, 1956), 75–81.
————. "Musica da Camera," in: Guido M. Gatti, ed., *La Musica* (Torino: Unione Tipografico, 1966), Parte prima: *Enciclopedia Storica* I, 685–702.
Mozart, Wolfgang Amadeus. *The Letters of Mozart and His Family*, trans. and ed. by Emily Anderson, 2nd ed. prepared by A. Hyatt King and Monica Carolan, 2 vols. London: Macmillan; New York: St. Martin's Press, 1966.
————. *Thomas Attwoods Theorie- und Kompositionsstudien bei Mozart*, Erich Hertzmann, Cecil B. Oldman, Daniel Heartz, and Alfred Mann, eds. Kassel: Bärenreiter, 1965. Also, *Kritische Bericht. (Neue Ausgabe Sämtlicher Werke*, Ser. X, Supplement).
Mracek, Jaroslav John Stephen. *Seventeenth-Century Instrumental Dances in Uppsala, University Library "I Mhs 409": A Transcription and Study*, 2 vols. Ph.D. diss.: Indiana University, 1965.
Muffat, George. *An Essay on Thoroughbass*, Hellmut Federhofer, ed. [Rome]: American Institute of Musicology, 1961.
Munter, Friedrich. "Beethovens Bearbeitungen eigener Werke," *Neues Beethoven-Jahrbuch* VI (1935) 159–73.
Murphy, Arthur Loring. *The "Bicinia Variorum instrumentorum" of Johann Chris-toph Pezel*. Ph.D. diss.: Florida State University, School of Music, 1959. (UM: 59–1761).
Neighbour, Oliver Wray. "New Consort Music by Byrd," *The Musical Times* CVIII/1492 (June 1967), 506–8.
Nelson, Everett Franklin. *An Introductory Study of the English Three-Part String Fancy*, 2 vols. Ph.D. diss.: Cornell University, 1960.
Nelson, Sheila. *The Violin Family*. London: Dennis Dobson, 1964.
Nettl, Paul. "Heinrich Franz Biber von Bibern," *Studien zur Musikwissenschaft: Beihefte der Denkmäler der Tonkunst in Österreich* XXIV (1960), 61–86.
Neumann, Friedrich. "Zur Frage der Echtheit der 'Romantischen Violin-sonaten'," *Mozart-Jahrbuch* (1965–66), 152–60.
Neumeyer, Fritz. "Beiträge zur Generalbasspraxis," *Hausmusik* Heft 1 (Janu-ary-February 1960) 5–11; Heft 2 (March-April 1960) 49–51; Heft 3 (May–June 1960), 80–7.
Newman, Joel. "Handel's Use of the Recorder," *The American Recorder* V/4 (November 1964), 4–9.
————. "*Jacobean Consort Music*, Some Commentary, from the Recorder Point of View," *The American Recorder* I/1 (Winter 1960), 5 & 22; I/3 (Summer 1960), 4.
————. "Some Ornaments in Renaissance Ensemble Music," *The American Recorder* VII/4 (Fall 1966), 10–11.
Newman, Sidney. "Mozart's G minor Quintet (K. 516) and its Relationship to the G minor Symphony (K. 550)," *The Music Review* XVII/4 (November 1956), 287–303.
Newman, William S. "Emanuel Bach's Autobiography" [includes translation], *The Musical Quarterly* LI/2 (April 1965), 363–72.
————. See: Bach, C.P.E.
————. "A Checklist of the Earliest Keyboard 'Sonatas' (1641–1738)," *Music Library Association Notes* XI/2 (March 1954), 201–12.

————. "Concerning the Accompanied Clavier Sonata," *The Musical Quarterly* XXXIII/3 (July 1947), 327–49.

————. "Further on the Nürnberg Music Publisher Johann Ulrich Haffner," *Acta Musicologica* XXXIV/4 (October–December 1962), 194–5.

————. "The Keyboard Sonatas of Benedetto Marcello," *Acta Musicologica* XXIX/1 (January–March 1957), 28–41.

————. "Postscript to 'The Keyboard Sonatas of Benedetto Marcello'," *Acta Musicologica* XXXI/3–4 (July–December 1959), 192–6.

————. "Ravenscroft and Corelli," *Music and Letters* XXXVIII/4 (October 1957), 369–70.

————. *The Sonata in the Baroque Era,* rev. ed. Chapel Hill: University of North Carolina Press, 1966.

————. *The Sonata in the Classic Era.* Chapel Hill : University of North Carolina Press, 1963.

————. *The Sonata since Beethoven.* Chapel Hill: The University of North Carolina Press, 1969.

————. "The Sonatas of Albinoni and Vivaldi," *Journal of the American Musicological Society* V/2 (Summer 1952), 99–113.

Newton, Richard. "Hommage à Marin Marais (1656–1728)," *The Consort* No. 9 (June 1952), 12–21.

————. "More about Marais," *The Consort* No. 10 (July 1953), 10-17.

Nimetz, Daniel. *The Wind Music of Carlo Besözzi.* Ph.D. diss.: University of Rochester, 1967.

Nolte, Ewald Valentin. *The Instrumental Works of Johann Pachelbel (1653–1706): An Essay to Establish His Stylistic Position in the Development of the Baroque Musical Art.* Ph.D. diss.: Northwestern University, 1954. (UM: 9264).

————. "The Paradox of the Peter Quintets," *The Moravian Music Foundation Bulletin* XII/1 (Fall 1967), 2–4.

Norton, Mary D. Herter. *The Art of String Quartet Playing; Practice, Technique and Interpretation,* preface by Isaac Stern. New York: Carl Fischer, 1925; reprint, New York: Simon & Schuster, 1962.

Norton, Richard Edward. *The Chamber Music of Giuseppe Torelli.* Ph.D. diss.: Northwestern University, 1967. (UM: 68–3207).

Noske, Frits. "Le Principe Structural Génétique dans l'Oeuvre Instrumental de Joseph Haydn," *Revue Belge de Musicologie* XII/1–4 (1958), 35–9.

Nutting, Geoffrey. "Jean-Marie Leclair, 1697–1764," *The Musical Quarterly* L/4 (October 1964), 504–14.

Obelkevich, Mary Rowen. "The Growth of a Musical Idea—Beethoven's Op. 96," *Current Musicology* XI (1971), 91–114.

Oberdoerffer, Fritz. "Changes of Instrumentation in the Chamber Music of the 18th Century," *Journal of the American Musicological Society* IV/1 (Spring 1951), 65–6.

————. *Der Generalbass in der Instrumentalmusik des ausgehenden 18. Jahrhunderts.* Kassel: Bärenreiter, 1939.

————. "Neuere Generalbassstudien," *Acta Musicologica* XXXIX/3–4 (July–December 1967), 182–201.

————. "Über die Generalbassbegleitung zu Kammermusikwerken Bachs und des Spätbarock," *Die Musikforschung* X/1 (January–March 1957), 61–74.

Orel, Alfred. "Das Autograph des Scherzos aus Beethovens Streichquartett op. 127," in Horst Heussner, ed., *Festschrift Hans Engel zum 70. Geburtstag* (Kassel: Bärenreiter, 1964), 274–80.

Ortiz, Diego. *Tratado de glosas sobre Clausulas y otros generos de puntos en la musica de violones, Roma 1553,* German trans. by Max Schneider. Kassel: Bärenreiter, 1967.

Page, Athol. *Playing String Quartets.* Boston: Bruce Humphries; London: Longmans, 1964.

Palisca, Claude V. *Baroque Music.* Englewood Cliffs, N.J.: Prentice Hall, 1968.

Palm, Albert. "J.J. de Momigny und sein Kompositorisches Werk," *Revue Belge de Musicologie* XVII/1–4 (1963), 39–92.

———. "Mozart Streichquartett d-Moll, KV 421, in der Interpretation Momignys," *Mozart-Jahrbuch* (1962–63), 256–79.

Pankaskie, Lewis Vincent. *Tonal Organization in the Sonata-Form Movements in Haydn's String Quartets.* Ph.D. diss.: University of Michigan, 1956. (UM: 21, 344).

Parrish, Carl. "Haydn and the Piano," *Journal of the American Musicological Society* I/3 (Fall 1948), 27–34.

Parsons, Pleasants Arrand. *Dissonance in the Fantasias and Sonatas of Henry Purcell.* Ph.D. diss.: Northwestern University, 1953. (UM: 6233).

Pauly, Reinhard G. *Music in the Classic Period.* Englewood Cliffs, N.J.: Prentice-Hall, 1965. (See Chapter 9, "Chamber Music, Divertimento, Serenade," 148–66).

Pearl, Mildred. *The Suite in Relation to Baroque Style.* Ph.D. diss.: New York University, 1957. (UM: 24,880).

Pellerite, James J. *A Handbook of Literature for the Flute,* 3rd ed. Bloomington, Indiana: Zalo Publications, 1970.

Pepper, William B. *The Use of the Keyboard in Representative English String Chamber Music of the Seventeenth Century.* M.A. thesis: University of Iowa, 1967.

Pfannkuch, Wilhelm. "Sonatenform und Sonatenzyklus in den Streichquartetten von Joseph Martin Kraus," in: Georg Reichert and Martin Just, eds., *Bericht über den internationalen Musikwissenschaftlichen Kongress Kassel 1962* (Kassel: Bärenreiter, 1963), 190–2.

Phelps, Roger P. *The History and Practice of Chamber Music in the United States from earliest times up to 1875.* Ph.D. diss.: The State University of Iowa, 1951. (The University of Rochester Press Microcard Publications in Music).

Pincherle, Marc. "Jean-Sébastien Bach et le violon," *Contrepoints* VII (1951), 47–62.

———. *Corelli, His Life, His Music,* trans. by Hubert E.M. Russell. New York: W.W. Norton, 1956.

———. "L'Exécution aux XVIIe et XVIIIe Siècles: Instruments à archet," in: Jan LaRue, ed., *International Musicological Society, Report of the Eighth Congress, New York: 1961* (Kassel: Bärenreiter, 1961), I, 220–31.

———. "Florid Ornamentation," *The Consort* No. 7 (July 1950), 21–5.

———. *Les Instruments du Quatuor.* Paris: Presses Universitaires de France, 1948.

———. *Jean-Marie Leclair l'Aîné.* Paris: La Colombe, 1952.

————. "On the Rights of the Interpreter in the Performance of 17th- and 18th-Century Music," *The Musical Quarterly* XLIV/2 (April 1958), 145–66.

————. *Antonio Vivaldi et la Musique Instrumentale,* 2 Vols. Paris: Librairie Floury, 1948.

————. *Vivaldi, Genius of the Baroque,* trans. by Christopher Hatch. New York: W.W. Norton, 1957. [Derived from preceeding work].

Pintacuda, Salvatore. *Biblioteca dell'Istituto Musicale "Nicolò Paganini." Catalogo del Fondo Antico.* Milan: Istituto Editoriale Italiano, 1966.

Planyavsky, Alfred. "Der Kontrabass in der Kammermusik," *Österreichische Musikzeitschrift* XIII/2 (February 1958), 57–63.

Platen, Emil. "Beethovens Streichtrio D-Dur, Opus 9 Nr. 2," in: Siegfried Kross and Hans Schmidt, eds., *Colloquium Amicorum Joseph Schmidt-Görg zum 70, Geburtstag* (Bonn: Beethovenhaus, 1967), 260–82.

Plath, Wolfgang."Überliefert die duboise Klavierromanze in As, KV. - Anh. 205, das verschollene Quintett-Fragment KV. - Anh. 54 (452a)?" *Mozart-Jahrbuch* (1965–66), 71–86.

Preston, Robert Elwyn. *The Forty-eight Sonatas for Violin and Figured Bass of Jean-Marie Leclair l'Aîné.* Ph.D. diss.: University of Michigan, 1959. (UM: 59–4972).

————. "Leclair's Posthumous Solo Sonata—an Enigma," *Recherches sur la Musique Française Classique* VII (1967), 154–63.

Priestman, Brian. "Catalogue Thématique des Oeuvres de Jean-Baptiste, John & Jacques Loeillet," *Revue Belge de Musicologie* VI/4 (1952), 219–74.

————. "An Introduction to the Loeillets," *The Consort* No. 11 (July 1954), 18–26.

Printz, Wolfgang Caspar. *Historische Beschreibung der edlen Sing- und Kling-Kunst (Dresden, 1960),* facsimile, Othmar Wessely, ed. Graz: Akademische Druck, 1964.

Proctor, George Alfred. *The Works of Nicola Matteis, Sr.,* 2 vols. Ph.D. diss.: University of Rochester, Eastman School of Music, 1960. (Microcard UR 5458).

Pruett, James Worrell. *The Works of Filippo Vitali.* Ph.D. diss.: University of North Carolina, 1962. (UM: 63–3512).

Quantz, Johann Joachim. *On Playing the Flute,* trans. and ed. by Edward R. Reilly. New York: The Free Press, 1966.

Rabey, Wladimir. "Der Originaltext der Bachschen Soloviolinsonaten und-partiten (BWV 1001–1006) in seiner Bedeutung für den ausführenden Musiker," *Bach-Jahrbuch* L (1963–64), 23–46.

Radcliffe, Philip. *Beethoven's String Quartets.* London: Hutchinson University Library, 1965.

Rahter, D., music publisher. *Violoncello-Musik und Kammermusikwerke. Vollständiges Verzeichnis mit ausführlichen Angaben über Inhalt der Werke, Tempi, Tonarten, Schwierigkeitsgrade, Besetzungen, Bearbeiter und Preise.* Leipzig: D. Rahter, H. Simrock & Anton J. Benjamin, 1931.

Rameau, Jean-Philippe. *Complete Theoretical Writings,* facsimile, Erwin R. Jacobi, ed., 6 vols. [Dallas]: American Institute of Musicology, 1967. (Miscellanea, 3).

Randall, J.K. "Haydn: string Quartet in D, op. 76, no. 5," *The Music Review* XXI/2 (May 1960), 94–105.

Rarig, Howard Raymond, Jr. *The Instrumental Sonatas of Antonio Vivaldi.* Ph.D. diss.: University of Michigan, 1958. (UM: 58–7779).

Rasmussen, Mary. "A Bibliography of Chamber Music Including Parts for Horn, as Compiled from Thirteen Selected Sources," *Brass Quarterly* II/3 (March 1959), 110–12; II/4 (June 1959), 147–57; III/1 (Fall 1959), 12–20; III/2 (Winter 1959), 73–81; III/3 (Spring 1960), 103–13; III/4 (Summer 1960), 155–65; VI/1 (Fall 1960), 18–29; IV/2 (Winter 1960), 64–74; IV/3 (Spring 1961), 133–41; IV/4 (Summer 1961), 159–67; Index [by Instrumentation] V/1 (Fall 1961), 18–33.

————. "A Bibliography of Chamber Music Including Parts for Trumpet or Cornetto, as Compiled from Sixteen Selected Sources," *Brass Quarterly* III/2 (Winter 1959), 49–66.

————. "Gottfried Reiche and his *Vier und zwantzig Neue Quatricinia* (Leipzig 1696), "*Brass Quarterly* IV/1 (Fall 1960), 3–17.

————, and Robert Gray. "A Bibliography of Chamber Music Including Parts for the Trombone," *Brass Quarterly* III/3 (Spring 1960), 93–102 & 113.

Ratner, Leonard. "Eighteenth-Century Theories of Musical Period Structure," *The Musical Quarterly* XLII/4 (October 1956), 439–54.

————. "Harmonic Aspects of Classic Form," *Journal of the American Musicological Society* II/3 (Fall 1949), 159–68.

Ratz, Erwin. "Die Originalfassung des B-Dur-Streichquartettes Op. 130/133 von Beethoven," *Österreichische Musikzeitschrift* VII/3 (1952), 81–7.

Ravizza, Victor, *Das instrumentale Ensemble von 1400–1550 in Italien (Wandel eines Klangbildes).* Ph.D. diss.: Bern University, 1967.

Rayner, Clare Grill. *A Little-Known Seventeenth-Century Composer, Christopher Gibbons (1615–1676),* 2 vols. Ph.D. diss.: Indiana University, 1962. (UM: 64–5483).

Reed, Carl Hadley. *Motivic Unity in Selected Keyboard Sonatas and String Quartets of Joseph Haydn.* Ph.D. diss.: University of Washington, 1966.

Reese, Gustave. *Music in the Renaissance,* revised ed. New York: W.W. Norton, 1959.

————. "The Origin of the English *In Nomine,*" *Journal of the American Musicological Society* II/1 (Spring 1949), 7–22.

Reeser, Eduard Hendrik. *Die Klaviersonate met Vioolbegeleiding in het Parijsche Muziekleven ten tijde van Mozart.* Rotterdam: W.L. & J. Brusse, 1939.

Refardt, Edgar. *Thematischer Katalog der Instrumentalmusik des 18. Jahrhunderts in den Handschriften der Universitatsbibliothek Basel.* Bern: Paul Haupt, 1957.

Reilly, Edward. "Further Musical Examples for Quantz's *Versuch,*" *Journal of the American Musicological Society* XVII/2 (Summer 1964), 157–69.

————, trans. and ed. See: Quantz, Johann Joachim.

————. *Quantz and His Versuch: Three Studies.* [n.p.]: American Musicological Society, 1971. [Available through Galaxy Music Corp.].

Reimann, Margarete. "Zur Deutung des Begriffs Fantasia," *Archiv für Musikwissenschaft* X (1953), 253–74.

Rendall, F. Geoffrey. *The Clarinet: Some Notes upon its History and Construction.* London: Williams and Norgate; New York: Philosophical Library, 1954.

Renner, Hans. *Reclams Kammermusikführer.* Stuttgart: Reclam-Verlag, 1955.

Richter, Johannes Friedrich. *Kammermusik-Katalog; Verzeichnis der von 1944 bis 1958 veröffentlichten Werke für Kammermusik und für Klavier vier- und sechshändig sowie für zwei und mehr Klaviere.* Leipzig: Friedrich Hofmeister, 1960.

Riemann, Hugo. *Beethoven's Streichquartette.* Berlin: Schlesinger, 1910.

Rinaldi, Mario. *Arcangelo Corelli.* Milan: Edizioni Curci, 1953.

——. *Catalogo Numerico Tematico delle Composizioni de Antonio Vivaldi.* Rome: Editrice Cultura Moderna, 1945. Parte Seconda: *Musica Strumentale da Camera.*

——. *Il Problema degli Abbellimenti nell' op. V di Corelli.* Sienna: Ticci, 1947.

——. "Sull' Autenticità della 'Ciaccona' di Tommaso Antonio Vitali," *La Rassegna Musical* XXIV/2 (April–June 1954), 129–34.

——. *Antonio Vivaldi.* Milan: Istituto d'Alta Cultura, 1943.

Robertson, Alec., ed. *Chamber Music.* Harmondsworth, Middlesex, and Baltimore: Penguin Books, 1957.

Roeseler, Albrecht. "Die Kammermusik," in: Paul Schaller and Hans Kühner, eds., *Mozart, Aspekte* (Olten, Freiberg im Breisgau: Walter-Verlag, 1956), 130–33.

Roncaglia, Gino. "Le Composizioni strumentali di Alessandro Stradella," *Rivista Musicale Italiana* XLIV/2 (1940), 81–105; XLIV/4 (1940), 337–50; XLV/1 (1941), 1–15.

Ronga, Luigi. *Gerolamo Frescobaldi.* Torino: Fratelli Bocca, 1930.

Rose, Gloria. "Agazzari and the Improvising Orchestra," *Journal of the American Musicological Society* XVIII/3 (Fall 1965), 382–93.

——. "Another Approach to Thorough-bass," *Fontes Artis Musica.* XIV/3 (September–December 1967), 118–9.

Rosenblum, Myron. "The Viola d'Amore and its Literature," *The Strad* LXXVIII/931 (November 1967), 250–53 & 277.

Rothschild, Germaine de. *Luigi Boccherini: His Life and Work,* trans. by Andreas Mayor. London: Oxford University Press, 1965.

Roy, Klaus G. "The So-Called Violin Sonatas of Haydn," *Bulletin of the American Musicological Society,* Nos. 11–13 (September 1948), 38–40.

Ruhnke, Martin. "Telemann-Forschung 1967. Bemerkungen zum 'Telemann-Werke-Verzeichnis'," *Musica* XXI/1 (1967), 6–10.

Saam, Joseph. *Zur Geschichte des Klavierquartetts bis in die Romantik.* Ph.D. diss.: Munich, Ludwig-Maximilians-Universität, 1932; Strassburg: Heintz, 1933.

Sachs, Curt. *The History of Musical Instruments.* New York: W.W. Norton, 1940.

——. *Rhythm and Tempo.* New York: W.W. Norton, 1953.

Sachs, Joel Alan. *Johann Nepomuk Hummel and his Chamber Music.* M.A. thesis: Columbia University, 1965.

——. *Hummel in England and France: A Study in the Intellectual Musical Life of the Early Nineteenth Century.* Ph.D. diss.: Columbia University, 1968.

Sachse, Hans-Martin. *Franz Schuberts Streichquartette.* Münster: Max Kramer, 1958.

Sadie, Stanley J. *British Chamber Music, 1720–1790,* 3 vols. Ph.D. diss.: Cambridge University, 1957.

——. "The Chamber Music of Boyce and Arne," *The Musical Quarterly* XLVI/4 (October 1960), 425–36.

——. "Concert Life in Eighteenth Century England," *Proceedings of the Royal Musical Association* LXXXV (1958–59), 17–30.

————. "The Wind Music of J.C. Bach," *Music and Letters* XXXVII/2 (April 1956), 106–17.

Sainsbury, John S., ed. *A Dictionary of Musicians from the Earliest Times,* 2 vols. London: 1825; reprint, with introduction by Henry George Farmer, New York: Da Capo, 1966.

Saint-Foix, Georges de. "Les Six Sonates, dites 'romantiques,' pour piano et violon, de Mozart," *La Revue Musicale* XXII/199 (April 1946), 81–9.

Salmen, Walter. *Haus- und Kammermusik: Privates Musizieren im gesellschaftlichen Wandel zwischen 1600 und 1900.* Leipzig: Veb Deutscher Verlag für Musik, 1970. *(Musikgeschichte in Bildern,* IV, Pt. 3).

Sartori, Claudio. *Bibliografia della musica strumentale italiana stampata in Italia fino al 1700.* 2 vols. Florence: Leo S. Olschki, 1952–68. *(Biblioteca di bibliografia italiana,* 56).

————. "Le quarantaquattro Edizioni italiane delle sei Opere di Corelli," *Rivista Musicale Italiana* LV/1 (January–March 1953), 29–53.

————. "Sono 51 (fino ad ora) le edizioni italiane della opere di Corelli e 135 gli esemplari noti," in: *Collectanea Historiae Musicae* (Florence: Leo S. Olschki, 1956), II, 379–89.

Sauzay, Eugéne. *L'Ecole de l'Accompagnement, ouvrage faisant suite à l'étude sur le quatuor.* Paris: Firmin Didot frères, 1869.

————. *Haydn, Mozart, Beethoven: Étude sur le Quatuor.* Paris: L'auteur, 1861.

Schenk, Erich. "Beobachtungen über die modenesische Instrumentalmusikschule des 17. Jahrhunderts," *Studien zur Musikwissenschaft: Beihefte der Denkmäler der Tonkunst in Österreich* XXVI (1964), 25–46.

Schenker, Heinrich. "Beethoven zu seinem opus 127," *Tonwille* IV/1 (1924), 39–41.

Schilling, Hans Ludwig. "Zur Instrumentenwahl in der Continuopraxis," *Schweizerische Musikzeitung* XCVIII/1 (January 1958), 6–9.

Schlossberg, Artur. *Die italienische Sonata für mehrere Instrumente im 17. Jahrhundert.* Ph.D. diss.: Heidelberg, 1932.

Schmid, Ernst Fritz. "Mozart and Haydn," *The Musical Quarterly* XLII/2 (April 1956), 145–61.

Schmieder, Wolfgang. *Thematisch-systematisches Verzeichnis der musikalischen Werke von Johann Sebastian Bach.* Leipzig: Breitkopf & Härtel, 1950.

Schmitz, Hans-Peter. *Die Kunst der Verzierung im 18. Jahrhundert; instrumentale und vocale Musizierpraxis in Beispielen.* Kassel: Bärenreiter, 1955.

————. *Querflöte und Querflötenspiel in Deutschland während des Barockzeitalters.* Kassel: Bärenreiter, 1952.

Schnapper, Edith B., ed. *The British Union Catalogue of Early Music printed before the year 1801: A Record of the Holdings of over One Hundred Libraries throughout the British Isles.* 2 vols. London: Butterworth Scientific Publications, 1957.

Schneider, Otto, and Anton Algatzy. *Mozart-Handbuch: Chronik, Werk, Bibliographie.* Vienna: Brüder Hollinek, 1962.

Schoenbaum, Camillo. "Die Kammermusikwerke des Jan Dismas Zelenka," in: Georg Reichert and Martin Just, eds., *Bericht über den Internationalen Musikwissenschaftlichen Kongress Wien, Mozartjahr 1956* (Graz–Köln: Hermann Böhlaus, 1958), 552–7.

Schrade, Leo. *Monteverdi: Creator of Modern Music.* New York: W.W. Norton, 1950; reissue, 1970.

Schrammek, Winfried. "Die musikgeschichtliche Stellung der Orgeltriosonaten von Joh. Seb. Bach," *Bach-Jahrbuch* XLI (1954), 7–28.

Schultz, Max. "Francesco Corbetta und das Generalbass-Spielen," *Die Musikforschung* IV/4 (1951), 371–2.

Schumann, Otto. *Schumanns Kammermusikbuch.* Wilhelmshafen: H. Hübener, 1951.

Schwarting, Heino. "Uber die Echtheit dreier Haydn-Trios," *Archiv für Musikwissenschaft* XXII/3 (September 1965), 169–82.

Schwartz, Boris. "Beethoven and the French Violin School," *The Musical Quarterly* XLIV/4 (October 1958), 431–47.

———. *French Instrumental Music between the Revolutions (1789–1830).* Ph.D. diss.: Columbia University, 1950. (UM: 1897).

Seaman, Gerald. "The First Russian Chamber Music," *The Music Review* XXVI/4 (November 1965), 326–37.

Serrins, David. *The Validity of Textbook Concepts of Sonata Form in the Late String Quartets of Haydn and Mozart.* M.A. thesis: University of North Carolina, 1950.

Shand, David A. *The Sonata for Violin and Piano from Schumann to Debussy (1851–1917).* Ph.D. diss.: Boston University, 1948.

Shanet, Howard. "Why did J.S. Bach Transpose his Arrangements?" *The Musical Quarterly* XXXVI/2 (April 1950), 180–203.

Shaw, Gertrude Jean. *The Violoncello Sonata Literature in France during the Eighteenth Century.* Ph.D. diss.: Catholic University of America, 1963. (UM: 63–6559).

Sheldon, David Alden. *The Chamber Music of Johann Friedrich Fasch.* Ph.D. diss.: Indiana University, 1968. (UM: 68–13,704).

Siegele, Ulrich. "Noch einmal: Die Violinsonate BWV 1024," *Bach-Jahrbuch* XLIII (1956), 124–39.

Siegmund-Schultz, W., and others. *Georg Philip Telemann–Leben und Werk.* Magdeburg, Arbeitskreis: G.P. Telemann im Deutschen Kulturbund, 1968.

Silbert, Doris. "Ambiguity in the String Quartets of Joseph Haydn," *The Musical Quarterly* XXXVI/4 (October 1950) 562–73.

Simon, Edwin J. "Sonata into Concerto: A Study of Mozart's first seven Concertos," *Acta Musicologica* XXXI/3–4 (July–December 1959), 170–85.

Sites, Caroline O. *Benedetto Marcello's Chamber Cantatas.* Ph.D. diss.: University of North Carolina, 1959. (UM: 59–6448).

Skempton, Alec. "The Instrumental Sonatas of the Loeillets," *Music and Letters* XLIII/3 (July 1962), 206–17.

Sleeper, William Allen. *Harmonic Style of Four-Part Viol Music of Jenkins, Locke, and Purcell.* Ph.D. diss.: University of Rochester, Eastman School of Music, 1964. (UM: 66–2364).

Slim, H. Colin. *The Keyboard Ricercar and Fantasia in Italy, ca. 1500–1550, with Reference to Parallel Forms in European Lute Music of the Same Period,* 2 vols. Ph.D. diss.: Harvard University, 1961.

Smith, Helen Margaret. *F.M. Veracini's "Il Trionfo della prattica musicale."* Ph.D. diss.: Indiana University, 1963. (UM: 64–5496).

Smith, William Charles. *A Bibliography of the Musical Works published by John Walsh during the years 1695–1720*. London: Printed for the Bibliographical Society at the University Press, Oxford, 1948.

——, assisted by Charles Humphries. *Handel: A Descriptive Catalogue of the Early Editions*. London: Cassell, 1960; 2nd ed., 1970.

Smithers, Don. "Seventeenth-Century English Trumpet Music," *Music and Letters* XLVIII/4 (October 1967), 358–65.

Solar-Quintes, Nicolás A. "Nuevos documentos sobre Luigi Boccherini," *Anuario Musical* II (1947), 88–98.

——. "Nuevas Obras de Sebastián Durón y de Luigi Boccherini, y músicos del Infante Don Luis Antonio de Borbón," *Anuario Musical* XIII (1958), 225–59.

Somfai, László. "Albrechtsberger-Eigenschriften in der Nationalen Bibliothek Széchényi Budapest," *Studia Musicologica Academiae Scientiarum Hungaricae* I/1 (1961), 175–202, IV/1 (1963), 179–90.

——. "A Klasszikus Kvartetthangza's Megszületese Haydn Vonésnegyeseiben" [Birth of the Classical Quartet Sonority in Haydn's String Quartets], in: Bence Szabolcsi and Dénes Bartha, eds. *Haydn Emlékére*. Budapest: Academy Press, 1960. [Hungarian, with a summary in German].

——. "Zur Echtheitsfrage des Haydn'schen 'Opus 3'," *The Haydn Yearbook* III (1965), 153–63.

Sondheimer, Robert. *Haydn; A Historical and Psychological Study Based on his Quartets*. London: Edition Bernoulli, 1951.

Southern, Eileen. "Bass-Dance Music in Some German Manuscripts of the 15th Century," in Jan LaRue, ed., *Aspects of Medieval & Renaissance Music: A Birthday Offering to Gustave Reese* (New York: W.W. Norton, 1966), 738–55.

——. "Some Keyboard Basse Dances of the Fifteenth Century" *Acta Musicologica* XXXV (1963), 144–24.

Spivakovsky, Tossy. "Polyphony in Bach's Works for Solo Violin," *The Music Review* XXVIII/4 (November 1967), 277–88.

Stein, Franz Alois. *Verzeichnis der Kammermusikwerke von 1650 bis zur Gegenwart*. Bern: Francks Verlag, 1962.

Stevens, Denis. "Baroque Instrumental Music," in: Alec Robertson and Denis Stevens, eds., *The Pelican History of Music* (Baltimore and London: Penguin Books, 1963), II, 297–319.

——. "Purcell's Art of Fantasia," *Music and Letters* XXXIII/4 (October 1952), 341–45.

——. "Seventeenth-Century Italian Instrumental Music in the Bodleian Library," *Acta Musicologica* XXVI/3-4 (August–December 1954), 67–74.

——. *Thomas Tomkins 1572–1656*. London: Macmillan; New York: St. Martin's Press, 1957; reprint, with new preface and discography, New York: Dover, 1967.

——. "Unique Italian Instrumental Music in the Bodleian Library," in: *Collectanea Historiae Musicae* (Florence: Leo S. Olschki, 1956), II, 401–12.

Stevens, John. *Music and Poetry in the Early Tudor Court*. London: Methuen; Madison: University of Wisconsin Press, 1961.

Stierhof, Karl. "Die Viola und ihre Solo-Literatur," *Österreichische Musikzeitschrift* XVII/3 (March 1962), 125–9.

Stillings, Frank Stuart. *Arcangelo Corelli*. Ph.D. diss.: University of Michigan, 1957. (UM: 19,718).

Stover, Edwin L. *The Instrumental Music of G.B. Pergolesi*. Ph.D. diss.: Florida State University, School of Music, 1964. (UM: 65–306).

Strunk, W. Oliver. "Haydn's Divertimenti for Baryton, Viola, and Bass," *The Musical Quarterly* XVIII/2 (April 1932), 216–51.

———, ed. *Source Readings in Music History*. New York: W.W. Norton, 1950.

Studeny, Bruno. *Beiträge zur Geschichte der Violinsonate im 18. Jahrhundert*. Munich: Wunderhornverlag, 1911.

Subirá, José. *La Música en la Casa de Alba; Estudios Históricos y Biográficos*. Madrid: Establecimiento tipográfico, 1927.

———. "La Música de Cámara en la Corte Madrilena durante el siglo XVIII y principios del XIX," *Anuario Musical* I (1946), 181–94.

Suess, John G. *Giovanni Battista Vitali and the "sonata da chiesa."* Ph.D. diss.: Yale University, 1963.

Sutherland, Gordon. "The Ricercari of Jacques Buus," *The Musical Quarterly* XXXI/4 (October 1945), 448–63.

———. *Studies in the Development of the Keyboard and Ensemble Ricercare from Willaert to Frescobaldi*, 2 vols. Ph.D. diss.: Harvard University, 1942.

Sutton, Julia. *Jean-Baptiste Bésard's "Novus Partus,"* 2 vols. PhD. diss.: University of Rochester, Eastman School of Music, 1962. (UM: 63–245).

———. "The Lute Instructions of Jean-Baptiste Besard," *The Musical Quarterly* LI/2 (April 1965), 345–62.

———. "The Music of J.B. Besard's *Novus Partus*, 1617," *Journal of the American Musicological Society* XIX/2 (Summer 1966), 182–204.

Svensson, Sven Erik. *Joseph Haydns Strakkvartetter*. Stockholm: H. Geber, 1948.

Szigeti, Joseph. *The Ten Beethoven Sonatas for Piano and Violin*, Paul Rolland, ed. Urbana, Ill.: American String Teachers Association, 1965. [Distributed by Carl Fischer, New York].

Tartini, Giuseppe. *A Letter from the Late Signor Tartini to Signora Maddalena Lombardini (Now Signora Sirmen) Published as an Important Lesson to Performers on the Violin*, trans. by Dr. Burney. London: 1779; reprint, New York and London: Johnson Reprint Corp., 1967.

———. *Traité des Agréments de la Musique*, German trans.; English trans. by Cuthbert Girdlestone; facsimile of the original Italian text. Celle: Hermann Moeck, 1961.

———. *Traktata über die Musik, gemäss der wahren Wissenschaft von der Harmonie*, trans. into German by Alfred Rubeli. Düsseldorf: Gesellschaft zur Förderung der systematischen Musikwissenschaft, 1966.

———. *Treatise on the Ornaments of Music*, trans. and ed. by Sol Babitz; reprinted from the *Journal of Research in Music Education* IV/2 (Fall 1956). New York: Distributed by Carl Fischer, 1957.

Terry, Charles Sanford. *John Christian Bach*, 2nd ed. with a foreword by H. C. Robbins Landon. London: Oxford University Press, 1967. [Reissue of 1929 ed. with supplemental material].

Thayer, Alexander Wheelock. *Thayer's Life of Beethoven*, rev. and ed. by Elliot Forbes, 2 vols. Princeton: Princeton University Press, 1964.

Thompson, Clyde H. "Marin Marais's Pièces de Violes," *The Musical Quarterly* XLVI/4 (October 1960), 482–99.

Tichota, Jiří. "Deutsche Lieder in Prager Lautentabulaturen des beginnenden 17. Jahrhunderts," *Miscellanea musicologica* XX (1967), 83–99.

Tilmouth, Michael. *Chamber Music in England, 1675–1720.* Ph.D. diss.: Cambridge University (Christ's College), 1960.

————. "Nicola Matteis," *The Musical Quarterly* XLVI/1 (January 1960), 22–40.

————. "The Technique and Forms of Purcell's Sonatas," *Music and Letters* XL/2 (April 1959), 109–21.

Tobel, Rudolf von. *Die Formenwelt der Klassichen Instrumentalmusik.* Bern and Leipzig: Paul Haupt, 1935.

Tomek, Otto. *Das Strukturphänomen des verkappten Satzes a tre in der Musik des 16. und 17. Jahrhunderts.* Ph.D. diss.: Vienna, 1953.

Torrefranca, Fausto. *Le Origini Italiane del Romanticismo Musicale; i primitivi della sonata moderna.* Turin: Fratelli Bocca, 1930.

Tovey, Donald Francis. "Haydn's Chamber Music," in his: *The Main Stream of Music and Other Essays.* (London and New York: Oxford University Press, 1949), 1–64.

Traficante, Frank. *The Mansell Lyra Viol Tablature,* 12 vols. Ph.D. diss.: University of Pittsburgh, 1965.

Trimpert, Dieter Lutz. *Die Quatuors Concertants von Giuseppe Cambini.* Tutzing: Hans Schneider, 1967.

Trogden, Patricia A. *Melodic Structure in Corelli and Veracini: A Comparative Study of Corelli's Opus 5 and Veracini's Dissertazioni.* M.A. thesis: Mills College, 1965.

Truscott, Harold. "Schubert's D minor string Quartet," *The Music Review* XIX/1 (February 1958), 27–36.

Tyson, Alan. "Haydn and Two Stolen Trios," *The Music Review* XXII/1 (February 1961), 21–7.

————. "New Light on a Haydn Trio (XV:32)," *The Haydn Yearbook* I (1962), 203–5.

————. *Thematic Catalogue of the Works of Muzio Clementi.* Tutzing: Hans Schneider, 1967.

————, and H.C. Robbins Landon. "Who Composed Haydn's Op. 3?" *The Musical Times* CV (July 1964), 506–7.

Ulrich, Homer. *Chamber Music, the Growth and Practice of an Intimate Art,* 2nd. ed. New York: Columbia University Press, 1966.

Unverricht, Hubert. "Francesco Zannettis Streichtrios," in: Siegfried Kross and Hans Schmidt, eds., *Colloquium Amicorum; Joseph Schmidt-Görg zum 70. Geburtstag* (Bonn: Beethovenhaus, 1967), 410–27.

————. *Geschichte des Streichtrios.* Tutzing: Hans Schneider, 1969. (*Mainzer Studien zur Musikwissenschaft,* 2).

Valetta, Ippolito. *I Quartetti di Beethoven.* Milan: Bocca, 1943.

Van Ackere, Jules Emile. *De Kamermusich en het lied van Corelli tot Debussy.* Hosselt: Uitgevery Heideland, 1967.

Vaught, Raymond. "Mersenne's Unknown English Viol Player," *The Galpin Society Journal* XVII (February 1964), 17–23.

Veinus, Abraham. *The Concerto.* New York: Doubleday, Doran, 1944; reprint, New York: Dover, 1964.

Verchaly, André, ed., *Les Influences étrangères dans l'oeuvre de W.A. Mozart.* Paris: Editions du Centre National de la Recherche Scientifique, 1958.

Vidal, Antoine. *Les Instruments à Archet les Feseurs, les Jouers d'Instruments, leur Histoire sur le Continent Européen, Suivi d'un Cataloque général de la Musique de Chambre,* 3 vols. Paris: 1876–78; reprint, London: The Holland Press, 1961.

Viollier, Renée. "Les Sonates pour violon et les Sonates en trio d'Elisabeth Jacquet de La Guerre et de Jean-François d'Andrieu," *Schweizerische Musikzeitung* IX/1 (September 1951), 349–51.

Volek, Tomislav, and Marie Skalicka. "Vivaldis Beziehungen zu den böhmischen Ländern," *Acta Musicologica* XXXIX/1–2 (January–June 1967), 64–72.

Volk, Alois. *Ernst Eichner, sein Leben und seine Bedeutung für die Entwicklung der Kammermusik und der Solokonzerte. Ein Beitrag zur vorklassischen Stilperiode.* Ph.D. diss.: Cologne, 1943.

Wailes, Marylin. "Four Short Fantasies by Henry Purcell," *The Score* No. 20 (June 1957), 59–65.

Waldschmidt, Carl. *Georg Boehm, His Life and Works.* Ph.D. diss.: Northwestern University, 1962.

Waln, George E. *Materials for Miscellaneous Instrumental Ensembles.* Washington, D.C.: Music Educators National Conference, 1960.

Walter, Georg. *Katalog der gedruckten und handschriftlichen Musikalien des 17. bis 19. Jahrhunderts im Besitze der Allgemeinen Musikgesellschaft Zürich.* Zürich: Verlag der Allgemeinen Musikgesellschaft, 1960.

Warner, Richard Lyman. *The Vocal and Instrumental Technique of Orlando Gibbons.* Ph.D. diss.: University of Rochester, Eastman School of Music, 1949.

Warner, Robert. *The Fantasia in the Works of John Jenkins,* 2 vols. Ph.D. diss.: University of Michigan, 1951. (UM: 24,932).

———. "John Jenkins' Four-Part Fancy (Meyer, No. 14) in C minor: An enharmonic Modulation around the Key Circle," *The Music Review* XXVIII/1 (February 1967), 1–20.

Wasielewski, Joseph Wilhelm von. *The Violoncello and its History.* London and New York: Novello, Ewer, 1894; reprint, with a new introduction by Robert C. Lawes, Jr., New York: Da Capo Press, 1968.

Wattenbarger, James Albert. *The "Turmmusik" of Johann Pezel.* Ph.D. diss.: Northwestern University, 1957. (UM:23,932).

Wedig, Hans Josef. *Beethovens Streichquartett op. 18 Nr. 1 und seine erste Fassung: Erst vollständige Veröffentlichung des Werkes aus dem Beethovenhaus Bonn.* Leipzig: Quelle & Meyer, 1922.

Weidner, Robert W. *The early In Nomine, a Genesis of Chamber Music.* Ph.D. diss.: Eastman School of Music, 1960. (The University of Rochester Press Microcard Publications in Music).

———. "The Instrumental Music of Christopher Tye," *Journal of the American Musicological Society* XVII/3 (Fall 1964), 363–9.

Weigl, Bruno. *Handbuch der Violoncell-Literatur; Systematisch geordnetes Verzeichnis der solo- und instructiven werke für das Violoncell.* Vienna: Universal Edition, 1929.

Weinmann, Alexander. *Kataloge Anton Huberty (Wien) und Christoph Torricella.* Vienna: Universal Edition, 1962.

————. "Verzeichnis der Musikalien des Verlages Johann Traeg in Wien 1794-1818," *Studien zur Musikwissenschaft. Beihefte der Denkmäler der Tonkunst in Österreich* XXIII (1956), 135–83.

————. *Vollständiges Verlagsverzeichnis Artaria & Comp.* Vienna: Ludwig Krenn, 1952.

————. "Vollständiges Verlagsverzeichnis der Musikalien des Kunst und Industrie Comptoirs in Wien 1801-1819. Ein bibliographischer Beitrag," *Studien zur Musikwissenschaft, Beihefte der Denkmäler der Tonkunst in Österreich* XXII (1955), 217–52.

————. *Die Wiener Verlagswerke von Franz Anton Hoffmeister.* Vienna: Universal Edition, 1964.

Wessely-Kropik, Helen. *Lelio Colista, ein römischer Meister vor Corelli: Leben und Umwelt.* Vienna: Hermann Böhlaus, 1961.

————. "Henry Purcell als Instrumentalkomponist," *Studien zur Musikwissenschaft. Beihefte der Denkmäler der Tonkunst in Österreich* XXII (1955), 85–141.

Westrup, Jack Allan. *Purcell.* London: J.M. Dent, 1937; New York: Farrar, Straus, & Cudahy, 1947 (*Master Musicians Series*); New York: Collier Books, 1962.

————. "The Chamber Music," in: Gerald Abraham, ed., *The Music of Schubert* (New York: W.W. Norton, 1947), 88–110.

White, Mary Gray. *The Violin Sonatas of Francesco Maria Veracini: some aspects of Italian late Baroque instrumental style exemplified.* Ph.D. diss.: University of North Carolina, 1967.

Wilson, Michael. *The English Chamber Organ, History and Development 1650–1850.* Columbia, S.C.: University of South Carolina, 1968.

Winternitz, Emanuel. *Musical Instruments of the Western World,* photographs by Lilly Stunzi. New York and Toronto: McGraw-Hill, 1970.

Wirsta, Aristide. *Écoles de Violon au XVIIIe Siécle.* Paris: Thése de Doctorat d'Université, 1955.

Wirth, Helmut. "Kammermusik," in: Friedrich Blume, ed., *Die Musik in Geschichte und Gegenwart* (Kassel: Bärenreiter, 1958), VII, 478–99.

Wohlforth, Martha Curti. *Orlando Gibbons' Chamber Music.* M.A. thesis: City College of New York, 1967.

Wolff, Christoph. "Der Terminus 'Ricercar' in Bachs *Musikalischem Opfer,*" *Bach-Jahrbuch* LIII (1967), 70–81.

Young, Percy M. *Handel.* New York: Collier Books, 1963.

Zeyringer, Franz. *Literatur für Viola.* Hartberg: Julius Schönwetter, 1963.

————. *Ergänzungsband.* Kassel–Wilhelmshöhe: Bärenreiter Antiquariat, 1965.

Ziegler, Benno. *Placidus von Camerloher (1718–82),* Des Altbayerischen Leben und Werke. Freising: F.P. Datterer, 1919.

Zimmermann, Franklin B. *Henry Purcell 1659–1695: An Analytical Catalogue of his Music.* London: Macmillan; New York: St. Martin's Press, 1963.

————. *Henry Purcell 1659–1695, His Life and Times.* London: Macmillan; New York: St. Martin's Press, 1967.

Zobeley, Fritz, ed. *Die Musikalien der Grafen von Schonborn-Wiesentheid, Teil I: Das Repertoire des Grafen Rudolf Franz Erwein von Schönborn (1677–1754),* Band I: *Drucke aus den Jahren 1676 bis 1738.* Tutzing: Hans Schneider, 1967.

SCORES AND CRITICAL EDITIONS

Abaco, Evaristo Felice dall'. *Selected Works,* Adolf Sandberger, ed. Braunschweig: H. Litolff, 1900–1938. DENKMÄLER DER TONKUNST IN BAYERN, I (1900); IX, 1 (1908).

Abel, Karl Friedrich. *Kompositionen,* Walter Knape, ed. Cuxhaven: W. Knape, 1964. Ser. C: Streichquartette; Ser. D: Streichtrios.

Albrechtsberger, Johann Georg. *Instrumentalwerke,* O. Kapp, ed. Vienna: Artaria, 1909. DENKMÄLER DER TONKUNST IN ÖSTERREICH, Jg. XVI/2, Bd. 33.

Alte Meister des Violinspiels, Arnold Schering, ed. Leipzig: C.F. Peters, 1909.

AMERICAN RECORDER SOCIETY EDITIONS, Joel Newman, general ed. New York: Galaxy Music Corp., 1960–. [63 numbers to date].

Antes, John. *Three Trios, Op. 3, for two Violins and Violoncello,* Thor Johnson and Donald M. McCorkle, eds. New York: Boosey & Hawkes, 1961. THE MORAMUS EDITION OF THE MORAVIAN MUSIC FOUNDATION.

ANTHOLOGY OF MUSIC. *A collection of complete musical examples illustrating the history of music,* Karl Gustav Fellerer, ed. Cologne: Arno Volk, 1959–. [28 vols. to date] [German ed. as *Das Musikwerk*].

ANTICA MUSICA STRUMENTALE ITALIANA. Milan: Ricondi (Collegium Musicum Italicum), 1959–. [50 vols. to date].

ANTIQUA: *Eine Sammlung Alter Musik Meisterwerke des 13.–18. Jahrhunderts.* Mainz: B. Schott's Söhne, 1929–. [95 numbers to date].

Arnold, Cecily, and Marshall Johnson, eds. *The Consort Player,* London: Stainer & Bell, 1949 [Works transcribed for use in viol consort].

Attaingnant, Pierre, publisher. *Preludes, Chansons, and Dances for Lute, Paris: 1529–1530.* Daniel Heartz, ed. Neuilly-sur-Seine: Société de la Musique d'Autrefois, 1964.

Bach, Carl Philipp Emanuel. *Die sechs Sammlungen von Sonaten, freien Fantasien und Rondos für Kenner und Liebhaber,* Carl Krebs, ed. Newly edited by Lothar Hoffmann-Erbrecht. Leipzig: Breitkopf & Härtel, 1953.

Bach, Johann Christian. *Sechs Quintette, Op. 11,* Rudolf Steglich, ed. Hannover: Nagel, 1935. DAS ERBE DEUTSCHER MUSIK, 3; Abteilung Kammermusik, 1.

Bach, Johann Christoph Friedrich. *Ausgewählte Werke.* Bückeburg: Fürstliches Institut für Musikwissenschaftliche Forschung, 1920–22. VII, *Kammermusik* (1920).

Bach, Johann Sebastian. *Sonate c-moll für Violine und Generalbass (BWV 1024),* Rolf Van Leyden, ed. Basel: Ernst Reinhardt, 1955.

––––––. *Werke für Flöte,* Hans-Peter Schmitz, ed. Kassel: Bärenreiter, 1963. NEUE AUSGABE SÄMTLICHER WERKE, Ser. VI, Bd. 3.

––––––. *Werke für Violine,* Günter Hausswald and Rudolf Rudber, eds. Kassel: Bärenreiter, 1958. NEUE AUSGABE SÄMTLICHER WERKE, Ser. VI, Bd. 1. Also, *Kritischer Bericht.*

Beck, Hermann, ed. *Die Suite.* Cologne: Arno Volk, 1964. DAS MUSIKWERK, 26.

––––––. *The Suite,* trans. by Robert Kolben. Cologne: Arno Volk, 1966. ANTHOLOGY OF MUSIC, 26.

Beethoven, Ludwig van. *Klavierquintett und Klavierquartette*, Siegfried Kross, ed. Munich: Henle, 1961. BEETHOVEN WERKE, Ser. IV, Vol. 1.

———. *Klaviertrios II*, Friedhelm Klugmann, ed. Munich: Henle, 1961. BEETHOVEN WERKE, Ser. IV, Vol. 3.

———. *Streichquartette I, II*, Paul Mies, ed. Munich: Henle, 1961. BEETHOVEN WERKE, Ser. VI, Vols. 3 & 4.

———. *Streichquintette*, Johannes Herzog, ed. Munich: Henle, 1968. BEETHOVEN WERKE, Ser. VI, Vol.20.

———. *Streichtrios und Streichduos*, Emil Platen, ed. Munich: Henle, 1965. BEETHOVEN WERKE, Ser. VI, Vol. 6.

Biber, Heinrich Johann Franz von. *Acht Violinsonaten*, Guido Adler, ed. Vienna: Artaria, 1898. DENKMÄLER DER TONKUNST IN ÖSTERREICH, Jg. V/2, Bd. 11.

———. *Fidicinium Sacro-Profanum tam choro, quam foro pluribus fidibus concinnatum et concini aptum (1683)*, Erich Schenk, ed. Graz: Akademische Druck- und Verlagsanstalt, 1960. DENKMÄLER DER TONKUNST IN ÖSTERREICH, 97.

———. *Harmonia Artificiosa-Ariosa, Diversimode Accordata*, Paul Nettl and Friedrich Reidinger, eds. Vienna: Österreichischer Bundesverlag, 1956. DENKMÄLER DER TONKUNST IN ÖSTERREICH, 92.

———. *Sechzehn Violinsonaten mit ausgeführter Klavierbegleitung*, Erwin Lutz, ed. Vienna: Artaria, 1905. DENKMÄLER DER TONKUNST IN ÖSTERREICH, Jg. XII/2, Bd. 25.

———. *Sonatae Tam Aris Quam Aulis Servientes (1676)*, Erich Schenk, ed. Graz: Akademische Druck- und Verlagsanstalt, 1963. DENKMÄLER DER TONKUNST IN ÖSTERREICH, 106–7.

Boccherini, Luigi, *4 Quintettini, op. 30. 6 Quartettini, op. 33 piccola*. Rome: Del Turco, 1956.

———. *Sonate per Cembalo con Violino Obbligato, op. 5*, Enrico Polo, ed. Milan: Fondazione Eugenio Bravi, 1941. I CLASSICI MUSICALI ITALIANI, 4.

The Bottegari Lutebook, Carol MacClintock, ed. Wellesley, Mass.: Wellesley College, 1965. THE WELLESLEY EDITION, 8.

Buxtehude, Dietrich. *Instrumentalwerke*, Carl Johann Christian Stiehl, ed. Leipzig: Breitkopf & Härtel, 1903. DENKMÄLER DEUTSCHER TONKUNST, 11.

———. *Werke*. Oberleitung der Glaubensgemeinde. Klecken, Ugrino: Abteilung Verlag, 1925–37, 1958–. XVII, *Instrumentalwerke: Kammermusik*.

Byrd, William. *The Collected Vocal Works of William Byrd*, Edmund H. Fellowes, ed. London: Stainer & Bell, 1937–1950. *Psalmes Songs and Sonnets (1611)*, XIV; *Chamber Music for Strings*, XVII.

Caldara, Antonio. *Kammermusik für Gesang*, Eusebius Mandyczewski, ed.; reprint, Graz: Akademische Druck- und Verlagsanstalt, 1960. DENKMÄLER DER TONKUNST IN ÖSTERREICH, Jg. XXXIX, Bd. 75.

Camerloher, Placidus von. *Vier Sonaten für 2 Violinen und Klavier (oder Cembalo), Violoncello ad lib.*, Adolf Hoffmann, ed. Mainz: B. Schott's Söhne, 1939.

Capirola, Vincenzo. *Compositione [for lute]*, Otto Gombosi, ed. Neuilly-sur-Seine: Société de Musique d'Autrefois, 1955.

Cesti, Antonio. *4 Chamber Duets*, David L. Burrows, ed. Madison, Wisc.: A-R Editions, 1969. COLLEGIUM MUSICUM: YALE UNIVERSITY, 2nd Ser., 1.

Chilesotti, Oscar, ed. *Biblioteca di raritá musicali*, 9 vols. Milan: G. Ricordi, 1884–1915.

———. *Lautenspieler des XVI. Jahrhunderts*. Leipzig: Breitkopf & Härtel, 1891; reprint, 1926.

Colección de vihuelistas españoles del siglo XVI, transcription from the original by Eduardo M. Torner. Madrid: Orfeo Tracio, S.A., 1923.

CONSORTIUM: *Eine Spiel- und Kammermusik-Reihe*, Helmut Mönkemeyer, ed. Amsterdam: Heinrichshofen; New York: C.F. Peters, 1961–. [5 numbers to date].

Corelli, Arcangelo. *Les Oeuvres de Arcangelo Corelli*, Joseph Joachim and Friedrich Chrysander, eds., 5 vols. London: Augener, 1888–91.

CORONA. *Werkereihe für Schul- und Kammerorchester*, Adolf Hoffmann, ed. Wolfenbüttel: Möseler, 193–. [105 vols. to date].

Couperin, François. *Oeuvres completes*, Maurice Cauchie, ed. Paris: Editions de l'Oiseau Lyre, 1932–33. VII–X: *Musique de chambre*.

Crema, Joan Maria da. *Intavolatura di liuto. Libro primo de recercari, canzon francese, motetti, madrigali, pass'e mezzi, saltarelli,* transcribed into modern notation by Giuseppe Gullino. Florence: Edizioni Musicali ditta R. Maurri, 1955.

Dandrieu, Jean François. *Livre de Sonates en Trio 1705*, Renée Viollier, ed. Amsterdam: Heinrichshofen's Verlag; New York: C.F. Peters, 1963.

DENKMÄLER ALTPOLNISCHER MUSIK, Adolf Chybiński, ed. Warsaw: Wydawnictwo Muzyczne, 193–. [43 vols. to date].

DILETTO MUSICALE. Doblingers Reihe alter Musik. Vienna: Doblinger, 1957. [249 vols. to date].

The Dolmetsch Collection of English Consorts; eleven fantasies, airs, pavans, galliards, almains, etc. by 16th and 17th century composers. New York: G. Schirmer, 1944. Scored from the original version for viols by Arnold Dolmetsch, version for modern string instruments by Percy Aldridge Grainger, with bowing and fingering by Ottokar Cadek.

Dolmetsch, Mabel. *Dances of England and France form 1450 to 1600, with their music and authentic manner of performance.* London: Routledge and Paul, 1949.

English Instrumental Music of the 16th and 17th Centuries from manuscripts in the New York Public Library, Sydney Beck, ed. New York: New York Public Library, 1947–.

Ferand, Ernst Thomas, ed. *Die Improvisation in Beispielen aus neun Jahrhunderten abendländischer Musik.* Cologne: Arno Volk, 1956. DAS MUSIKWERK, 12.

———. *Improvisation in Nine Centuries of Western Music; an anthology with a historical introduction.* Cologne: Arno Volk, 1961. ANTHOLOGY OF MUSIC,12.

FLORES MUSICAE; *Oeuvres des musiciens des XVIIe et XVIIIe siècles,* Claude Crussard, ed. Lausanne: Foetisch, 1949–. [9 vols. to date].

FLORILEGIUM MUSICUM; *Ein Werkreihe Alter Musik.* Gustav Scheck & Hugo Ruf, eds. Lörrach, Baden: Deutscher Ricordi-Verlag, 1954–. [9 vols. to date].

Förster, Emanuel Aloys. *Zwei Quartette, Drei Quintette,* Karl Weigl, ed. Graz: Akademische Druck- und Verlagsanstalt, 1960. DENKMÄLER DER TONKUNST IN ÖSTERREICH, 67.

Franck, Melchior, and Valentin Haussmann. *Ausgewählte Instrumentalwerke,* Franz Bölsche, ed. Leipzig: Breitkopf & Härtel, 1904. DENKMÄLER DEUTSCHER TONKUNST, 16.

Friedrich II, der Grosse. *Musikalische Werke,* Ph. Spitta, ed. Leipzig: Breitkopf & Härtel, 1889, reprint, as: *The Musical Works of Frederick the Great,* 3 vols. New York: Da Capo Press, 1967.

Fux, Johann Joseph. *Sämtliche Werke.* Johann-Joseph-Fux-Gesellschaft, Graz. Kassel: Bärenreiter, 1959–. Ser. VI, *Instrumentalmusik,* I, 1964.

Gabrieli, Giovanni. *Opera Omnia,* Denis Arnold, ed. Rome: American Institute of Musicology, 1956–. [5 vols. to date].

Gastoldi, Giovanni Giacomo. *Balletti a cinque voci (1591),* Michel Sanvoisen, ed. Paris: Heugel, 1968. LE PUPITRE, 10.

Geiringer, Karl, ed. *Music of the Bach Family: An Anthology.* Cambridge, Mass.: Harvard University Press, 1955.

Geminiani, Francesco. *Twelve Sonatas for Violin and Piano,* Ross Lee Finney, ed. Northampton, Mass.: Smith College, 1935. SMITH COLLEGE MUSIC ARCHIVES, 1.

Giardini, Felice. *Quartetti Op. 23, Nr. 3 e 4,* Alberto Poltronieri, ed. Milan: 1941. I CLASSICI MUSICALI ITALIANI, 6.

———. *Sonate per Cembalo con Violino o Flauto Traversò, Op. 3,* Enrico Polo, ed. Milan: 1941. I CLASSICI MUSICALI ITALIANI, 3.

Gibbons, Orlando. *Fantasies in 3 parts, composed for viols.* London: Printed for the members of the Musical Antiquarian Society by Chappell, 1843. MUSICAL ANTIQUARIAN SOCIETY, 9.

Giegling, Franz, ed. *Die Solosonate.* Cologne: Arno Volk, 1959. DAS MUSIKWERK, 15.

———. *The Solo Sonata.* Cologne: Arno Volk, c. 1960. ANTHOLOGY OF MUSIC, 15.

DIE GITARRE IN DER HAUS- UND KAMMERMUSIK VOR 100 JAHREN (1780–1820), Heinrich Albert, ed. Leipzig: Zimmermann, 1921. [14 numbers].

GITARRE-KAMMERMUSIK, Karl Scheit, ed. Vienna, Wiesbaden: Doblinger, 19?–. [38 numbers to date].

Gluck, Christoph Willibald. *Triosonaten,* Friedrich Neumann, ed. Kassel: Bärenreiter, 1961. SÄMTLICHE WERKE, Abt. V: *Instrumental- und Vokalmusik,* 1.

Graziani, Carlo. *Sei Sonate per Violoncello e basso continuo Op. 3,* Giacomo Benvenuti and Enrico Polo, eds. Milan: 1943. I CLASSICI MUSICALI ITALIANI, 15.

Händel, Georg Friedrich. *Elf Sonaten für Flöte und bezifferten Bass,* Hans-Peter Schmitz and Max Schneider eds. Kassel: Bärenreiter, 1955. HALLISCHE HÄNDEL-AUSGABE, Ser. IV: *Instrumentalmusic,* 3.

———. *Sechs Sonaten für Violine und bezifferten Bass,* Johann Philipp Hinnenthal, ed. Kassel: Bärenreiter, 1955. HALLISCHE HÄNDEL-AUSGABE. Ser. IV: *Instrumentalmusik,* 4.

———. *Triosonaten op. 5, 1–7,* Walter Serauky, Siegfried Flesch, and Max Schneider, eds. Kassel: Bärenreiter, 1956, HALLISCHE HÄNDEL-AUSGABE. Ser. IV: *Instrumentalmusik,* 10.

Hammerschmidt, Andreas. *"Erster Fleiss,"* *Instrumentalwerke zu 5 und 3 Stimmen,* Helmut Mönkemeyer, ed. Kassel: Nagel, 1957. DAS ERBE DEUTSCHER MUSIK, 49; Abteilung Kammermusik, 7.

HAUSMUSIK. Vienna: Österreichischer Bundesverlag, 1947–. [186 numbers to date].

Haussmann, Valentin. See: Franck, Melchior.

Haydn, Joseph. HAYDN WERKE. Cologne: Joseph Haydn-Institut, 1958–. Under the direction of Jens Peter Larsen. *Barytontrios,* XIV, 2–5; *Divertimenti für gemischte Besetzung,* VIII; *Divertimenti für Streicherbesetzung,* X: *Kammermusik verschiedener Art ohne Klavier,* XVI; *Klavier-Divertimenti mit Begleitung,* XVII; *Klaviertrios,* XVIII; *Sonaten für Klavier mit Violine oder Flöte,* XIX; *Streichduos,* XIII; *Streichquartette,* XII; *Streichtrios,* XII; *Verschiedene Instrumentalmusik,* XXII; *Werke mit Baryton,* XIII.

———. *Divertimenti; Scherzandi,* H.C. Robbins Landon, ed. Vienna: Doblinger, 1961–.

———. *Pianoforte Trio in F sharp minor; Pianoforte Trio in A Major,* redistributed for the benefit of the violin and violoncello by Donald Francis Tovey. London and New York: Oxford University Press, 1951.

Haydn, Michael. *Instrumentalwerke,* L.H. Perger, ed. Vienna: Artaria, 1907. DENKMÄLER DER TONKUNST IN ÖSTERREICH, Jg. XIV/2, Bd. 29.

Henry VIII. *Music at the Court of Henry VIII,* John Stevens, ed. London: Stainer & Bell, 1962. MUSICA BRITANNICA, 18.

Hoffmann, Ernst Theodor Amadeus. *Musikalische Werke,* Gustav Becking, ed. Leipzig: C.F.W. Siegel's Musikalienhandlung, [1922–27], *Kammermusik,* II.

Holborne, Anthony. *Music for Lute and Bandora,* Masakata Kanazawa, ed. Cambridge, Mass.: Harvard University Press, 1967. HARVARD PUBLICATIONS IN MUSIC, 1.

Holzbauer, Ignaz, *Instrumentale Kammermusik,* Ursula Lehmann, ed. Kassel: Nagel, 1954. DAS ERBE DEUTSCHER MUSIK, 24; Abteilung Kammermusik, 4.

HORTUS MUSICUS, *die neue Ausgabenreihe erlesener Haus- und Kammermusik.* Kassel: Bärenreiter, 1936–. [206 numbers to date].

Jackman, James L., ed. *Fifteenth Century Basse Dances: Brussels Bibl. roy. Ms. 9085,* collated with Michel Toulouze's *L'Art et Instruction de bien Dancer.* Wellesley, Mass.: Wellesley College, 1964. THE WELLESLEY EDITION, No. 6.

Jenkins, John. *Fancies and Ayres,* Helen Joy Sleeper, ed. Wellesley, Mass.: Wellesley College, 1950. THE WELLESLEY EDITION, 1.

———. *Jacobean Consort Music,* Thurston Dart and William Coates, eds. London: Stainer & Bell, 1955. MUSICA BRITANNICA, 9.

———. *Three-part Fancy and Ayre Divisions, for 2 Trebles and a Bass to the Organ,* Robert Warner, ed. Wellesley, Mass.: Wellesley College, THE WELLESLEY EDITION, 10.

KAMMERSONATEN. Ausgewählte Werke alter Musik für ein Soloinstrument mit Begleitung. Leipzig: Breitkopf & Härtel, 1928–. [17 numbers to date].

Krebs, Johann Ludwig. *6 Kammersonaten für Flöte (Violine) und obligates Cembalo,* Bernhard Klein, ed. Leipzig: Peters, 1963.

Lawes, William, *Select Consort Music,* Murray Lefkowitz, ed. London: Stainer and Bell, 1963. MUSICA BRITANNICA, 21.

Leclair, Jean Marie. *Six Sonates pour Violon et Clavecin ou Piano*, Marc Pincherle, ed. Monaco: Editions l'Oiseau-Lyre, 1952.
——. *Sonatas for Violin and Piano, Op. 9, Nos. 1,4,6.* New York: Carl Fischer, 1960.
——. *Sonatas for violin and basso continuo, op. 5, op. 9, op. 15,* Robert E. Preston, ed. Madison, Wisc.: A-R Editions, 1968–. RECENT RESEARCHES IN THE BAROQUE ERA, 4 & 5. Part I: op. 4, sonatas I–V; Part II: op. 5, sonatas VI–XII.
Legrenzi, Giovanni. *Sonate da chiesa, opus 4 and opus 8 (1656–1663),* Albert Seay, ed. Paris: Heugel, 1968. LE PUPITRE, 4.
Le Roux, Gaspard. *Pièces de Clavecin (1705),* Albert Fuller, ed. New York: Alpeg Editions, 1959.
Locatelli, Pietro Antonio. *Sei Sonate da Camera per Violino e Basso dall' Op. 6,* Giacomo Benvenuti and Enrico Polo, eds. Milan: Fondazione Eugenio Bravi, 1956. I CLASSICI MUSICALI ITALIANI, 14.
Mannheimer Kammermusik des 18. Jahrhunderts, Hugo Riemann, ed. Braunschweig: H. Litolff, 1900–38. DENKMÄLER DER TONKUNST IN BAYERN, 15 & 16.
Massaino, Tiburtio. *Drei Instrumentalcanzonen (1608),* Raffaello Monterosso, ed. Graz: Akademische Druck- und Verlagsanstalt, 1964. DENKMÄLER DER TONKUNST IN ÖSTERREICH, 110.
MOECKS KAMMERMUSIK, Celle: Hermann Moeck, 1939–. [203 vols. to date].
Mondonville, Jean-Joseph Cassanea de. *Les Pièces de Clavecin avec Voix ou Violon, oeuvre 5,* facsimile, with preface by Marc Pincherle. London: H. Baron, 1966.
——. *Sonates en trio, Op. 2 (1734),* Roger Blanchard, ed. Paris: Heugel, 1967. LE PUPITRE, 3.
MONUMENTS OF RENAISSANCE MUSIC, Edward E. Lowinsky, ed. Chicago: University of Chicago Press, 1964, I: *Musica nova, accommodata per cantar et sonar sopra organi, et altri strumenti, composta per diversi eccellentrissimi musici. Venice, 1540,* H. Colin Slim, ed.: forward by Edward E. Lowinsky.
Morley, Thomas, *The First Book of Consort Lessons, 1599 and 1611,* Sydney Beck, ed. New York: published for the New York Public Library by C.F. Peters, 1959.
Mozart, Wolfgang Amadeus. *Klaviertrios,* Wolfgang Plath and Wolfgang Rehm, eds. Kassel: Bärenreiter, 1966. NEUE AUSGABE SÄMTLICHER WERKE. Ser. VIII: *Kammermusik:* Werkgruppe 22, Abteilung 2.
——. *Quartette mit einem Blasinstrument,* Jaroslav Pohanka, ed. Kassel: Bärenreiter, 1962. NEUE AUSGABE SÄMTLICHER WERKE. Ser. VIII: *Kammermusik:* Werkgruppe 20, Abteilung 2.
——. *Quartette und Quintette mit Klavier und mit Glasharmonika,* Hellmut Federhofer, ed. Kassel: Bärenreiter, 1957. NEUE AUSGABE SÄMTLICHER WERKE. Ser. VIII: *Kammermusik:* Werkgruppe 22, Abteilung 1.
——. *Quintette mit Bläsern,* Ernst Fritz Schmid, ed. Kassel: Bärenreiter, 1958. NEUE AUSGABE SÄMTLICHER WERKE. Ser. VIII: *Kammermusik:* Werkgruppe 19, Abteilung 2.
——. *Sonaten und Variationen für Klavier und Violine,* Eduard Hendrik Reeser, ed. Kassel: Bärenreiter, 1964–65. NEUE AUSGABE SÄMTLICHER WERKE. Ser. VIII: *Kammermusik:* Werkgruppe 23, Bd. 1 & 2.

————. *Streichquartette*, Ludwig Finscher, ed. Kassel: Bärenreiter, 1961–62. NEUE AUSGABE SÄMTLICHER WERKE. Ser. VIII: *Kammermusik:* Werkgruppe 20, Abteilung 1, Bd. 2 & 3.

————. *Streichquartette und Quartette mit einem Blasinstrument,* Karl Heinz Füssl, Wolfgang Plath, and Wolfgang Rehm, eds. Kassel: Bärenreiter, 1966. NEUE AUSGABE SÄMTLICHER WERKE. Ser. VIII: *Kammermusik:* Werkgruppe 20, Abteilung 1.

————. *Streichquintette,* Ernst Hess and Ernst Fritz Schmid, eds. Kassel: Bärenreiter, 1967. NEUE AUSGABE SÄMTLICHER WERKE. Ser. VIII: *Kammermusik:* Werkgruppe 19, Abteilung 1.

————. *The Ten Celebrated String quartets; First Authentic Edition in Score, Based on Autographs in the British Museum and on Early Prints,* Alfred Einstein, ed. London: Novello & Co., 1945. PUBLICATION OF THE PAUL HIRSCH MUSIC LIBRARY, 12.

————. *Trio (nr. 8) für Klavier, Violine und Violoncello, KV 442,* Karl Marguerre, ed. Wiesbaden: Breitkopf & Härtel, 1968.

Muffat, Georg. *Armonico Tributo (1682),* Erich Schenk, ed. Vienna: Österreichischer Bundesverlag, 1953. DENKMÄLER DER TONKUNST IN ÖSTERREICH, 89.

Music for String Instruments by 18th Century Masters, Josef Marx, ed. New York: McGinnis & Marx, 1948–.

Music for Wind Instruments by 18th Century Masters, Josef Marx, ed. New York: McGinnis & Marx, 1946–. [13 numbers to date.].

MUSICA ANTIQUA BOHEMICA. Prague: Editio Artia, 1949–. [60 numbers to date].

MÚSICA HISPANA. Barcelona: Instituto Español de Musicología, Consejo Superior de Investigationes Científicas, 1952–. Ser. c. Música de cámara.

MUSICA INSTRUMENTALIS; *eine neue Werkreihe für Melodieinstrumente,* Egon Kraus, ed. Zurich: Musikverlag zum Pelikan, 1954–. [7 vols. to date].

MUSICA RARA. London: Musica Rara, 195–. [234 numbers to date].

MUSICHE VOCALI E STRUMENTALI SACRE E PROFANE, SEC, XVII–XVIII–XIX, Bonaventura Somma, ed. Rome: Edizione de Santis, 1941–. [28 vols. to date].

MUSIKSCHÄTZE DER VERGANGENHEIT. Berlin: Chr. Friedrich Verlag, 1928–. [72 numbers to date].

DAS MUSIKWERK; *eine Beispielsammlung zur Musikgeschichte,* Karl Gustav Fellerer, ed. Cologne: Arno Volk, 1951–. [35 vols. to date]. [English ed. as ANTHOLOGY OF MUSIC].

MUSIQUES FRANÇAISES [Old French Music]. Georges Migot, ed. Geneva: Editions du Siècle Musical, 1948–. 22 vols.

NAGELS MUSIK-ARCHIV. Hannover: Adolph Nagel, 1927–. [228 numbers to date].

Österreichische Lautenmusik im XVI. Jahrhundert, Adolf Koczirz, ed. Vienna: Artaria, 1911. DENKMÄLER DER TONKUNST IN ÖSTERREICH, Jg. XVIII/2, Bd. 37.

Österreichische Lautenmusik zwischen 1650 und 1720, Adolf Koczirz, ed. Vienna: Artaria, 1918. DENKMÄLER DER TONKUNST IN ÖSTERREICH, Jg. XXV/2, Bd. 50.

ORGANUM. Reihe 3, *Kammermusik.* Leipzig: F. Kistner & C.F.W. Siegel, ca.1924–. [68 numbers to date].

Parthenia In-Violata or Mayden-Musicke for the Virginalls and Bass-Viol, Selected by Robert Hole. Facsimile of the unique copy in the New York Public Library; historical introduction by Thurston Dart; bibliographical note by Richard J. Wolfe; foreword by Sydney Beck. New York: The New York Public Library, 1961.

――――. Thurston Dart, ed. New York: C.F. Peters, 1961. *Pegasus Kammermusik Ausgaben.* Amsterdam: Heinrichshofen, 19?–.

Pepusch, Johan Christopher. *Sechs Triosonaten für Violine, Oboe und Basso continuo,* Lothar Hoffmann-Erbrecht, ed. Leipzig: Breitkopf & Härtel, 1957. MITTELDEUTSCHES MUSIKARCHIV, Reihe 2: *Kammermusik,* Heft 1–2.

Pergolesi, Giovanni Battista. *Opera omnia.* Francesco Caffarelli, ed. Rome: Gli Amici della Musica da Camera, 1939–42, V, *Sonate a tre per violini e basso continuo;* XXI, *Sonate e concerti;* XXII, *Arie da camera.*

Perlen alter Kammermusik deutscher und italienischer Meister, Arnold Schering, ed. Leipzig: C.F. Kahnt, 19?–. [Intraden, Suiten, etc.]

Peuerl, Paul. *Neue Paduanen (1611), Weltspiegel (1613), Ganz Neue Paduanen (1625); Isaac Posch: Musikalische Tafelfreud (1621).* Vienna: Universal-Edition A.G., 1929. DENKMÄLER DER TONKUNST IN ÖSTERREICH, Jg. XXXVI/2, Bd. 70.

Playford, John. *Musick's Recreation on the Viol, Lyra-way (1682),* with a historical introduction in English and German by Nathalie Dolmetsch. London: Hinrichsen, ca.1965.

LE PUPITRE: *Collection de musique ancíenne,* François Lesure, ed. Paris: Heugel et Cie, 1967–. [24 numbers to date].

Purcell, Henry. *Complete Works,* published by the Purcell Society. London: Novello & Co., 1878–. V, *12 Sonatas of 3 parts,* for stringed instruments and pianoforte (1893); VII, *10 Sonatas of 4 parts,* for stringed instruments and pianoforte (1896); XXXI, *Fantasias and other instrumental music,* (1959).

Radino, Giovanni Maria. *Intavolatura di balli per sonar di liuto,* Giuseppe Gullino, ed. Florence: Edizioni Musicali ditta R. Maurri, 1949.

Rameau, Jean-Philippe. *Pièces de Clavecin,* with the composer's original appended texts unabridged and with several facsimile reproductions, Erwin R. Jacobi, ed., 3rd, rev. ed. Kassel: Bärenreiter, 1966.

――――. *Pièces de Clavecin en Concert avec un Violon ou Flute et une Viole ou Deuxième Violon,* with the composer's original "Notices" and with several facsimile reproductions. Kassel: Bärenreiter, 1961.

Reusner, Essias, and Silvius Leopold Weiss. *Lautenmusik des 17/18 Jahrhunderts,* Hans Neemann, ed. Braunschweig: Litolff, 1939. DAS ERBE DEUTSCHER MUSIK, Reihe 1, 12.

Rosetti, Francesco Antonio [Franz Anton Rössler]. *Ausgewählte Kammermusikwerke nebst einem Instrumentalkonzert,* Oscar Kaul, ed. Braunschweig: H. Litolff, 1900–38. DENKMÄLER DER TONKUNST IN BAYERN, 25.

Roman, Johan Helmich. *Assaggi A Violino Solo,* Ingmar Bengtsson and Lars Frydén, eds. Uppsala: Almqvist & Wiksell, 1958. MONUMENTA MUSICAE SVECICAE, 1.

――――. *Sonata a tre.* Stockholm: A.B. Nordiska Musikförlaget, 1935. SVENSKA SAMFUNDET FÖR MUSIKFORSKNING, 1.

Rosenmüller, Johann. *Sonate da camera,* Karl Nef, ed. Leipzig: Breitkopf & Härtel, 1904. DENKMÄLER DEUTSCHER TONKUNST, 18.

Rossi, Salamon. *Sinfonie, Gagliarde, Canzone 1607–1608,* Fritz Rikko and Joel Newman, eds. New York: Mercury Music, 1965.

Rossini, Gioacchino Antonio. *Quaderni Rossiniani,* Pesaro: La Fondazione Rossini, 1954–. I, *Sei sonate a quattro,* (1954); VI, *Musica da camera,* (1957).

Rust, Friedrich Wilhelm. *Werke für Klavier und Streichinstrumente,* R. Czach, ed. Wolfenbüttel: G. Kallmeyer, 1939. DAS ERBE DEUTSCHER MUSIK, Mitteldeutschland, 1.

Sammartini, Giovanni Battista. *The Symphonies of G.B. Sammartini,* Bathia Churgin, ed. Cambridge, Mass.: Harvard University Press, 1968–. [1 vol. to date]. HARVARD PUBLICATIONS IN MUSIC, 2.

Scarlatti, Domenico. *Sonatas for Violin and Clavier,* Lionel Salter, ed. Formerly published as solo harpsichord sonatas. Edited from mss. at Biblioteca Marciana, Venice. London: Augener, 1940–50.

Schein, Johann Hermann. *Banchetto Musicale 1617. 20 Suiten zu 5 Stimmen,* Dieter Krickeberg, ed. Kassel: Bärenreiter, 1967. NEUE AUSGABE SÄMTLICHER WERKE, 9.

Schenk, Erich, ed. *Die Italienische Triosonate.* Cologne: Arno Volk, 1955. DAS MUSIKWERK, 7.

———. *The Italian Trio Sonata.* Cologne: Arno Volk, 1959. ANTHOLOGY OF MUSIC, 7.

Schenk, Johann. *Le Nymphe di Pheno für zwei Solo-Gamben,* Karl Heinz Pauls, ed. Kassel: Nagel, 1956. DAS ERBE DEUTSCHER MUSIK, 44; Abteilung Kammermusik, 6.

Schmelzer, Johann Heinrich. *Duodena Selectarum Sonatarum (1659),* Erich Schenk, ed. Graz: Academische Druck- und Verlagsanstalt, 1963. DENKMÄLER DER TONKUNST IN ÖSTERREICH, 105.

———. *Sonatae Unarum Fidium (1664): Violinsonaten,* Erich Schenk, ed. Vienna Österreichischer Bundesverlag, 1958. DENKMÄLER DER TONKUNST IN ÖSTERREICH, 93.

Schobert, Johann. *Ausgewählte Werke,* Hugo Riemann, ed. Leipzig: Breitkopf & Härtel, 1909. DENKMÄLER DEUTSCHER TONKUNST, 39.

———. *Sechs Sinfonien für Cembalo mit Begleitung von Violine und Hörnern ad lib. Op. 9 & Op. 10,* Gustav Becking and Walter Kramolisch, eds. Kassel: Johann Philipp Hinnenthal, 1960. DAS ERBE DEUTSCHER MUSIK, Sonderreihe, 4.

SCHOTT'S SERIES OF EARLY LUTE MUSIC. London: Schott & Co., *c.*1954–. [3 vols. to date].

Schubert, Franz Peter. *Neue Ausgabe sämtlicher Werke,* published by the Internationalen Schubert-Gesellschaft. Kassel: Bärenreiter, 1964–. Ser. VI, Kammermusik. 1, Nonette. Oktette; 2, Streichquintette; 3, Streichquartette; 4, Streichtrios; 5, Kammermusik mit Klavier (dazu Stimmen).

Schultz, Helmut, ed. *Deutsche Bläsermusik vom Barock bis zur Klassik.* Kassel: Nagel, 1941, 1961. DAS ERBE DEUTSCHER MUSIK, 14; Abteilung Kammermusik, 2.

Spohr, Louis. *Ausgewählte Werke,* Friedrich Otto Leinert, ed. Kassel and Basel: Bärenreiter, 195?–.

Steffani, Agostino. *Eight songs for solo voice with one or two woodwinds (flute, recorder or oboe) and continuo,* Gertrude Parker Smith, ed. Northampton, Mass.: Smith College, 1950. SMITH COLLEGE MUSIC ARCHIVES, 11.

Telemann, Georg Philipp. *Kammermusik ohne Generalbass, 1735,* Günter Hausswald, ed. Kassel: Bärenreiter, 1955. MUSIKALISCHE WERKE, 6–8.

———. *Sechs Suiten für Querflöte, Violine, und Basso continuo,* Johann Philipp Hinnenthal, ed. Kassel: Bärenreiter, 1955. MUSIKALISCHE WERKE, 9.

———. *Tafelmusik,* Johann Philipp Hinnenthal, ed. Kassel: Bärenreiter, 1959–63. MUSIKALISCHE WERKE, 12–14.

———. *Zwölf methodische Sonaten für Querflöte (Violine) und Basso continuo, Hamburg, 1728 & 1732,* Max Seiffert, ed. Kassel: Bärenreiter, 1955. MUSIKALISCHE WERKE, 1.

———. *Zwölf Pariser Quartette,* Walter Bergmann, ed. Kassel: Bärenreiter, 1965. MUSIKALISCHE WERKE, 18–19.

———. *Pariser Quartet Nr. 1–3,* Walter Bergmann, ed. Kassel: Bärenreiter, 1968.

Thesaurus Musicus, Ferenc Brodszky, general ed. Budapest: Zenemükiado Vällalat, 195–. [Available through Boosey & Hawkes].

Tiroler Instrumentalmusik im 18. Jahrhundert, Walter Senn, ed. Vienna: Universal, 1949. DENKMÄLER DER TONKUNST IN ÖSTERREICH, 86.

Tye, Christopher. *The Instrumental Music,* Robert Weidner, ed. New Haven, Conn: A-R Editions, 1967. RECENT RESEARCHES IN THE MUSIC OF THE RENAISSANCE, 3.

Viadana, Lodovico. *Cento Concerti Ecclesiastici, opera duodecima, 1602. Parte Prima: Concerti a una voce con l'organo,* Claudio Gallico, ed. Kassel: Bärenreiter, 1964. MONUMENTI MUSICALI MANTOVANI, Ser. I, Numero I.

Vierdanck, Johann. *Spielmusik für zwei und drei Violinen oder andere Melodieinstrumente,* Hans Engel, ed. Kassel: Bärenreiter, 1930. DENKMÄLER DER MUSIK IN POMMERN: Pommersche Meister des 6. bis 18. Jahrhunderts, 1.

Vitali, Giovanni Battista. *Artifici Musicali, Op. 13,* Louise Rood and Gertrude P. Smith, eds. Northampton, Mass.: Smith College, 1959. SMITH COLLEGE MUSIC ARCHIVES, 14.

Vitali, Tommaso Antonio. *Concerto di Sonate, Opus 4, For Violin, Violoncello, and Continuo,* Doris Silbert, Gertrude Parker Smith and Louise Rood, eds. Northampton, Mass.: Smith College, 1954. SMITH COLLEGE MUSIC ARCHIVES, 12.

Vivaldi, Antonio. *Le Opere di Antonio Vivaldi,* Gian Francesco Malipiero, ed. Rome: Edizioni Ricordi, 1947–. [500 vols. to date].

Walther, Johann Jakob. *Scherzi da Violino Solo con il Basso continuo 1676,* Gustav Beckmann, ed. Hannover: Nagel, 1953. DAS ERBE DEUTSCHER MUSIK, 17; Abteilung Kammermusik.

Wasielewski, Joseph Wilhelm von. *Anthology of Instrumental Music from the End of the Sixteenth to the End of the Seventeenth Century,* new introduction by John Suess. New York: Da Capo Press, 1973. (Reprint of *Instrumentalsätze vom Ende des XVI, bis Ende des XVII, Jahrhunderts.* Berlin: Leo Liepmannssohn, ca. 1874.)

Weiss, Silvius Leopold. See: Reusner, Essias.

WERKE AUS DEM 18. JAHRHUNDERT, Robert Sondheimer, ed. Berlin and Basel: Edition Bernoulli, 1922–39. [52 numbers].

Werner, Gregor Joseph. *Musikalischer Instrumental-Kalender, für zwei Violinen und Basso continuo,* Fritz Stein, ed. Kassel: Nagel, 1956. DAS ERBE DEUTSCHER MUSIK, 31; Abteilung Kammermusik, 5.

The Wickhambrook Lute Manuscript, transcribed and ed. by Daphne E.R. Stephens. New Haven: Yale University, 1963. COLLEGIUM MUSICUM, 4.

Wiener Instrumentalmusik ver 1750, Wilhelm Fischer, ed. Vienna: Artaria, 1912. DENKMÄLER DER TONKUNST IN ÖSTERREICH, Jg. XIX/2, Bd. 39.

Wiener Instrumentalmusik um 1750, Karl Horwitz and Karl Riedel, eds. Vienna: Artaria, 1908. DENKMÄLER DER TONKUNST IN ÖSTERREICH, Jg. XV/2, Bd. 31.

Wiener Lautenmusik im 18. Jahrhundert, Karl Schnürl, ed. Vienna: Universal, 1942. DENKMÄLER DER TONKUNST IN ÖSTERREICH, 84.

Wiener Tanzmusik in der zweiten Hälfte des siebzehnten Jahrhunderts, Paul Nettl, ed. Vienna: Artaria, 1921. DENKMÄLER DER TONKUNST IN ÖSTERREICH, Jg. XXVIII/2, Bd. 56.

ZEITSCHRIFT FÜR SPIELMUSIK. Celle: Hermann Moeck [n.d.]. [296 numbers to date].

ZRODLA DO HISTORII MUZYKI POSKIEJ. Krakow: Polskie Wydawnictwo Muzyczne, 19?–. [7 vols. to date].

INDEX

Aaron, Pietro, 35
Abel, Karl Friedrich, 81
Absorption of parts, see *Canzone*
"*A cappella* era," use of organ in, 18
Acciaccatura, 50
Accompagnando, see Figures
Acoustics, 5
Adagio, character of the, 95, 103 ff.; ornamentation of the, 111 ff.
Addition of parts, factor in formation of trio sonata, 35 ff., 42 f.
Ad libitum part, 45, 124, 131, 134 ff.
Agazzari, Agostino, quoted, 15 f., 20
Alberti, Domenico, "Alberti bass," 50 f., 135
Albicastro, Henrico, 68
Albinoni, Tommaso, 96n
Albrechtsberger, Johann Georg, 145
Alembert, Jean le Rond d', 11 f.
Alla Camera, see Instrumentation, solo
Alla mente, see Improvisation
Allegri, Gregorio, *Symphonia*, 83
Allegro, character of the, 96 ff., 101-106, 167; ornamentation of the, 111; omission of first, 119
Allemande, 10 f., 94 f., 100, 102 f.
Alternative "Bases" for Excerpt from Corelli's Sonata, Op. 2, No. 3 (mus. ex. from Burney, *A General History of Music*), 94
Alternativo, second minuet of Haydn's Op. 2, No. 3, 159
Amadino, music publishers, 35
Ancelet, quoted, 66, 74
Anerio, Felice, 21
Antoniotto, Giorgio, quoted, 7 f., 103, 106
Anweisung zum Violinspielen (Hiller), 63
Apothéose de Lulli (Couperin le Grand), 52
Appoggiatura, 110, 139
Aria style (Air), transfer to instrumental music, 54, 101 ff., 110, 119, 123, 132 f., 147
Arioso style, in instrumental music, 106, 157n, 162
Ariosti, Attilio, 76
Arm viol, *see* Viola da braccio

Arnold, Samuel, 65n
Arpeggio, a subdivision of *Brechung*, 34; composed, 47, 50 f., 60, 74, 78, 95 f., 113, 128, 135, 144, 151, 160, 162 f.; improvised, 49 f., 129
Artaria, Domenico, 164
Art de toucher le clavecin, L' (Couperin le Grand), 53
Arte de Tañer Fantasia (Sancta Maria), 17
Artusi, Giovanni Maria, 35
Asplmayr, Franz, 152
Attaingnant, Pierre, 23
Avison, Charles, quoted, 59 f., 66, 69, 82, 89, 104, 146 f.

Bach, Carl Philipp Emanuel, 123, 125 f., 143; quoted, 47 f., 52; discussion of tempo rubato, 114; influence on Haydn, 149, 156; sonatinas, 152
Bach, Johann Sebastian, 44, 47, 109, 131; as an accompanist, 28; attacked by Scheibe, 53 f.; unaccompanied solos, 62, 76 f., 137; use of recorder and flute, 64 f.; use of meter-signatures, 106 f.; works for obbligato clavier and melodic instrument, 124-128, 130
Bagpipe, 12, 162
Balleto, 91 f.
Banchetto musicale (Schein), 20
Banchieri, Adriano, 18, 21
Baroque style, musical ornamentation, 111; thematic construction, 115 f.; voluminous sound, 121
Bassani, Giovanni Battista, 92, 99
Bassevi, Jacopo, 77
Bass gamba, *see* Viol, bass
Basso continuo, see Thorough bass
Bassoon, 12, 16, 43, 54, 65, 70 f., 80-83, 89, 117, 139
Bass part, harmonic function of, 17, 21, 25, 40, 44, 76, 117, 127, 152; melodic activity in, 21, 23, 34, 37, 39 f., 95, 97 f., 144; ornamentation of, 50, 79; division of, 78 ff., 85 f., 121; in tempo rubato, 114; *see also* Drum bass; Lazy bass; Organ bass

INDEX